faith first

Legacy Edition

SCHOOL

Grade Six

RCL✷
Benziger®

Cincinnati, Ohio

This book reflects the
new revision of the

ROMAN
MISSAL

THIRD EDITION

"The Ad Hoc Committee to Oversee the Use of the Catechism, United States Conference of Catholic Bishops, has found this catechetical series, copyright 2007, to be in conformity with the *Catechism of the Catholic Church*."

NIHIL OBSTAT
Rev. Msgr. Robert M. Coerver
Censor Librorum

IMPRIMATUR
† Most Rev. Charles V. Grahmann
Bishop of Dallas

October 31, 2005

The Nihil Obstat and Imprimatur are official declarations that the material reviewed is free of doctrinal or moral error. No implication is contained therein that those granting the Nihil Obstat and Imprimatur agree with the contents, opinions, or statements expressed.

Send all inquiries to:
RCL Benziger
8805 Governor's Hill Drive
Suite 400
Cincinnati, Ohio 45249

Toll Free   877-275-4725
Fax   800-688-8356

Visit us at www.RCLBenziger.com
            www.FaithFirst.com

20536   ISBN 978-0-7829-1121-3 (Student Book)

20546   ISBN 978-0-7829-1127-5 (Teacher Guide)

4th printing.
Manufactured for RCL Benziger in Cincinnati, OH, USA.
March 2012.

ACKNOWLEDGMENTS

Scripture excerpts are taken or adapted from the *New American Bible with Revised New Testament and Psalms* Copyright © 1991, 1986, 1970, Confraternity of Christian Doctrine, Washington, DC. Used with permission. All rights reserved. No part of the *New American Bible* may be reproduced by any means without the permission of the copyright owner.

Excerpts are taken or adapted from the English translation of the *Roman Missal* © 2010, ICEL International Committee on English in the Liturgy, Inc.; the English translation of the Act of Contrition from *Rite of Penance* © 1974, ICEL; the English translation of *Rite of Baptism for Children* © 1969; the English translation of *Rite of Confirmation,* Second Edition © 1975, ICEL; *Pastoral Care of the Sick* © 1982, ICEL; *Ordination of Deacons, Priests and Bishops* © 1975, ICEL; the English translation of *A Book of Prayers* © 1982, ICEL; the English translation of *Book of Blessings* © 1988, ICEL; *Catholic Household Blessings and Prayers* (revised edition) © 2007, United States Conference of Catholic Bishops, Washington, D.C. All rights reserved.

Excerpts are taken or adapted from English translation of *Gloria Patri, Kyrie Eleison, Nicene Creed, Apostles' Creed, Sanctus and Benedictus, Agnus Dei,* and *Te Deum Laudamus* by the International Consultation on English Texts (ICET).

Faith First Legacy Edition Development Team

Developing a religion program requires the gifts and talents of many individuals working together as a team. RCL Benziger is proud to acknowledge the contributions of these dedicated people.

Program Theology Consultants
Reverend Louis J. Cameli, S.T.D.
Reverend Robert D. Duggan, S.T.D.

Advisory Board
Judith Deckers, M.Ed.
Marina Herrera, Ph.D.
Elaine McCarron, SCN, M.Div.
Reverend Frank McNulty, S.T.D.
Reverend Ronald J. Nuzzi, Ph.D.

Contributing Writers
Student Book and Teacher Guide
Reverend Louis J. Cameli
Christina DeCamp
Judith Deckers
Jack Gargiulo
Mary Beth Jambor
Michele Norfleet
Marie Raffio
Susan Stark

Director of Creative Development
Jo Rotunno

National Catechetical Consultant
Kate Sweeney Ristow

Managing Editor
Susan Smith

Art & Design Director
Lisa Brent

Electronic Page Makeup
Laura Fremder, Manager
Marti Ewing

Production Director
Jenna Nelson

Designers
Pat Bracken
Tricia Legault

Project Editors
Patricia A. Classick
Steven M. Ellair
Craig W. O'Neill

Web Site Producers
Joseph Crisalli
A. C. Ware

General Editor
Ed DeStefano

President/Publisher
Maryann Nead

Contents

We Celebrate: The Liturgical Seasons

We Pray

Dear God,
We are looking forward to an exciting journey in sixth grade. Thank you for calling us to faith and for the opportunity to learn more about you and your love for us this year. With your help, we will grow and accept more responsibility as Christians. Help us to treat all those we meet with justice and care. Amen.

Welcome to Faith First!

My Life

- Where were you baptized?

  St. Rose of Lima

- Who first taught you about Jesus?

  My Mom

- Where is it easy for you to pray?

  My room

- What is a holy place that you would like to visit?

  Rome

God's Plan of Salvation

Just as the story of your life happens over time, so has the story of God's love for his people unfolded in history. This year you will learn many new things about God and the story of his people. Complete the activities on the next page to see what you already know and to find out the kinds of things you will learn this year.

We Believe

God revealed his name to Moses in a voice heard from a burning bush. What is the name God revealed, and what does it mean? Look on page 28 to check your answer.

Name
yhwh

Meaning
_I r y_

We Worship

Many centuries after the time of Moses, God anointed David, son of Jesse, as king of God's people. David also wrote poems that are part of the Bible. Many of them were used in worship by the Israelites. You will learn what these poems are called on page 179.

Psalms

We Live

David's poems and songs are part of the wisdom books of the Bible. Another of the wisdom books contains short sayings such as this one:

Better a dry crust with peace,
than a house full of feasting with strife.

What is the name of this book of the Bible? You can find the answer on page 292.

proverbs

We Pray

Jesus teaches us that we can call God Father, just as he did. Did you know that there are two versions of the Our Father in the New Testament? Which Gospel has the longer version that we pray today? Look on page 332 to check your answer.

Matthew

The Lord Is My Shepherd

The leader, holding the Bible high for all to see, walks at the head of a procession to the prayer space.

All make the sign of the cross together.

LEADER: Lord, we gather today to honor the gift of your word. We remember your love for us and that you are always with us.

ALL: **The Lord is my shepherd,**
I shall not want.

LEADER: A reading from the Second Book of Samuel.
Proclaim 2 Samuel 7:9–10a, 16.
The word of the Lord.

ALL: **Thanks be to God.**

LEADER: Even though I walk in the
dark valley
I fear no evil; for you are
at my side.

ALL: **The Lord is my shepherd,**
I shall not want.

LEADER: Only goodness and kindness
follow me
all the days of my life;
And I shall dwell in the house
of the LORD
for years to come.

ALL: **The Lord is my shepherd,**
I shall not want.

BASED ON PSALM 23:1, 4, 6

Come forward and reverence the Bible.

Unit 1 • We Believe

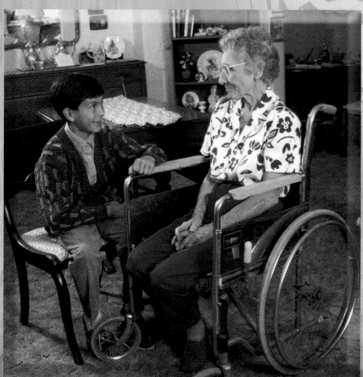

What do we profess in the creeds of the Church?

11

Getting Ready

What I Have Learned

What is something you already know about these faith terms?

The prophets

I don't

Know

Jesus Christ, Savior of the world

He died for

_us._

Kingdom of God

Where we go

when we die

Words to Know

Put an X next to the faith terms you know. Put a ? next to the faith terms you need to know more about.

Faith Vocabulary

- ☒ faith
- ☒ creed
- ? Covenant
- ? oral tradition
- ? Redemption
- ? Immaculate Conception
- ? Revelation
- ☒ original sin
- ? Salvation
- ? Incarnation

Questions I Have

What questions would you like to ask about God's plan of Salvation?

_____

_____

_____

_____

A Scripture Story

Saint Paul dictating to a scribe

What do you know about the New Testament letters of Saint Paul the Apostle?

The Gift of Faith

1

We Pray

Praise the LORD from the
  earth, . . .
You mountains and all hills.
PSALM 148:7, 9

**We thank you, Father,
for making yourself
known to us through
your Son, Jesus Christ.
Amen.**

*Who do you know better today
than you did a year ago?
How did you get to know this
person well?*

Getting to know someone
well takes time and effort.
The more people show and
tell us about themselves, the
more we can get to know
them. Coming to know God
is something like that.

*What are some of the ways you
come to know God?*

13

God's Own Word to Us

Faith Focus

How do we access God's light that shines within all of us?

Faith Vocabulary

Divine Revelation. God making himself and the divine plan of creation and salvation known over time.

Sacred Tradition. The passing on of the Gospel in the Church through the power and guidance of the Holy Spirit.

Have you ever worked at a computer? You know it contains a lot of information and other helpful data. Sometimes, though, it is a challenge to access this data. Knowing God is sometimes like that for some people too.

God's Word Within Us

God writes his word on our hearts, plants his love deep in our souls. Jeremiah the Prophet shared this truth about God and ourselves when he wrote:

[God said:] I will give them a heart with which to understand that I am the LORD. They shall be my people and I will be their God, for they shall return to me with their whole heart.
JEREMIAH 24:7

Whether we are happy or sad, successful or in trouble, God's word is always there. His word placed within us is at work in everyone. It acts like the sun to light up our days and like the moon to help us see at night.

Now our challenge is to access and understand the light of God's word. Here are some ways that will help us:

- Pray to the Holy Spirit. The Holy Spirit is our helper and teacher. He is the One who helps us truly understand all that God makes known to us and has revealed to us in Jesus Christ. The Holy Spirit dwells in our hearts and gives us the grace to call God "Abba," our Father.
- Come to know Jesus Christ personally. In giving us his Son, Jesus, God the Father gave us himself. Everything he wants to say to us can be found in Jesus Christ.

- Grow in our understanding of **Divine Revelation** through the prayerful reading of Sacred Scripture, the inspired Word of God.

    All scripture is inspired by God and is useful for teaching, for refutation, for correction, and for training in righteousness, so that one who belongs to God may be competent, equipped for every good work.   2 TIMOTHY 3:16

- Study **Sacred Tradition** and the teachings of the Church. Sacred Tradition and Sacred Scripture make up a single source, or deposit, of the Revelation. Together they are like a mirror in which the Church contemplates God.

- Listen to the preaching and teaching of the popes and bishops. In the name of Christ, they teach us and guide us in living our faith. They help us understand Divine Revelation more clearly and accurately and live it in practical ways.

Why did God place his word within our heart?

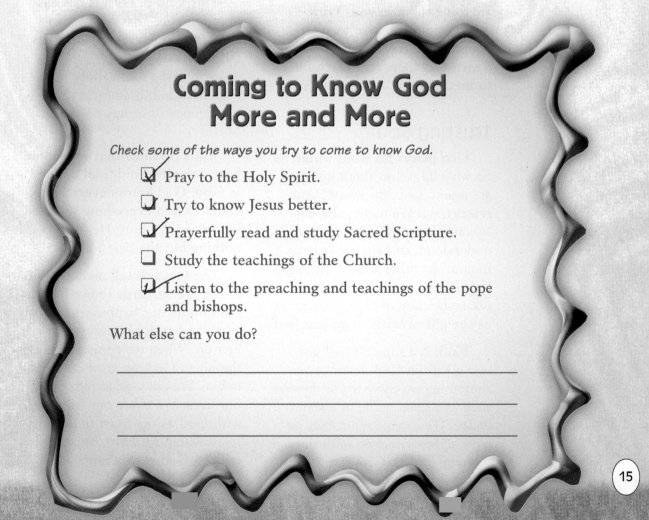

Coming to Know God More and More

Check some of the ways you try to come to know God.

☑ Pray to the Holy Spirit.

☑ Try to know Jesus better.

☑ Prayerfully read and study Sacred Scripture.

☐ Study the teachings of the Church.

☑ Listen to the preaching and teachings of the pope and bishops.

What else can you do?

_____

_____

_____

Faith Vocabulary

faith. A supernatural gift and power from God; the gift of God's invitation to us that enables us to know and believe in him, and the power God gives us to freely respond to his invitation.

Who are the teachers or relatives you trust and admire completely? You know that they care about what is best for you and that they will guide you well. You know that they will not do anything to harm you. What response do you give to such people? You trust them. You depend on them and reach out to them to give you guidance.

Trusting God

God places his word within us. So what do we do about it? We are free to say, "So what?" and reject God. We might also say, "Okay, God, there is a lot I don't understand; so help me believe in you." In other words, we can try to grow in confidence and understanding of God, who gives us the gift of **faith** to do just that.

Faith is a supernatural gift, or a gift from God. It is not something we can earn or deserve, such as a good grade or a scout badge. We cannot claim that we have achieved a deep faith through our own efforts. Growing in faith

does not work that way. We must pray for the grace to truly come to know God and respond to his gift to know and believe in him and all that he has revealed.

This kind of faith is not easy or automatic. That is why the Letter to the Hebrews describes faith this way:

> Faith is the realization of what is hoped for and evidence of things not seen.
> HEBREWS 11:1

Jesus revealed that we should have complete and total faith in God. God knows everything about us and everything we need before we ask him. He wants nothing but the best for us.

The Gospels tell us that Jesus' whole life on earth showed us that God wants our happiness now on earth and with him forever in heaven. When we come to believe this about God, we grow in our faith in him. We put God at the center of our lives. We value our friendship with God as the most important relationship we have. This is what faith in God is all about.

The Israelites were powerless slaves in Egypt, where Pharaoh's army was the strongest in the world. Nonetheless, Moses and Miriam were willing to believe that God somehow would deliver them to a new homeland that he had promised to them.

Moses and Miriam were willing to believe in God when all the odds were against them. They knew God would keep his word to them. God did. Successfully, the Israelites journeyed from slavery to freedom.

God invites us to believe in him as Moses and Miriam did. Like Moses and Miriam we are free to say yes or no. We are also free to ask God questions, as Moses did, so we can grow in our faith and trust in God.

Miriam

A Story of Faith

Moses and Miriam both were willing to submit their lives in faith to God. Recall what you have learned about the story of Moses and the Israelites.

How would you define faith?

Faith-Filled People

Miriam

Miriam the Prophet was the sister of Moses and Aaron. After the Israelites crossed the Red Sea during the Exodus, Miriam gathered the women of Israel. With tambourine in hand, she led the women in song and dance as she sang, "Sing to the LORD, for he is gloriously triumphant" (Exodus 15:21).

Growing in Faith

Describe someone who has helped you grow in your faith. What did this person do to help you? How did you respond to this person?

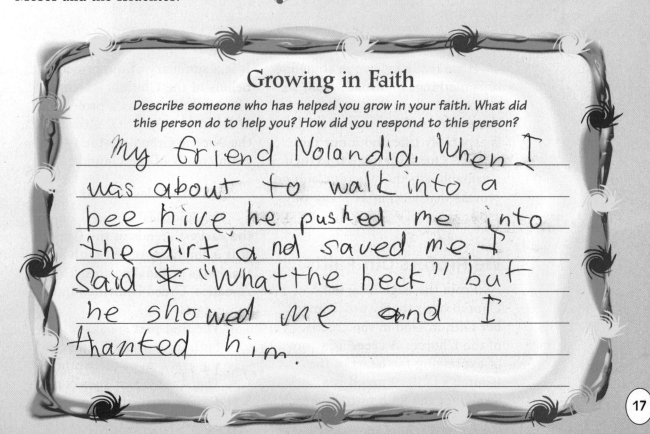

My friend Noland did. When I was about to walk into a bee hive, he pushed me into the dirt and saved me. I said "What the heck" but he showed me and I thanked him.

Faith Vocabulary

creed. A statement of beliefs, a profession of faith; a summary of the principal beliefs of the Church.

If we really believe in someone or something, we usually want to tell others about that person or share that truth with others. That is especially true about our faith in God. Our faith in God is such a valuable gift that we proclaim or profess that faith in as many ways as we can.

We Profess Our Faith

From the beginning the Church has proudly proclaimed her faith in God in the creeds of the Church. A **creed** is a way of expressing the heart of the Church's faith. A creed is a symbol of the faith of the Church.

It is a summary of the principal beliefs of the Church, which is often proclaimed as a profession of faith. The Apostles' Creed and the Nicene Creed are the two main creeds of the Church.

Apostles' Creed

The Apostles' Creed is one of the earliest creeds of the Church. It is a summary of the faith and teachings of the Apostles. The Apostles' Creed is divided into three parts.

- The first part speaks of our faith in God the Father and the creation of the world.
- The second part speaks of Jesus Christ, the Son of God,

18

and our Redemption—or the saving activity of God through Christ delivering humanity from sin.

- The third part speaks of God the Holy Spirit and our sanctification. Our sanctification is the gift of sharing in God's life and love and living and growing in friendship and communion with him with the help of the Holy Spirit.

The Nicene Creed

The Nicene Creed is the creed we most often pray at Mass. When we proclaim the Nicene Creed at Sunday Mass, the grace of the Holy Spirit helps us give our hearts in faith and trust to God the Holy Trinity. We unite ourselves with the Church throughout the world.

QUESTION *What are the main beliefs of the Church in the Apostles' Creed?*

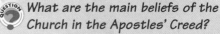
Our Catholic Identity

Nicene Creed

The creed we usually profess at Mass on Sundays was written by the Church at the Council of Nicaea in 325 and the Council of Constantinople in 381. This creed clearly states that the Father, Son, and Holy Spirit are one God in three Persons. Jesus Christ is true God and true man. He is equally God as the Father and the Holy Spirit are.

Symbols of Our Faith

In the circles create symbols that represent each part of the Apostles' Creed. Describe each symbol with a statement of belief.

The cross shows sacrafice

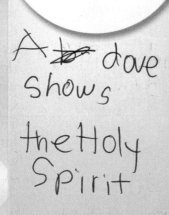

A ~~b~~ dove shows the Holy Spirit

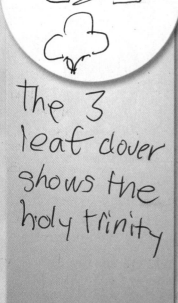

the 3 leaf clover shows the holy trinity

Our Church Makes a Difference

World Youth Day

Every two to three years Catholic youth from all over the world gather together to profess and share their faith in Jesus Christ. They gather at the invitation of the pope to grow in their faith and friendship with Jesus and to live their faith within their communities.

In 2005 Pope Benedict XVI gathered with Catholic youth from all over the world in Cologne, Germany. This was the ninth World Youth Day. The previous eight World Youth Days were celebrated in 1987 in Buenos Aires, Argentina; in 1989 in Santiago de Compostela, Spain; in 1991 in Czestochowa, Poland; in 1993 in Denver, United States of America; in 1995 in Manila, Philippines; in 1997 in Paris, France; in 2000 in Rome, Italy; and in 2002 in Toronto, Canada.

During World Youth Day celebrations, Catholic youth celebrate their faith. They deepen their understanding of the teachings and practices of the Catholic Church and discuss ways to live their faith. They return to their countries and parishes filled with commitment to live the Gospel with inspired enthusiasm. They return home to build up the kingdom of justice and peace announced by Jesus Christ.

 What are some ways your parish brings youth together to celebrate, grow in, and live their faith?

Twentieth World Youth Day
Cologne, Germany, August 2005

What Difference Does Faith Make in My Life?

The Holy Spirit continuously invites you to grow in your faith and friendship with God. He helps you live the gift of faith with your whole heart.

Write three statements. Write one that expresses your faith in God the Father; a second, your faith in Jesus, God the Son; and a third, your faith in the Holy Spirit. Then describe how that faith helps you make decisions each day.

I Believe in God

1 I believe God made the Earth.

2 I believe that Jesus lived,

3 I believe the Holy Spirit is real.

My Faith Choice

I profess my faith in God the Holy Trinity each day both by my words and by my actions. This week I will profess my faith in God by

_____

_____ .

We Believe in God

Leader: At Baptism we first profess our faith in God with the Church.
Let us pray this profession of faith, which is taken from the
rite of Baptism.
Let us profess our faith.
Do you reject sin
so as to live in the freedom of God's children?

All: I do.

Leader: Do you reject the glamour of evil,
and refuse to be mastered by sin?

All: I do.

Leader: Do you reject Satan,
father of sin and prince of darkness?

All: I do.

Leader: Do you believe in God,
the Father almighty, creator of heaven and earth?

All: I do.

Leader: Do you believe in Jesus Christ,
his only Son, our Lord,
who was born of the Virgin Mary,
was crucified, died, and was buried,
rose from the dead,
and is now seated at the right hand of the Father?

All: I do.

Leader: Do you believe in the Holy Spirit,
the holy catholic Church,
the communion of saints,
the forgiveness of sins,
the resurrection of the body,
and the life everlasting?

All: I do.

Leader: This is our faith. This is the faith of the Church.
We are proud to profess it, in Christ Jesus our Lord.
FROM THE "PROFESSION OF FAITH," RITE OF BAPTISM FOR CHILDREN 57

We Remember

What I Have Learned

Match each term in column A with its meaning in column B.

Column A

_a_ 1. faith

_e_ 2. Holy Trinity

_b_ 3. Nicene Creed

_c_ 4. Redemption

_d_ 5. sanctification

Column B

a. our acceptance of God and our willingness to receive his Revelation

b. the gift of sharing in God's life and love

c. the saving activity of God through Christ delivering humanity from sin

d. a summary of the principal beliefs of the Church

e. the mystery of one God in three divine Persons

Answer the following.

6. Name some of the ways we can grow in our understanding of God's revelation of himself to us.

   We can donate to the needy.

7. Describe the three main parts of the Apostles' Creed.

   The three main parts of the creed are parts of the creed

8. Explain why the Church expresses her faith in creeds.

   The Church express her faith in creeds because they profess faith that way.

Growing in Faith

One important thing I learned this week is

~~Pray~~ _listen To God_

This is important because

I pray

What will people see me doing as I live my faith choice this week?

~~I pray~~ _Donate money to poor_

This Week . . .

In chapter 1, "The Gift of Faith," your child learned more about the gift of faith. God reaches out to us and invites us to come to know and believe in him. He invites us to make him the center of our lives and to discover the experience and meaning of true happiness. God created us to know, love, and serve him and to be happy with him now on earth and forever in heaven. The whole life of Jesus Christ on earth most clearly and fully reveals that divine invitation.

For more on the teachings of the Catholic Church on the gift of faith, see *Catechism of the Catholic Church* paragraph numbers 26–38, 50–95, and 144–197.

Sharing God's Word

Read together Jeremiah 24:7. Emphasize that God created us with his word in our hearts and his love deep in our souls.

Praying

In this chapter your child prayed a profession of faith based on the "Profession of Faith" in the rite of Baptism. Read and pray together this prayer on page 22.

Making a Difference

Choose one of the following activities to do as a family or design a similar activity of your own.

- Learn the Apostles' Creed by heart. Make a puzzle to help you. Write the creed on a piece of paper. Then cut the paper into small pieces. Assemble the puzzle to become more familiar with the words of the Apostles' Creed.

- Talk about the things that your family "gives its heart to." Identify which of those things are signs that God is at the center of the life of your family. Discuss how these things are signs to others that you are followers of Christ.

- Read together Exodus 15:1–18. Talk about how much Moses, Miriam, and the Israelites trusted God.

For more ideas on ways your family can live your faith, visit the "Faith First for Families" page at **www.FaithFirst.com**. You will find the "About Your Child" page helpful as your sixth grader begins a new year.

God's Own Word to Us

We Pray

Your word is a lamp
  for my feet,
  a light for my path.
            PSALM 119:105

Lord God, send the Holy
Spirit to open our minds
and hearts to your holy
word. May we share the
good news of your love
with all we meet.   Amen.

*How do you find the information
that you need?*

Think of a project you have
had to do recently. Maybe you
went to the library and did
research on the Internet, or
interviewed people. There are
many ways to grow in
understanding and living the
gift of faith.

*Why is reading and praying the
Bible vital to your life of faith?*

Going to the Source

Faith Focus

How did God communicate about himself through the Bible?

Faith Vocabulary

inspiration of the Bible.
The Holy Spirit guiding the human writers of Sacred Scripture so that they would faithfully and accurately communicate the word of God, who is the principal author of the Scriptures.

When we want to study history, we turn to a history book. When we do a science project, we use a science book. Of course, we can use the Internet to learn many things too. However, when we want to learn about God, we can go to God's own word to us. We can read the Bible, or Sacred Scripture. Through the Sacred Scripture God continues to talk to us about himself and his love for us.

God's Inspired Word

The Bible is the inspired Word of God. This means that God acted through human authors so that they wrote what he wanted. We call this the **inspiration of the Bible.** The various human writers of Sacred Scripture only wrote the truths about God and his saving love for us that he revealed for our Salvation. The Bible contains seventy-three books. These are found in the Old Testament and the New Testament.

Antique illustrated Bible on walls of Mexican mission; San Javier, Baja California, Mexico

Old Testament

The forty-six books of the Old Testament are often grouped this way.

- The Pentateuch, or the first five books of the Bible, tells of God revealing himself and making the Covenant with his people. These five books of the Old Testament are also called the written Torah. The word *torah* means "guide" or "teaching." The Pentateuch, or Torah, contains the basic laws revealed to the Israelites that would guide them in living the Covenant.
- The sixteen historical books tell of how God's people sometimes lived the Covenant well and at other times did not.
- The seven wisdom books share advice on how to live the Covenant.
- The eighteen prophetic books remind God's people to be faithful to the Covenant and that he will always be faithful to them.

New Testament

The twenty-seven books of the New Testament are grouped this way.

- The four written accounts of the Gospel are the heart of Sacred Scripture because Jesus Christ is their center.
- The Acts of the Apostles tells the story of the early Church.
- The thirteen epistles, or letters, of Saint Paul help us understand the Church's faith in Jesus and how to live that faith.

- Eight other letters in the New Testament also help us understand and live our faith.
- The Book of Revelation encourages Christians to remain faithful to Jesus Christ when they suffer because of their faith in him, trusting in his faithfulness to them.

QUESTION What does it mean to say the Bible is the inspired Word of God?

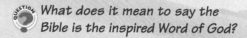
Reading the Bible

Locate and read the following passages in your Bible. Describe what each tells us about God's love for us.

1. Genesis 1:27 _He made us all with diffrent kinds of talents._

2. 1 Samuel 17:32–37 _We are filled with lots of courage._

3. Mark 11:20–26 _Forgive people so God can forgive you._

4. Philippians 4:4–9 _Be happy because the Lord is near._

Faith Focus

What does the name that God gives to himself tell us about him?

Faith Vocabulary

YHWH. The Hebrew letters for the name of God that he revealed to Moses.

Moses and the Burning Bush,
Leslie Xuereb,
contemporary French artist

When we tell our name to another person, we give them a part of our true selves. God freely chose to share his name with Moses and the Israelites. The Pentateuch gives us the account of God revealing his name to Moses.

God Reveals His Name

One day while Moses was tending sheep, he saw a bush that was in flames but was not being consumed by the fire. Curious, Moses walked toward this strange sight. As he approached the burning bush, he heard a voice coming from the bush, saying:

"Moses! Moses! . . . I am the God of your father, . . . the God of Abraham, the God of Isaac, the God of Jacob. . . . Come, now! I will send you to Pharaoh to lead my people, the Israelites, out of Egypt."

EXODUS 3:4, 6, 10

You can just imagine how confused Moses must have been. So he asked:

"[W]hen I go to the Israelites and say to them, 'The God of your fathers has sent me to you,' if they ask me, 'What is his name?' what am I to tell them?"

EXODUS 3:13

God replied:

"I am who am. . . . This is what you shall tell the Israelites: I AM sent me to you."

EXODUS 3:14

Through this Old Testament story God shares his name with Moses, with the Israelites, and with all people. He says, "I am who am." In Hebrew that name is **YHWH.**

By naming himself YHWH, God is making it known that he is always with all people. Wherever we are, God is always there for us.

Hebrew letters for the divine name

In thinking about the divine name, these are some of the things we have come to know and believe about God:

- God is a mystery who will never be fully grasped.
- God says, "I will be with you."
- God is always faithful to his people.
- God enters history in a loving way.

- God is close to his people.
- God knows his people and their needs.
- God is ready to stand by his people in their times of trouble.

 What did God reveal about himself at the burning bush?

READING THE BIBLE

Look up and read Matthew 3:17 in your Bible.
[Matthew = Book of the Bible; 3 = chapter of the book; 17 = verse of the chapter]

Write what the passage reveals about Jesus.

It reveals that ~~God~~ Jesus is the son of God and God is pleased with the doing of Jesus.

Faith Focus

How does the Covenant unfold in the Bible?

Faith Vocabulary

Covenant. The solemn commitment of fidelity that God and God's People made with one another, which was renewed in Christ, the new and everlasting Covenant.

It is important to share over and over again the important events in the life of our family. Sharing the stories of these events helps us understand and pass them on from generation to generation. This helps us know who we are as a family and what makes our family unique.

The Covenant

The **Covenant** is the most important event in the history of God's people. The story of the Covenant begins in the very first book of the Bible and unfolds with more and more detail throughout the Bible. Here are some of those details found in the Old Testament:

- God promised that from Eve's descendants would come one who would conquer the tempter, the devil. God said:

  "He [the descendant] will strike at your head, while you [the serpent] strike at his heel."
  GENESIS 3:15

- God entered the Covenant with Noah and all living things. God promised that the Covenant will remain in force as long as the world lasts. He said to Noah and to his sons with him:

  "See, I am now establishing my covenant with you and your descendants after you and with every living creature. . . . This is the sign that I am giving for all ages to come, of the covenant."
  GENESIS 9:12

- God promised Abraham that he would be the father of a great people, saying:

  "I will make of you a great nation,
  and I will bless you;
  I will make your name great,
  so that you will be a blessing."
  GENESIS 12:2

- At Mount Sinai God promised Moses and the Israelites that he would be their God. They promised that they would be his people and live the Law he revealed to them. God said:

> "[I]f you hearken to my voice and keep my covenant, you shall be my special possession, dearer to me than all other people, though all the earth is mine. You shall be to me a kingdom of priests, a holy nation."
> EXODUS 19:5–6

- The prophets reminded God's people to live the Covenant and announced a new and everlasting

Covenant. Through Jeremiah the Prophet, God said:

> I will make with them an eternal covenant, never to cease doing good to them.
> JEREMIAH 32:40

Jesus is the new and everlasting Covenant. In him God's final Covenant with the world has been made.

QUESTION *What do we learn about God from the biblical accounts of the Covenant?*

Abraham

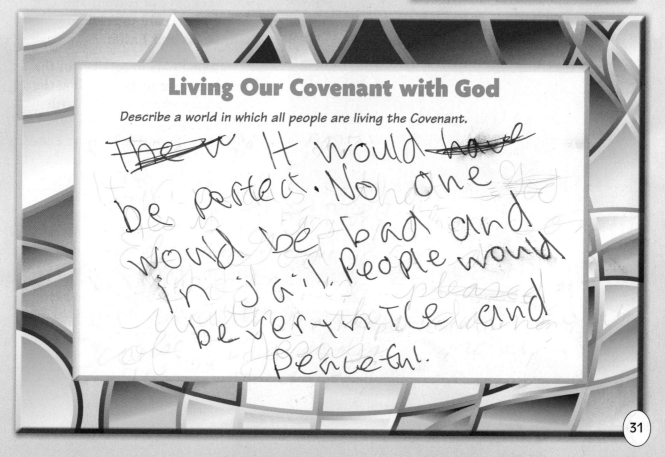

Living Our Covenant with God

Describe a world in which all people are living the Covenant.

It would be perfect. No one would be bad and in jail. People would be very nice and peaceful.

Services of the Word

Bible reading and faith sharing are vital to the faith life of Catholics. We gain a great deal of inspiration and understanding of our faith by reading Sacred Scripture quietly to ourselves or by prayerfully reading the Scriptures and sharing our faith as a group. Reading the Scriptures makes us aware of God's presence with us. It guides us in living the Covenant God has made with us in Jesus.

The Church encourages us to take part in Scripture services, or services of the word, on the vigils of solemn feasts, such as Pentecost, on Sundays, and on holy days. Taking part in these services on the weekdays of Advent and Lent helps us prepare to celebrate Christmas and Easter.

Taking part in services of the word and prayerfully reading the Scriptures either alone or with other people connects the Word of God with our daily lives. The Word of God truly becomes "a light for [our] path" (Psalm 119:105). We make living the Commandments and the Beatitudes come alive in the world. We become lights in the world as Jesus commanded us to be.

QUESTION *What will you do to set time aside to read the Bible often each week?*

What Difference Does Faith Make in My Life?

God is always communicating his word to us. When you prayerfully read the Scriptures alone or with others, God himself speaks to all the People of God, the Church, and to you.

Write three ways your life could be changed by reading, listening to, and studying the Bible.

The Word of the Lord

My life could be changed by reading the Bible because I will know more about God. Listening to the Bible makes me hear God's voice. When I study the Bible I will have more knowledge.

My Faith Choice

This week I will read and listen to God's word and share my thoughts and feelings with him. I will

read the Bible more often.

Your Word Is a Light for My Path

Lectio divina is an important form of prayer of the Church. It is a form of meditation. Follow these steps. Spend quiet time with God, reading and listening to his word.

1. Sit quietly. Be aware that God is present with you. The Holy Spirit dwells within you.

2. Imagine yourself someplace where you can talk and listen to God.

3. Open your Bible to a favorite passage. Sign your forehead, lips, and chest over your heart with a small sign of the cross.

4. Prayerfully and reverently read the passage you selected.

5. Take time to talk and listen to God. Say, "Your word, Lord, is a light for my path" (based on Psalm 119:105).

6. After a few quiet moments, ask the Holy Spirit, "What is your word saying to me?" Write down any key words or phrases that you remember.

7. Make a faith decision and put God's word into action.

We Remember

What I Have Learned

1. Write a brief paragraph describing the Church's teaching about Sacred Scripture. Use these faith terms.

> Bible   inspiration of the Bible
>
> canon of Scripture

The Bible has the inspiration of the Bible ~~The canon of Scripture is also in a part of the Bible.~~

The ~~inspires~~ Holy Spirit communicates with writers to write the word of God in the Bible

Answer the following.

2. What does it mean to say that Sacred Scripture is God's own word to us?

It means God is talking to us through the Bible.

3. What does God tell us through the story of Moses and the burning bush?

That I he would be with us at all times

4. How did God fulfill his promise of a new and everlasting Covenant?

He ~~gave~~ sent Jesus to us to save us from our sins

To Help You Remember

1. The Holy Spirit guided, or inspired, the human writers of Sacred Scripture to faithfully and accurately communicate the Word of God.

2. Through the Bible God reveals himself and his loving plan of goodness for the world and for all people.

3. The Bible tells the story of the Covenant that God and his people freely entered into.

Growing in Faith

One important thing I learned this week is

God is with us where ever we are

This is important because

We will have hope.

What will people see me doing as I live my faith choice this week?

I will be brave

This Week . . .

In chapter 2, "God's Own Word to Us," your child learned more about the gift of Sacred Scripture, the Bible. Sacred Scripture is the inspired Word of God. The heart of Sacred Scripture is the Gospel because Jesus Christ, the Incarnate Word of God, is the heart and fullness of God's Revelation. The Holy Spirit guided, or inspired, the human writers of Sacred Scripture to faithfully and truthfully communicate God's word. The Bible contains the forty-six books of the Old Testament and the twenty-seven books of the New Testament named by the Church to be the inspired Word of God. These books are listed in and make up the canon of Scripture.

For more on the teachings of the Catholic Church on the mystery of God's word to us revealed in Sacred Scripture, see *Catechism of the Catholic Church* paragraph numbers 101–133.

Sharing God's Word

Read together 1 Thessalonians 2:13 and 2 Timothy 3:16–17. Emphasize that the Bible is the inspired Word of God.

Praying

In this chapter your child prayed a lectio divina, or a prayer of meditation. Read and pray together this prayer on page 34.

Making a Difference

Choose one of the following activities to do as a family or design a similar activity of your own.

- This week use Bible stories for your family prayer. Invite a different family member to choose the story each day, and read it as part of your grace before meals.

- Watch television as a family. Carefully listen to the events that are making the headlines. Now imagine that you are a prophet. Discuss what you would tell the people.

- Create and decorate a special place in your home to display a Bible. Open the Bible each day to a favorite Bible story.

For more ideas on ways your family can live your faith, visit the "Faith First for Families" page at www.FaithFirst.com. Click on "Bible Stories" and discuss the Bible story as a family this week.

Living the Covenant
A Scripture Story

We Pray

Happy are those whose hope is in the LORD God.

BASED ON PSALM 146:5

Father, send the Holy Spirit to those you send into the world to announce the Gospel. Amen.

Who in your school has been chosen to represent the views of the students to the teachers? How do they know what to say?

Ambassadors represent their countries. They speak, not for themselves, but for the governments of the nations they represent. Biblical prophets were chosen by God to speak in his name to the Israelites.

Name some of the prophets in the Bible about whom you have learned.

Byzantine art of six unnamed Old Testament prophets

Bible Background

Faith Focus

What were the names of the prophets? What were some of their primary concerns?

Faith Vocabulary

fidelity. A word meaning "faithfulness," the virtue of keeping our promises and fulfilling our responsibilities to God and to other people.

hope. The theological virtue by which we desire and trust that God will fulfill all his promises, especially the promise of eternal happiness.

The prophets in the Bible all shared a common calling. You might say that they were God's ambassadors. They spoke to God's people not in their own name but in the name of God. In other words, God chose to speak through the prophets' words and actions to his people.

The Prophets

The canon of Scripture contains the teachings of eighteen prophets. The prophetic books include the writings of the major prophets (Isaiah, Jeremiah, and Ezekiel), the twelve minor prophets, and the books of Baruch, Lamentations, and Daniel. The major prophets have the longest prophetic books. The minor prophets have shorter works represented in the Bible.

Often a prophet simply preached their message. At other times, the message was delivered in a more dramatic way, such as by wearing a yoke that was used to control oxen. This really got the attention of their listeners. The message of the prophets centered on the two themes of fidelity to the Covenant and hope in the future.

Fidelity

The prophets often spoke about the **fidelity** (and infidelity) of the Israelites to the Covenant. Over and over again they admonished the Israelites when they failed to meet their responsibilities and were unfaithful to the promises that they made to God.

When addressing the issue of fidelity (or infidelity), the prophets focused on the three themes of true worship, the relationship of God's people with other nations, and doing works of justice for people, especially for the poor and weak. The very first chapter of the Book of the Prophet Isaiah helps us understand these three themes.

- **True worship.** The prophet Isaiah told the people that they had forgotten to worship God from their hearts. (See Isaiah 1:11.)

- **Relationship with other nations.** Isaiah warned the people that they had become like pagan nations. (See Isaiah 1:10.)

- **Doing works of justice.** Isaiah also told the people to act justly and, in a special way, to help the poorest and weakest people. (See Isaiah 1:17.)

The Scroll of Isaiah, Chapter 6:7–7:15, Dead Sea Scrolls

Hope

The prophets often invited the Israelites to place their **hope** in God. While God's people were not always faithful to him, he would always be faithful to them. He would send them his faithful servant. (See Isaiah 53:11.)

Above all, the poor and humble will be signs of this hope. Such holy women as Sarah, Rebecca, Rachel, Miriam, Deborah, Hannah, Judith, and Esther kept this hope of Israel's salvation alive. All these promises were fulfilled in Jesus Christ. In him we place our hope.

 What things can you do to live a life of hope?

Isaiah the Prophet,
sixteenth-century icon

A Prophet's Message for Today

What can we do today about these three issues from the prophet Isaiah?

1. True worship ___Go to Church and pray a lot.___

2. Relationship with other nations ___You can make peace with them.___

3. Doing works of justice ___Help the bad people be good.___

Reading the Word of God

Faith Focus

How did God challenge and bring hope to his people during the Exile?

Faith Vocabulary

Exile. The time in the history of God's people when many of them were forced to leave their homeland and live in the country of their conquerors.

There was a time in the history of God's people when they seemed to have very little hope. It was a time of great infidelity of the Israelites to the Covenant. It was a time known as the **Exile.**

The Prophet Baruch

During the Exile God's people were forced to leave their homeland and live in the country of their conquerors, the Assyrians and Babylonians. During this time of suffering, God sent the prophet Baruch and other prophets to speak to his people in Babylon.

Baruch's message is found in the Book of Baruch. This six-chapter book contains different kinds of writing. This passage is part of a poem called "Praise of Wisdom in the Law of Moses."

Hear, O Israel, the
   commandments of life:
listen, and know prudence!
How is it, Israel,
   that you are in the land of
    your foes,
   grown old in a foreign
    land, . . .
You have forsaken the fountain
   of wisdom!
   Had you walked in the way
    of God,
   you would have dwelt in
    enduring peace.
Learn where prudence is,
   where strength, where
    understanding;
That you may know also
   where are length of days,
    and life,
   where light of the eyes, and
    peace.

Who has found the place of
    wisdom,
    who has entered into her
        treasuries? . . .
Yet he who knows all things
    knows her;
    he has probed her by his
        knowledge—
He who established the earth
    for all time,
    and filled it with four-footed
        beasts; . . .
Before whom the stars at
    their posts
    shine and rejoice;
When he calls them, they
    answer, "Here we are!"
    shining with joy for their
        Maker.
Such is our God;
    no other is to be compared
        to him:
He has traced out all the way
    of understanding,
    and has given her to Jacob,
        his servant,
    to Israel, his beloved son.

She is the book of the precepts
    of God,
    the law that endures forever;
All who cling to her will live,
    but those will die who
        forsake her.
Turn, O Jacob, and receive her:
    walk by her light toward
        splendor.

    BARUCH 3:9–15, 32–38; 4:1–4

In this poem, Baruch was
speaking to the people who were
suffering terribly. Taken from
their homes in Jerusalem, they
were forced to walk many miles
away to the foreign country of
Babylon. Baruch tried to help
them understand how this had
happened and how they could
find true happiness. They should
have hope. God would always be
faithful to them.

**What does Baruch say about
wisdom?**

Old Testament Prophets	
836 B.C.	JOEL
780 B.C.	JONAH
765 B.C.	AMOS
760 B.C.	ISAIAH
755 B.C.	HOSEA
740 B.C.	MICAH
630 B.C.	NAHUM
625 B.C.	ZEPHANIAH
609 B.C.	HABAKKUK
609 B.C.	JEREMIAH
609 B.C.	BARUCH
586 B.C.	EZEKIEL
586 B.C.	DANIEL
586 B.C.	OBADIAH
520 B.C.	HAGGAI
520 B.C.	ZECHARIAH
400 B.C.	MALACHI

Acting Wisely

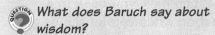

*Think about choices you have made that resulted in
unhappiness. Describe one of those choices. What can
you do to make better choices?*

One choice is when
I made my brother
mad. I can make better
choices by not being
mean

Understanding the Word of God

Faith Focus

What is the meaning of Baruch's message to his exiled people?

Faith Vocabulary

prudence. One of the four moral virtues, a virtue that helps us know what is truly good for us and how to choose the right way of achieving that good.

wisdom. One of the seven Gifts of the Holy Spirit, which helps us know God's plan of creation and salvation and make moral decisions according to that divine plan.

End of Exile, illustrated manuscript of Flavius Josephus, Jewish historian born in A.D. 37

When have you been in a situation when you let things get out of control and the situation became too difficult for you to handle—when things seemed hopeless? Perhaps someone pointed out to you what you did wrong, advised you to work at correcting what you did wrong, and assured you, "Work at it and things will improve." Baruch's message to the Israelites was something like that.

Baruch's Challenge

Baruch told the Israelites that they had brought this tragedy upon themselves. It was the consequence of their own choices.

In so many words, Baruch told them that their own bad choices had sent them into exile. They did not act wisely. He said:

Had you walked in the
way of God,
you would have dwelt in
enduring peace.
BARUCH 3:13

Baruch's message did not end there. The prophet gave the Israelites hope for the future. He told them that they needed to act with prudence and wisdom. Such decisions would return them to their homeland, and they would live in peace.

Baruch, mosaic

Prudence

Prudence is a blend of good judgment and self-control. It is the ability to realize that bad judgment can lead to bad consequences. God's people did not act prudently when they turned their backs on God and broke his law. They thought worshiping the false gods of their neighbors would bring them power and wealth. They were wrong. The real consequence of their decision was this: They lost their homeland.

Wisdom

Baruch speaks of God's **wisdom** as a person. He writes:

All who cling to her will live, but those will die who forsake her.   Baruch 4:1

The prophet urges God's people to realize that if they are looking for life, they can find it only in God's word. They need to turn to God and keep their eyes fixed on him. When they do, they will leave their sadness behind and come into God's wonderful light.

How might people today be acting in a way similar to the people in Baruch's time?

✝ **Our Catholic Identity**

Apostolate of the Laity

All laypeople share in the apostolate, or work, of the Church. The laity are all the baptized who are not ordained or members of a religious community. You are a member of the laity, or laypeople, of the Church. You have the responsibility to be a messenger of the Gospel in your school and place where you live, on the athletic field or dance studio—wherever you are. The Church needs you.

Baruch's Message

What was Baruch's message to the people?

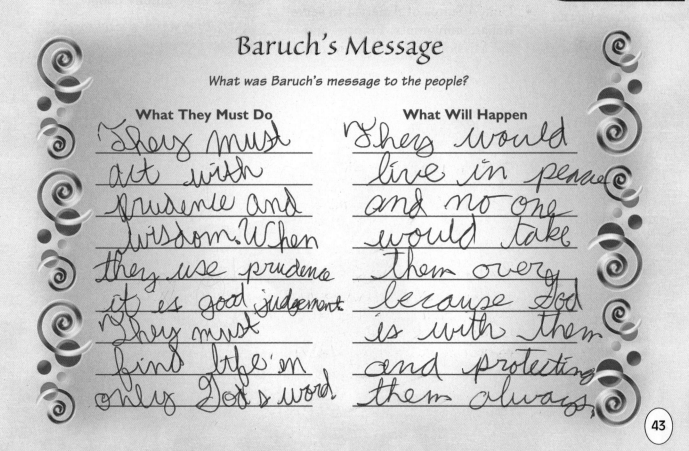

What They Must Do	What Will Happen
They must act with prudence and wisdom. When they use prudence it is good judgement. They must find life in only God's word.	They would live in peace and no one would take them over because God is with them and protecting them always.

Saint Frances Cabrini (1850–1917), who emigrated from Italy to the United States in 1889 and became a naturalized citizen in 1909

Messengers of Hope

Saint Frances Xavier Cabrini, "Mother Cabrini," was the first citizen of the United States of America to be named a saint. When she was young, geography was her favorite subject in school, and she dreamed of becoming a missionary.

In 1874, at the age of twenty-four, Frances organized the Missionary Sisters of the Sacred Heart at the invitation of her bishop. Later, Pope Leo XIII asked her and the Missionary Sisters to travel to the United States of America to serve Italian immigrants. Frances and the Missionary Sisters arrived in New York City on March 31, 1889. For the next twenty-eight years, they worked together to build hospitals, orphanages, and schools across the United States from New York to Chicago to Seattle.

Today the Missionary Sisters work in Argentina, Brazil, Chile, Panama, Spain, France, and Italy, as well as the United States. They are often joined by the Cabrini Mission Corps to continue the work begun by Mother Cabrini. The Cabrini Mission Corps is a group of laypeople, both single and married. They volunteer for a minimum of one year in the United States and a minimum of eighteen months overseas. Together the Missionary Sisters of the Sacred Heart and the Cabrini Mission Corps live as signs of hope among people.

 How can you be a messenger of hope to people?

Cabrini Missioners, Baguio City, Philippines

What Difference Does Faith Make in My Life?

The Holy Spirit gives you the gift of wisdom. When people see you doing what is good, when you make wise choices, you are showing people that God is at the center of your life. Your choices benefit both yourself and other people too.

Describe a time when you have needed to make an important choice about living your Catholic faith. Tell who helped you and how that person helped you make a wise choice.

Practicing Wisdom

Wise Choice I Made

to not argue with anyone at all.

Who Helped Me

My parents and brother helped me.

Wisdom Shared with Me

Never pick on someone ever.

My Faith Choice

This week I will think about what my choices to live the Catholic faith are saying to others. Before I make a decision to say or do something, I will

think before I say.

Words of Hope

Leader: Isaiah the Prophet spoke words of hope to the people of Israel living in exile. The Hebrew name Isaiah means "YHWH is salvation." Jesus, the Savior of the world, is the hope of all Christians.

Let us listen to these words of hope spoken to us by God through his prophet Isaiah.

Reader: A reading from the book of the prophet Isaiah.

> Comfort, give comfort to my people,
>   says your God.
> Speak tenderly to Jerusalem, and proclaim to her
>   that her service is at an end,
>   her guilt is expiated;
> Indeed, she has received from the hand of the LORD
>   double for all her sins.
>
> ISAIAH 40:1–2

The word of the Lord.

All: Thanks be to God.

Leader: Let us pray together and express the hope we have in Jesus Christ, the Savior of the world.

All: O my God,
relying on your infinite goodness
    and promises,
we hope to attain forgiveness of
    our sins and life everlasting in
    the eternal kingdom
through the merits of Jesus Christ,
    our Lord and Redeemer. Amen.

We Remember

What I Have Learned

Circle T if the statements are true and F if the statements are false. Make the false statements true.

1. The promises God made through the prophets of the Old Testament were fulfilled in Jesus Christ. **(T)** F

2. Baruch the Prophet told the Israelites that they brought the tragedy of the Exile upon themselves. **(T)** F

3. The consequence of the Israelites' decision to abandon the Covenant was their new wealth and power. T **(F)**

4. God always remains faithful, even to those who are unfaithful to him. T F

5. Wisdom is the cardinal virtue, or habit, of a person blending good judgment and self-control.  T F

Answer the following.

6. What work did the prophets do among God's people?

   They tell God's word to keep them faithful

7. What does Baruch say about God's wisdom?

   God's wisdom is very strong and very good.

8. Where does Baruch say the people can find life?

   People ~~could had~~ had to use wisdom and prudence

To Help You Remember

1. Fidelity to God and hope in his fidelity to his promises were central themes of the prophets.

2. Baruch the Prophet came to God's people during the Exile and promised God would remain faithful to them.

3. Baruch's message focused on living the virtues of wisdom and prudence as the source of happiness and peace.

Growing in Faith

One important thing I learned this week is

God is very nice.

This is important because

God is in our heart.

What will people see me doing as I live my faith choice this week?

I will be nice to them

This Week . . .

In chapter 3, "Living the Covenant: A Scripture Story," your child discovered the important role of the prophets, in particular the prophet Baruch, in the life of God's people. The central focus of the prophets' message to God's people was the double-edged message of fidelity and hope. The prophets constantly called people to be faithful to the Covenant as God was always faithful to them. This divine fidelity was always the source of hope, no matter how terrible the suffering God's people experienced.

For more on the teachings of the Catholic Church on the prophets and the virtue of hope, see *Catechism of the Catholic Church* paragraph numbers 64, 201, 214, and 1817–1821.

Sharing God's Word

Read together Baruch 3:9–15, 4:1–4. Emphasize that Baruch tried to help God's people understand that they could find true happiness by remaining faithful to God.

Praying

In this chapter your child prayed an act of hope. Read and pray together this prayer on page 46.

Making a Difference

Choose one of the following activities to do as a family or design a similar activity of your own.

- Think about a time when your family had hope because of your faith in God's love and faithfulness. Describe how that hope helped you at that time.

- Baruch brought a message of hope to the people. Talk about ways that your family can bring hope to each other and to others.

- Actions speak louder than words. Decide on one way that your family can show others that God is at the center of your lives. Make a conscious effort to implement your decision. Profess your faith in God in both words and actions.

For more ideas on ways your family can live your faith, visit the "Faith First for Families" page at **www.FaithFirst.com**. This week pay special attention to "Questions Kids Ask."

The Mystery of God

We Pray

As the heavens tower over
  the earth,
 so God's love towers
  over the faithful.
                              PSALM 103:11

God and Father of all
gifts, we praise you. You
are the source of all we
have and are.   Amen.

*Why do people enjoy solving
mysteries?*

Mysteries capture our
imagination. Usually, if we
have enough time and insight,
we can solve most mysteries.
God is a mystery unlike any
other mystery. We can never
fully know God, never fully
understand God and his ways.

*What is the most important thing
you have come to believe about
the mystery of God?*

Faith Vocabulary

Holy Trinity. The mystery of one God in three divine Persons—God the Father, God the Son, God the Holy Spirit.

When we speak of the mystery of God, we mean much more than a puzzle. God is like and, at the same time, unlike anyone or anything we know. We can never fully know God. Saint Augustine of Hippo put it this way: "If you understood him, it would not be God."

The Mystery of Mysteries

We can get a glimpse of the mystery of God by looking at the wonders of creation: the unique design of fingerprints, the magnificence of a sunset, the delicate tracings of a flower petal, the rhythms of the seasons, and especially, the innocence and beauty of a newly born infant. All the wonders of creation tell us how wonderful and powerful God is.

While we can come to know on our own that God exists, we really cannot come to know much about the mystery of who God is without his revealing himself. God has revealed, or unveiled, the mystery of who he is.

God has revealed that he is:

- Faithful—the One who is always faithful to his people (see Exodus 34:6);
- Truth—all his promises come true (see Deuteronomy 7:9);
- Love—God is love (see 1 John 4:8, 16).

Holy Trinity

The Holy Trinity

God has revealed these qualities, or attributes, and many others about himself. Each divine attribute helps us come to know something about God. But who has God revealed himself to be? God has revealed himself to be the **Holy Trinity**, the mystery of one God in three divine Persons: Father, Son, and Holy Spirit. That Divine Revelation has been passed on to us in Sacred Scripture and the Sacred Tradition of the Church. The mystery of the Holy Trinity is at the very center of the faith of the Church.

Many other mysteries of faith have their beginning in this mystery of mysteries. For example, the story of the human family begins with God creating us out of love. Then, after we had sinned, the Father sent the Son, who became fully human and like us in all ways but sin so that we could become sharers in his divinity. The Father and the Son have sent the Holy Spirit to make us holy, or sanctify us, and to reconcile us with God who created us.

 How would you explain the mystery of the Holy Trinity to a friend?

Give Praise to God

In each blank section of the triangle write one word of praise to each divine Person of the Holy Trinity.

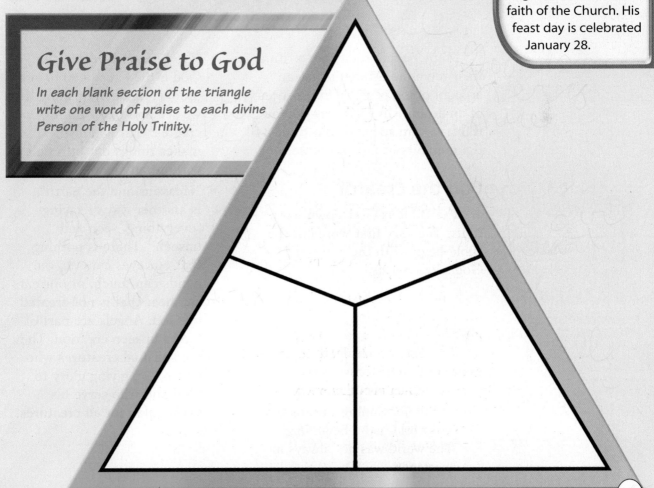

Faith Vocabulary

soul. The spiritual dimension of the human person that never dies, or is immortal.

Hand, symbol of God the Father and Creator

Many people today are writing their memoirs. Memoirs are an account of the personal experiences of an author. In what way do you think we can speak of the Bible as the memoirs of God's people?

God the Creator

The Bible is God's own word to us. The very first words of the Bible begin with the story of God's love for us.

In the beginning . . .
God created the heavens
and the earth.   GENESIS 1:1

If we listen carefully to these words of Scripture, we can hear God telling us about himself.

- "In the beginning" means that the world had a beginning. The world was not always in existence.

- "God created" means that God is the Creator who, out of love, made everything that we see and know. Only God creates; that is, only he makes things out of nothing without any help.

- "Heavens and the earth" is another way of saying "everything, seen and unseen." There is nothing that our eyes can see, our hands can touch, or our ears can hear that is not created by God. Angels are part of God's unseen creation. They are spiritual creatures who never stop giving glory to God and who serve his saving plan for all creatures.

- In the Apostles' Creed we profess our faith "in God, the Father almighty, Creator of heaven and earth." God the Father not only created the universe out of love, he also keeps it in existence by his Word, the Son, and by the Holy Spirit, the giver of life.

Images of God

In God's plan of creation, human beings have an extraordinary and unique place. The greatness of every person is founded in this revealed truth:

God created man in his image;
in the divine image he
created him;
male and female he
created them.

GENESIS 1:27

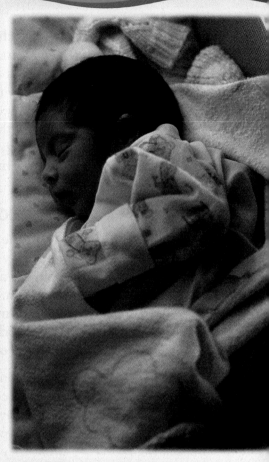

When we reflect on this, it helps us understand who we are and who other people are. God shares his love and life with everyone. Each person is created with a **soul** that bears the imprint of God's image. Our soul is the innermost spiritual part of us. It is immortal, or never dies. It gives us the ability to share in his life and love forever. When we choose to live as images of God, we tell others about his love. We give honor and glory to God.

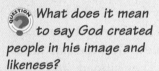 **What does it mean to say God created people in his image and likeness?**

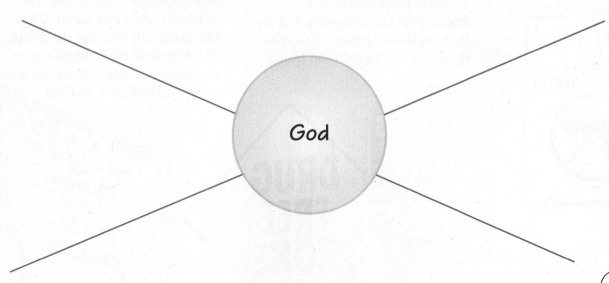

Sharing God's Love

Write on the lines ways that we can act that show we are images of God.

God

Faith Focus

What was the sin of our first parents at the dawn of creation?

Faith Vocabulary

original sin. The sin of Adam and Even, by which they and all people lost the state of original holiness, and by which death, sin, and suffering entered the world.

temptation. Everything that tries to move us to do or say something we know is wrong or from doing something good we know we can and should do, all that moves us away from living a holy life.

Watching and listening to the news certainly, more often than not, tells us that something is wrong with creation. God certainly did not create a world filled with violence, hunger, suffering, sickness, and so many other forms of evil.

Sin and Evil

In the beginning God created humanity in a state of original holiness and justice, or friendship with him. **Sin** and evil, the Bible tells us, made their way into the good world of God's creation through **original sin.**

Original sin is the sin Adam and Eve committed by freely turning away from God's love and friendship. They freely chose to do what they knew God did not want them to do. They sinned, and by their sin the original holiness and justice human beings received from God was lost for them and for all humans, except Mary, the Mother of Jesus.

The biblical story of humanity's fall from grace and original holiness begins with the **temptation** of Eve by a snake, or serpent. The Bible describes this temptation by putting these words in the mouth of the serpent: "you will be like gods" (Genesis 3:5). Adam and Eve gave in to this temptation and sinned. They chose to do what they knew was against the will of God.

> Now the serpent was the most cunning of all the animals that the LORD God had made. The serpent asked the woman, "Did God really tell you not to eat from any of the trees in the garden?" The woman answered the serpent: "We may eat of the fruit of the trees in the garden; it is only about the fruit of the tree in the middle of the garden that God said, 'You shall not eat it or even touch it, lest you die.' "
>
> GENESIS 3:1–4

Their sin was a combination of disobedience, pride, ambition, and selfishness.

The loss of original holiness has become part of our fallen human nature. Every human person now shares in the effects of original sin. The world and all of us in the human family are marked by sin and suffer from the effects of original sin. From the very first moment of our existence, or conception, we need to be reconciled with God.

The New Adam

God saw what happened. He promised, from the very beginning, to make things well again. He promised to save humanity from sin.

> Then the LORD God said to the serpent:
> "Because you have done this, . . .
> I will put enmity between you
>   and the woman,
>   and between your offspring
>   and hers;
> He will strike at your head,
>   while you strike at his heel."
> GENESIS 3:14, 15

Jesus Christ is the One God promised would come and set things right again. He is the Son of God who became a man, lived on earth, and was raised from the dead to save us and redeem us from sin and death. In Jesus Christ we have been healed, or reconciled, with God, with one another, and with all creation. Saint Paul writes:

> [T]hrough one person sin entered the world, and through sin, death. . . .
>
> But the gift is not like the transgression. For if by that one person's transgression the many died, how much more did the grace of God and the gracious gift of the one person Jesus Christ overflow for the many."
> ROMANS 5:12, 15

Saint Paul was sharing with us who Jesus is and the meaning of his work on earth. Adam and Eve, by their disobedience, brought sin and death into the world. By his obedience, Christ, the new Adam, brings life to the world. He is the Son of Mary, the new Eve.

 What can you do that shows you believe Jesus Christ is our Savior?

Our Catholic Identity

Christian Art

Michelangelo was a painter and a sculptor who expressed his faith through his art. You may have learned about the Sistine Chapel when Pope Benedict the XVI was elected the 265th pope. Michelangelo's fresco of the creation of Adam is on the ceiling of the Sistine Chapel.

Turning Back to God

Name three things that you believe are sinful. How does someone who is involved in these sins become separated from God? How can they be united again with God?

Sin	Separation	United with God

Our Church Makes a Difference

Mosaics

Art can help us come to know the mystery of the loving presence of God within us and among us. Long before we had Bibles for everyone to read, Christians used art to help people "hear" the story of creation and Redemption.

Mosaics are one of the earliest forms of art used by Christians. The creation of mosaics is an art form consisting of pressing colored pieces of glass called tesserae into soft plaster to form pictures. Mosaics help us enter the mystery of God. They give drama and life to scenes from the Bible that reveal the story of God's love for us. Often decorating the ceilings and walls of churches, they instruct the faithful concerning the majesty and mystery of God, and the lives of Jesus and of Mary and the other saints.

Mosaics and other forms of Christian art, like all the sacramentals of the Church, help us respond in faith to the mystery of the one God, who is Father, Son, and Holy Spirit. They invoke in us a sense of wonder and awe for God. They spark a desire within us to spread the story of God's love by striving to be his living images in the world.

> **QUESTION** *What other art forms inspire and teach us about God? What art in your parish helps you remember God's love for you and for all people?*

Theotokos and Child, Byzantine icon

Detail of Christ Bearing His Cross from the Stations of the Cross War Memorial, Dublin, Ireland

Holy Spirit, mosaic within bronze sculpture

What Difference Does Faith Make in My Life?

God always manifests his love. God never stops giving you signs of his love. If you look closely, there are many clues that give you a glimpse into the mystery of God.

Make a collage of words and pictures of people, places, things, and events that have come to be signs of God and his love for you.

Signs of the Mystery of God

My Faith Choice

This week I will try to show that I am made in the image and likeness of God. I will be a sign of God's love by

_____

_____ .

Give Thanks to God

Leader: The Psalms are prayer-songs of the people of God. Many of the Psalms praise God for his creation. The Church prays the Psalms every day.

Let us pray this Psalm antiphonally by alternating saying the verses aloud.

All: **Come and see the works of God, awesome in the deeds done for us.**

Group 1: Shout joyfully to God, all you on earth;
Group 2:   sing of his glorious name.
All: **Come and see the works of God, awesome in the deeds done for us.**

Group 1: All on earth fall in worship before you;
Group 2:   they sing of you, sing of your name!
All: **Come and see the works of God, awesome in the deeds done for us.**

Group 1: Bless our God, you peoples;
Group 2:   loudly sound his praise.
All: **Come and see the works of God, awesome in the deeds done for us.**

Group 1: [God] has kept us alive
Group 2:   and not allowed our feet to slip.
All: **Come and see the works of God, awesome in the deeds done for us.**

Group 1: Blessed be God, who did not refuse me
Group 2:   the kindness I sought in prayer.
All: **Come and see the works of God, awesome in the deeds done for us.**

PSALM 66:1, 2, 4, 5, 8, 9, 20

We Remember

What I Have Learned

Decipher the hidden message. *Complete the sentences. Unscramble the highlighted letters to discover the belief about God that is at the center of our faith.*

1. God has revealed himself to be the
   _ _ _ ◯ _ ◯◯ of one God in three
   divine Persons.

2. Divine _ _ _ _ _ _ _ _ ◯ _ ◯ is God
   making himself and his plan of creation and
   Redemption known over time.

3. _ _ _ _ ◯ _ _ _ is God making everyone
   and everything, seen and unseen, out of nothing and
   without any help.

4. _ _ _ _ ◯ _ _ _ sin is the name given to
   the first sin.

5. The central belief about God is the mystery of the

   — — — — — — — — .

Answer the following.

6. What does it mean to say that God is a mystery?

   _____

   _____

   _____

7. Why are humans God's greatest creation?

   _____

   _____

   _____

8. How did Jesus save us from sin and death?

   _____

   _____

   _____

To Help You Remember

1. God is the mystery of mysteries who has revealed himself and his plan of creation and Redemption.

2. All creation is destined for the glory of God.

3. Original sin broke the first Covenant uniting creation and God. In Jesus, the final Covenant, God's plan has been restored and creation is reconciled with God.

Growing in Faith

One important thing I learned this week is

_____

_____

_____.

This is important because

_____

_____

_____.

What will people see me doing as I live my faith choice this week?

_____

_____

_____

This Week . . .

In chapter 4, "The Mystery of God," your child learned more about the mystery of God and the divine plan of creation. God is the mystery of mysteries. While we can come to know God exists on our own, we really cannot come to know much about the mystery of who God is and his plan for the world without God's revelation of himself. God has revealed himself to be the Holy Trinity, or one God in three Persons—God the Father, God the Son, and God the Holy Spirit. God created people in his image and likeness to live in happiness and friendship with him. By sinning Adam and Eve broke that original Covenant God made with creation. We call that sin *original sin*. Jesus Christ, the new Adam, restored us to friendship with God and redeemed us from sin and death.

For more on the teachings of the Catholic Church on the mystery of God and the divine plan of creation, see *Catechism of the Catholic Church* paragraph numbers 51–67, 199–227, 232–260, 279–314, 325–349, 355–379, and 385–412.

Sharing God's Word

Read together Exodus 34:6, Deuteronomy 7:9, and 1 John 4:8, 16. Emphasize that through Sacred Scripture God reveals who he is and his plan of loving goodness for the world.

Praying

In this chapter your child prayed a prayer based on Psalm 66. Read and pray together this prayer on page 58.

Making a Difference

Choose one of the following activities to do as a family or design a similar activity of your own.

• Invite family members to take turns completing the sentence, "God is . . ." Continue until no one is able to complete the sentence. Distribute art materials and create table mats displaying words and phrases your family used to describe God.

• Recall that all people are created in the image and likeness of God. Share ideas about how your family is an image of God.

• Religious art helps us come to know God. This week when you take part in Mass, look at the works of art in your church. Talk about how each work of art helps you come to know God.

For more ideas on ways your family can live your faith, visit the "Faith First for Families" page at **www.FaithFirst.com**. This week take time to read an article from "Just for Parents."

Jesus Christ, the Son of God

We Pray

Hear me, LORD, and
    answer me, . . .
save your servant who
    trusts in you.

PSALM 86:1, 2

**Lord God, send your
blessing upon all
who believe in your Son.
May their faith grow
stronger.   Amen.**

*What is one important promise
that you have made? Why was it
easy or difficult to keep?*

Think about the important role
that making and keeping
promises has in our lives.
Making and keeping promises
also plays an important role in
the Bible. We can describe the
Bible as "The Story of the
Promise."

*What is the biggest promise
made in the Bible?*

Cross commemorating site where
Captain Pedro Menendez de
Aviles, Spanish explorer, landed
in 1565 to found Saint Augustine
(Florida), oldest city in America

God Fulfills His Promises

Faith Vocabulary

Salvation. The deliverance of humanity from the power of sin and death by God through Jesus Christ who "died for our sins in accordance with the Scriptures."

When we play a game, we promise to play by the rules. When we take part in a class project, we make promises to do our part responsibly. The leaders of our towns, cities, states, and country make a solemn promise to uphold the Constitution and lead us fairly and justly.

God's Promise

God's promises to his people and the fulfillment of his promises are at the heart of the Bible. You might say that all of God's promises in the Bible are part of one big promise. They fulfill the promise first made at creation—the promise to send a savior.

God renewed that promise to Noah, to Abraham and Sarah, to Moses and the Israelites, and to the kings and prophets of his people of the old, or first, Covenant.

Jesus, the New Covenant

All of God's promises in the Old Testament and all the events surrounding them point to Jesus Christ. He is the One who Mary, John the Baptist, Simeon and Anna, and the Jewish people of Jesus' time were hoping would come. In him all God's promises are fulfilled. Jesus did not abolish the Law and the Covenant of Sinai. He fulfilled and perfected them. Jesus said:

"Do not think that I have come to abolish the law or the prophets. I have come not to abolish but to fulfill. Amen, I say to you, until heaven and earth pass away, not the smallest letter or the smallest part of a letter will pass from the law, until all things have taken place." MATTHEW 5:17–18

Jesus is the new and everlasting Covenant. At the Last Supper, Jesus took the cup of wine, showed it to his disciples, and said, "This cup is the new covenant in my blood." 1 CORINTHIANS 11:25

Jesus is the new Covenant. He is the center of **Salvation.** In him all God's promises are fulfilled. He is the Savior of all people.

But what about those who have not heard of Jesus? The answer to that question is very important.

Last Supper

God wants everyone to share in his love both now and forever. The Catholic Church teaches:

[Salvation] holds true not for Christians only but also for all [people] of good will in whose hearts grace is active invisibly.

CHURCH IN THE MODERN WORLD 22

Through the grace of the Holy Spirit, God works quietly and mysteriously to draw all people to himself even those who have not heard of Jesus. All can be saved who seek to know, love, and serve God with all their heart.

 Why is Christ important to all members of the human race?

Fresco of Jesus on ceiling with smaller portrait of Mary and infant Jesus on nearby alcove, St. Andrews Church, Chicago, Illinois

Salvation Is for Everyone

Write the names of Christians and non-Christians you know who are signs of God's love. Tell what they did.

Names	Signs of God's Love

Faith Vocabulary

Incarnation. The term the Church uses to name the faith of the Church that the Son of God became fully human in all things except sin, while remaining fully divine.

Think about your experiences of coming to know a new classmate or teammate, a new member of the band or choir or science club. It takes time to come to know people. Sometimes we never really come to know a person much at all.

Peter's Confession of Faith

While Jesus lived on earth and did the work his Father sent him to do, not everyone came to believe he was the Savior and Messiah. Some people were confused and hesitant to believe. Others were hostile.

On one occasion Jesus and his disciples were traveling through an area of Palestine known as Caesarea Philippi. Caesarea Phillipi was about 150 miles north of Jerusalem in the far northern section of Palestine. The people who lived there were mostly Gentiles, or non-Jews. While they were there Jesus asked his disciples:

"Who do people say that the Son of Man is?" They replied, "Some say John the Baptist, others Elijah, still others Jeremiah or one of the prophets." He said to them, "But who do you say that I am?" Simon Peter said in reply, "You are the Messiah, the Son of the living God."

MATTHEW 16:13–16

The Gospel story of Simon Peter's confession of faith in Jesus is the foundation of what the Holy Spirit has led the Church to believe about Jesus:

Jesus Is Lord

Saint Paul the Apostle wrote, "And no one can say, 'Jesus is Lord,' except by the holy Spirit" (1 Corinthians 12:3). When we say, "Jesus is Lord," we are expressing our faith that Jesus is truly God.

Jesus and His Disciples,
Ethiopic art

Jesus Is the Son of the Living God

Jesus is the second Person of the Holy Trinity. Jesus is intimately one with the Father in the Holy Spirit. Jesus revealed:

"Whoever believes in me believes not only in me but also in the one who sent me, and whoever sees me sees the one who sent me."

JOHN 12:44–45

Jesus Is True God and True Man

The Son of God became truly and fully human without giving up his divinity. The Son of God became like us in all things but sin. (See Hebrews 4:15.) We call this the mystery of the **Incarnation**.

The Word became flesh and made his dwelling among us, and we saw his glory, the glory as of the Father's only Son.

JOHN 1:14

Jesus Is Messiah and Savior

Jesus is the One whom God promised to send to deliver his people and to lead them to faithfully live the Covenant. He is the Messiah and Savior, the Redeemer of the world. Jesus is the one and only Mediator, or "go-between," who links God and the human family. He alone reconciles humanity with God.

For there is one God.
There is also one mediator between God and the human race,
Christ Jesus, himself human, who gave himself as ransom for all.   1 TIMOTHY 2:5–6

Each Sunday, moved by the grace of the Holy Spirit and drawn by the Father, we profess our faith in Jesus Christ and confess with Peter, "You are the Messiah, the Son of the living God" (Matthew 16:16).

 In what ways can you profess your faith in Jesus?

A MEDITATION

1. Find a quiet place. Close your eyes and relax.

2. Imagine yourself at the Jordan River at the baptism of Jesus. (Read Matthew 3:13–17.)

3. Describe the scene.

4. Imagine Jesus talking to you after his baptism. Share your thoughts with Jesus.

5. Record some of your thoughts.

Faith Focus

Why are the Passion, death, Resurrection, and Ascension of Jesus so important to us?

Faith Vocabulary

Paschal Mystery.
The Passion, death, Resurrection, and glorious Ascension of Jesus Christ: the "passing over" of Jesus from death into a new and glorious life.

The Risen Lord

The Paschal Mystery

The center of the work the Father sent Jesus to do on earth is called the **Paschal Mystery.** The word *paschal* comes from a Hebrew word meaning "the passing over." The Paschal Mystery is Jesus' passing over from life on earth through his Passion, death, Resurrection, and Ascension to a new and glorified life with the Father.

The Crucifixion and Descent of Jesus to the Dead

Jesus sacrificed his life by freely accepting death on the cross and being buried. The dead Christ went down to the dead and opened the gates of heaven for all the just who had gone before him and for those who would come after him.

The Resurrection

Three days after he died and was buried, Jesus was raised from the dead with a new and glorified body. All four accounts of the Gospel clearly teach that the Resurrection of Jesus took place. It is at the heart of our faith in Christ.

I handed on to you as of first importance what I also received: that Christ died for our sins in accordance with the scriptures; that he was buried; that he was raised on the third day in accordance with the scriptures; that he appeared to Cephas [Peter], then to the Twelve. After that, he appeared to more than five hundred brothers at once, most of whom are still living, though some have fallen asleep. After that he appeared to James, then to all the apostles. Last of all . . . he appeared to me. . . . [I]f Christ has not been raised, your faith is vain.

1 CORINTHIANS 15:3–8, 17

The Ascension and Exaltation

Forty days after the Resurrection, the Risen Christ ascended to the Father in heaven, God's domain, where he reigns gloriously at the right hand of the Father.

> Then [Jesus] led them [out] as far as Bethany, raised his hands, and blessed them. As he blessed them he parted from them and was taken up to heaven. They did him homage and then returned to Jerusalem with great joy, and they were continually in the temple praising God.
>
> LUKE 24:50–53

From there, Christ, who is hidden from our eyes, will come again in glory at the end of time to judge the living and the dead (see Matthew 25:31–46). Through Christ's Ascension and exaltation in glory, all humanity has been given an unbreakable promise of everlasting life of happiness with the Trinity, with the angels, and with Mary and all the other saints.

> They will look upon his face, and his name will be on their foreheads. Night will be no more, nor will they need light from the lamp or sun, for the Lord God shall give them light, and they shall reign forever and ever.
>
> REVELATION 22:4–5

This great mystery of God's love for us is the center of the Gospel, or Good News. Through the Paschal Mystery all things have been justified, or made right, in Christ with God. Christ is the firstborn from the dead. Through him we are saved and will rise to life everlasting.

 What is the importance of the Paschal Mystery in the divine plan of Salvation?

Symbols of Faith in Christ

The ⤢ (fish) is an ancient Christian symbol for Jesus Christ, Son of God, Savior. Reflect on the meaning of the Paschal Mystery. Draw a symbol that expresses your faith in the Paschal Mystery.

Saint Paul of the Cross

The Passion, death, and Resurrection are the heart of the Gospel. For Paolo (Paul) Francesco Daneo, Saint Paul of the Cross, the Passion and Resurrection of Christ was the greatest work of divine love.

The times during which Paul lived were filled with neglect for the poor, hungry, and sick. Paul believed this was a sign that people had forgotten the suffering and death of Jesus. They were ungrateful for God's love. Paul wrote, "The world lives unmindful of the sufferings of Jesus which are the miracle of miracles of the love of God."

Saint Paul of the Cross decided to make people more aware of the Passion of Christ and the power of the love of God working in the world. Dressed in a black robe, he traveled up and down Italy and founded the "Barefoot Clerks of the Cross and the Passion," or the Passionists to work with him. Today, there are more than two thousand Passionists who preach the message of the cross to a suffering world in fifty-two nations on all five continents. They see Jesus in people who are suffering. They believe that when they help the suffering, they are helping Jesus who said, "Amen, I say to you, whatever you did for one of these least brothers [or sisters] of mine, you did for me" (Matthew 25:40).

QUESTION How might Christians today reach out to people who are suffering and share their faith in the Passion, death, and Resurrection of Jesus?

Saint Paul of the Cross (1694–1775)

Working with the poor in Costa Rica (below) and HIV children in Jamaica (right)

What Difference Does Faith Make in My Life?

Each day you have many opportunities to profess your faith in Jesus Christ either by word or by your actions. Sometimes this is easier to do than at other times. Always the Holy Spirit, the Advocate, is with you to help you.

You will soon be interviewed by a reporter for a Catholic magazine for an article about people living their faith in Jesus. Choose a situation from your life that you will share with the reporter. Write notes for your interview on the pages of this planner.

Living Our Faith in Jesus

My Faith Choice

When I am faced with a difficult decision about living my faith, I will ask myself what Jesus would do. Then I will

_____

_____ .

Scripture-based Stations of the Cross

The Stations of the Cross is a prayer of meditation. This Scripture-based version of the Stations has been given to us by Pope John Paul II. It differs slightly from the traditional Stations, which can be found on page 395. Prayerfully journey the way of the cross with Jesus. Meditate on each of these Stations. Quietly say this prayer after each Station: "We adore you, O Christ, and we bless you. By your holy cross you have saved us and set us free."

Jesus in Garden of Gethsemane

Peter's denial of Jesus

12. Jesus is on the cross, with his mother and Saint John at the foot of the cross.
13. Jesus dies on the cross.
14. Jesus is placed in the tomb.

1. Jesus is in the Garden of Gethsemane.
2. Jesus, betrayed by Judas, is arrested.
3. Jesus is condemned by the Sanhedrin.
4. Jesus is denied by Peter.
5. Jesus is judged by Pilate.
6. Jesus is scourged and crowned with thorns.
7. Jesus takes up his cross.
8. Jesus is helped by Simon Cyrene to carry his cross.
9. Jesus meets the women of Jerusalem.
10. Jesus is crucified.
11. Jesus promises Redemption to the good thief.

Mary and John at foot of cross

We Remember

What I Have Learned

1. Circle the five faith words hidden in this heart. Choose two of the faith words you circled and share a brief description of each with a partner .

```
J K L M E R S V      O F R B H S T
Q S A L V A T I O N G H O P D S W X V M F
T P E H B D S V B I N C A R N A T I O N R
M C R U C I F I X I O N C N A T I X L
O P B N R E S U R R E C T I O N W
A B A S C E N S I O N C R T X
N U I O D E S C B M N
K I H Y D
```

Explain each of the following statements.

2. The Bible can be called "The Story of the Promise."

_____

_____

_____

3. Jesus Christ is true God and true man.

_____

_____

_____

4. The Paschal Mystery of Jesus stands at the center of the Gospel.

_____

_____

_____

_____

To Help You Remember

1. Jesus is the Savior of the world.

2. The Church professes her faith in Jesus Christ, the Son of the living God, who is Lord, Messiah, and the one Mediator between God and humanity.

3. The Paschal Mystery is at the center of the work the Father sent Jesus to do.

Growing in Faith

One important thing I learned this week is

_____

_____

_____.

This is important because

_____

_____

_____.

What will people see me doing as I live my faith choice this week?

_____

_____

_____

This Week . . .

In chapter 5, "Jesus Christ, the Son of God," your child learned more about the mystery of Salvation in Jesus Christ. God's plan of Salvation began at creation with the promise that a child of Eve would overcome sin and death and reconcile humanity with God. In Jesus Christ, the Son of Mary, the new Eve, that plan was fulfilled. Through the Paschal Mystery—through Christ's passing over from life through his Passion, death, Resurrection, and Ascension to a new and glorified life with his Father—humanity has been saved and redeemed in Christ. Humankind has received the promise of eternal life and happiness.

For more on the teachings of the Catholic Church on the mystery of Jesus Christ and God's plan of Salvation, see *Catechism of the Catholic Church* paragraph numbers 410–412, 430–451, 461–469, and 512–679.

Sharing God's Word

Read together Hebrews 9:15–28. Emphasize that Jesus, the Savior of the world, alone reconciles the human family with God.

Praying

In this chapter your child prayed the scriptural Stations of the Cross. Read and pray together the Stations of the Cross on page 70 or the traditional form of the Stations of the Cross on page 395.

Making a Difference

Choose one of the following activities to do as a family or design a similar activity of your own.

- Talk about some of the choices your family has made. How are these choices signs of your faith in Jesus Christ?

- Standing up for our faith can sometimes be difficult. Why? When would you be willing to stand up for your faith?

- When we pray the Sign of the Cross we profess our faith in Jesus who freely died on the cross to save us from sin and death. This week, pray the Sign of the Cross every time you begin to pray.

For more ideas on ways your family can live your faith, visit the "Faith First for Families" page at **www.FaithFirst.com**. This week share some of the ideas on the "Gospel Reflections" page as a family.

God's Plan
of Salvation
A Scripture Story

We Pray

Let this be written
for the next generation,
for a people not yet born,
that they may praise
the LORD. PSALM 102:19

**Lord our God, may Mary,
the Apostles, and all the
saints help us on our way
of Salvation. Amen.**

*What have you learned from
reading about someone's life?*

Anne Frank wrote an
extraordinary series of letters
that we can read in *The Diary
of Anne Frank*. These letters
pass on the story of the
Holocaust for generations to
come. The letters, or epistles,
in the New Testament pass on
to us the Church's faith in
Jesus Christ.

*What is something you know
about Jesus from reading one of
the New Testament letters?*

The Great Theatre in Ephesus,
Turkey. In New Testament
times Ephesus was a chief port
of Asia with a population of
250,000 people.

Bible Background

Faith Focus

Why were the letters in the New Testament written?

Faith Vocabulary

epistles. Lengthy and formal type of letters found in the New Testament.

Saint Paul Arriving at Malta, Peter Muller (1637–1701), Dutch painter

The New Testament Letters

From the first drawings found in caves to the latest gadgets that deliver e-mail anywhere anytime, people have always communicated with one another with drawings and symbols. Letters have been the most common form of written communication throughout history. Some of the most widely read letters are found in the New Testament.

The New Testament letters are sometimes called **epistles**. The letters and epistles written in Jesus' time represent a similar kind of writing, but there is a difference between them. An epistle was a longer and a more formal type of letter. When someone had an idea and wanted to explain it in detail, they might write an epistle.

Letters, on the other hand, were usually more personal and exchanged between people who knew each other well. Our friends normally write us letters. They may want to send their good wishes and keep in touch or they simply may want to write a letter because they need our advice on a specific matter.

The Letters of Saint Paul

Many letters Saint Paul the Apostle wrote are found in the New Testament. Often the people to whom Paul wrote were people who came to believe in Jesus Christ through his preaching. Paul wrote to encourage, support, and instruct his friends. Philippians 1:3–7 is an example of a personal note from Saint Paul to the early Church in Philippi.

74

Philippi was located in eastern Macedonia (Greece). It was the first city in what is today Europe in which the Gospel was preached.

In his letters Saint Paul sometimes addressed a problem that a particular church was facing. For example, in 1 Corinthians 11:17–34 he addressed the problem of inappropriate behavior during the celebration of the Eucharist.

At other times Saint Paul used his letters as a means to remind people of the faith of what he preached to them—especially if they were in danger of falling away from the truth. For example, in Galatians 4:8–11, Saint Paul admonished Christians for placing their trust in false gods.

There are other letters in the New Testament not written by Saint Paul, such as the three letters of John, the letter of James, and the letters of Peter. The teachings of all the letters in the New Testament are essential for deepening our understanding and living our faith in Jesus Christ.

QUESTION *How can reading the letters in the New Testament help us today?*

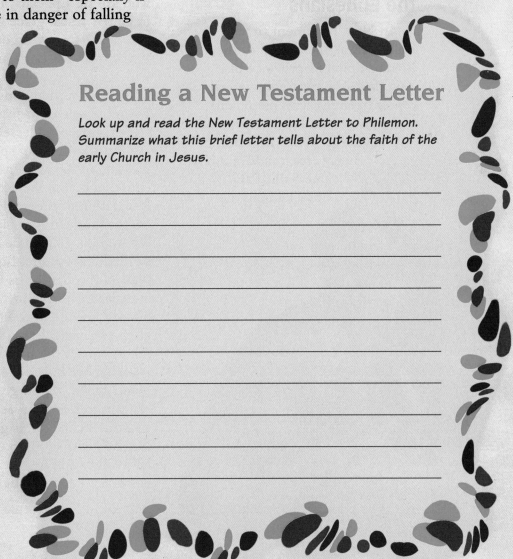

Reading a New Testament Letter

Look up and read the New Testament Letter to Philemon. Summarize what this brief letter tells about the faith of the early Church in Jesus.

_____

_____

_____

_____

_____

_____

_____

_____

Faith Focus

What is the message of the opening part of the Letter to the Ephesians?

MACEDONIA
Black Sea
Rome
GALATIA
Athens
Ephesus
Antioch
Mediterranean Sea
Damascus
Jerusalem
JUDEA
LIBYA   EGYPT

The Letter to the Ephesians

In New Testament times Ephesus was the capital of the Roman Empire's province of Asia. It was a great commercial center, teeming with merchants, tradespeople, and sailors from all over the world. Into this noisy crossroads of a city came Saint Paul proclaiming the Gospel.

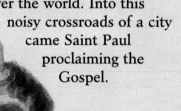

Saint Paul stayed there for two years before the local silversmiths forced him to flee. They were angry that their trade in shrines to a pagan goddess had suffered due to the growth of the Church.

Read and discover Saint Paul's opening words to the Ephesians. Paul, an apostle of Christ Jesus by the will of God, to the holy ones who are [in Ephesus] faithful in Christ Jesus: grace to you and peace from God our Father and the Lord Jesus Christ.

Blessed be the God and Father of our Lord Jesus Christ, who has blessed us in Christ with every spiritual blessing in the heavens, as he chose us in him, before the foundation of the world, to be holy and without blemish before him. In love he destined us for adoption to himself through Jesus Christ, in accord with the favor of his will, for the praise of the glory of his grace that he granted us in the beloved.

In him we have redemption by his blood, the forgiveness of transgressions, in accord with the riches of his grace that he lavished upon us. In all wisdom and insight, he has made known to us the mystery of his will in accord with his favor that he set forth in him as a plan for the fullness of times, to sum up all things in Christ, in heaven and on earth. . . .

In him you also, who have heard the word of truth, the gospel of your salvation, and have believed in him, were sealed with the promised holy Spirit, which is the first installment of our inheritance toward redemption as God's possession, to the praise of his glory. EPHESIANS 1:1–14

This letter was probably written by disciples of Saint Paul. It shares with the Church in Ephesus the heart of the faith in Christ that Saint Paul the Apostle preached.

 What was God's plan for us since before the foundation of the world?

Encouraged to Live Our Faith

In the left column write adjectives you would use to describe the faith shared in the Letter to the Ephesians. In the right column describe how the language in the letter inspires you to live your faith in Jesus Christ.

Understanding the Word of God

Faith Focus

How can we apply the teachings of the Letter to the Ephesians to our lives today?

Have you ever written a thank-you note to a friend? Did you want to make sure that your friend understood exactly what you wrote? Did you want your note to mean something special to your friend—a letter that he or she would never forget? The Letter to the Ephesians was written very carefully, including chapter 1, verses 1–14.

Greeting

The first two verses of the Letter to the Ephesians are the greeting. The writer of the letter is identified—"Paul, an apostle of Christ Jesus by the will of God."

Many today acknowledge that Saint Paul may not have personally written this letter, and it may have been written by a disciple of Saint Paul who used Paul's name to get his readers' attention. Then those who are receiving the letter are named, "the holy ones who are in Ephesus." The greeting closes with a prayerful wish: "grace to you and peace from God our Father and the Lord Jesus Christ."

Prayer of Praise and Thanksgiving

Verses 3 to 14 are a long prayer of praise and thanksgiving to God. The letters in the New Testament and other letters in the ancient world often began with a prayer of thanks.

- Verses 3–10. God is praised and thanked for what he has done in Jesus Christ: God the Father *chose* and *adopted* the Ephesians as his very own through Jesus Christ. God *redeemed* them, or saved them from sin through the blood of Jesus Christ. Finally, God *revealed* to them the plan that he had for them in Jesus Christ.

- Verses 11–14. The gift of the Holy Spirit is "the first installment of our inheritance toward redemption as God's possession." God's life in us has only just begun. In the future we will share in God's life forever.

A Letter for Us Today

The Letter to the Ephesians was written two thousand years ago, but in a very real sense, it is also written to us today. We are chosen by God. We are adopted as God's sons and daughters. We are redeemed in Christ. We are temples of the Holy Spirit.

The story of the Ephesians is our story. We believe in Jesus Christ. And we have been sacramentally sealed with the promised Holy Spirit, who continues to work with us as we proceed along life's bumpy road. In the end, the work that God the Father has begun in Christ, the Incarnate Son of God, and continues through the Holy Spirit, will be completed.

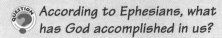

According to Ephesians, what has God accomplished in us?

Pastoral Letters

The writing of pastoral letters is one way the bishops of the United States communicate with Catholics and non-Catholics. Through pastoral letters bishops instruct the faithful on Catholic teachings, worship, social concerns, and other topics that are important to the people.

Let's Live Our Faith

You are a youth editor of the advice column "Let's Live Our Faith" in your diocesan newspaper. How would you respond to these youth?

"My best friend has been spreading false rumors about me at school. He is saying that the only reason I make Honor Roll is that I cheat on tests. He doesn't know that I know that he is behind the rumors. It really hurts me. But I am afraid to say anything because I don't want to lose him as a friend."

Jared

"I have a problem that most sixth graders don't have. I want to be a missionary when I grow up. When I told my parents, they said that they didn't think it was a good idea. They wanted me to be a doctor like my grandfather and my mother. 'We have a family tradition of doctors,' they said. 'Look at all the good you could do for people as a doctor.'"

Teri

Dear Jared,

_____

_____

_____

_____

_____

Dear Teri,

_____

_____

_____

_____

_____

_____

Our Church Makes a Difference

Catholic Newspapers

For almost two hundred years the Catholic press has served Catholics in the United States. The *United States Catholic Miscellany* (1822–1861) and the *Truth Teller* (1825–1855) were two of the earliest Catholic newspapers published in the United States. Bishop John England established the *United States Catholic Miscellany*, which today is the *Catholic Miscellany*, to instruct Catholics of the Diocese of Charleston, South Carolina, in the teachings of the Catholic Church. The *Truth Teller* was established in New York to foster religious freedom for Catholics.

The *Pilot*, which is the newspaper published by the Archdiocese of Boston, is the oldest existing Catholic newspaper in the United States. It was established on September 5, 1829, as the *Jesuit*, or *Catholic Sentinel*. The newspaper of the Archdiocese of Cincinnati, the *Catholic Telegraph*, which was established in 1831, is also one of the earliest Catholic newspapers being published today.

Many parishes in the United States provide each family with a copy of its diocesan newspaper. This helps Catholic families grow in their understanding of the teachings of the Catholic Church. It also provides families and Catholic community leaders with the information they need to make informed decisions about living the Catholic faith.

QUESTION Does your diocese publish a newspaper? If so, what is its name? How does your parish communicate with its members?

United States Catholic Miscellany photo courtesy of the Diocese of Charleston Archives

The *Tidings*, published by the Roman Catholic Archdiocese of Los Angeles, California

What Difference Does Faith Make in My Life?

From its beginning the Church has shared her faith through letters. The Holy Spirit invites and helps you to share your faith with others.

Think about several things you can say or do to share your faith in Jesus. Compose an outline of a letter you might write to share your faith.

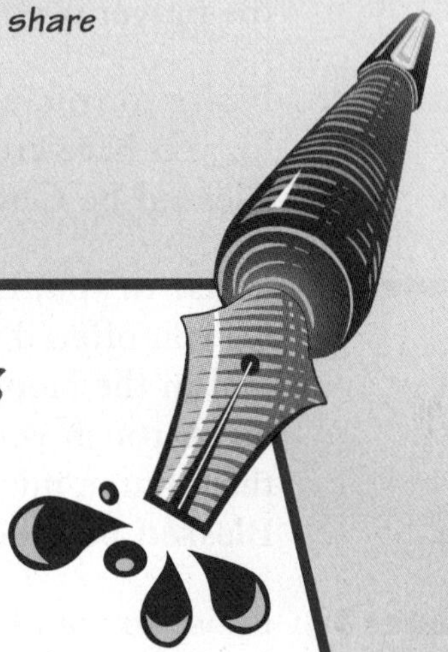

Sharing Faith in Jesus

_____

_____

_____

_____

_____

_____

_____

_____

_____

_____

My Faith Choice

This week I will try to share my faith in Jesus. I will

_____

_____.

A Prayer of Praise

Leader: The Letter to the Ephesians gives praise to God the Father for the blessings he has bestowed on us in Jesus Christ. In Baptism we are joined to Christ and made sharers in the mystery of Salvation. Let us join our voices and give praise to God, using the prayer used for the blessing of water at Baptism.

Reader 1: Praise to you, almighty God and Father,
for you have created water to cleanse and to give life.
All: **Blessed be God.**

Reader 2: Praise to you, Lord Jesus Christ, the Father's only Son,
for you offered yourself on the cross,
that in the blood and water flowing from your side
and through your death and resurrection
the Church might be born.
All: **Blessed be God.**

Reader 3: Praise to you, God the Holy Spirit,
for you anointed Christ at his baptism in the waters
of the Jordan,
that we might all be baptized in you.
All: **Blessed be God.**

RITE OF CHRISTIAN INITIATION OF ADULTS

Leader: Let us proclaim our faith in the mystery of Salvation.
All: **Save us, Savior of the world,
for by your Cross and Resurrection
you have set us free.**

MEMORIAL ACCLAMATION ROMAN MISSAL

What I Have Learned

Define each term by using it in a sentence.

1. epistle _____

_____

2. letter _____

_____

3. Ephesians _____

_____

4. Redemption _____

_____

Answer the following.

5. Compare New Testament epistles to New Testament letters.

_____

_____

_____

6. Explain two reasons Saint Paul wrote his letters to the early Church.

_____

_____

_____

7. Describe the importance of the message of Ephesians 1:1–4 for Christians today.

_____

_____

_____

To Help You Remember

1. The New Testament letters deepen our understanding and love of our faith in Jesus Christ.

2. The Letter to the Ephesians was written to share with us the heart of Saint Paul's preaching about Jesus.

3. The message of Ephesians is as important for us today as it was for the members of the early Church to whom it was addressed.

Growing in Faith

One important thing I learned this week is

_____

_____

_____.

This is important because

_____

_____

_____.

What will people see me doing as I live my faith choice this week?

_____

_____

_____

This Week . . .

In chapter 6, "God's Plan of Salvation: A Scripture Story," your child learned more about Sacred Scripture, especially the literary genre of letter writing in the New Testament. The New Testament Letter to the Ephesians was studied. Your child learned that knowing both the audience and the writing style of a particular book of the Bible helps us better understand its content.

For more on the teachings of the Catholic Church on how to read Sacred Scripture, see *Catechism of the Catholic Church* paragraph numbers 101–133.

Sharing God's Word

Read together Ephesians 1:1–14. Emphasize that this passage is from a letter written to members of the early Church who were living in the city of Ephesus.

Praying

In this chapter your child prayed a prayer of praise. Read and pray together this prayer on page 82.

Making a Difference

Choose one of the following activities to do as a family or design a similar activity of your own.

- Write letters to family members or friends with whom you have not been in touch for a while. Be sure to include a note of thanks for their friendship.

- Take the time to page through the New Testament and review the names of the New Testament letters. Talk about how the Letter to the Ephesians and the other New Testament letters encourage us to live as followers of Christ.

- Write a letter to each other encouraging one another to live as followers of Christ.

For more ideas on ways your family can live your faith, visit the "Faith First for Families" page at **www.FaithFirst.com**. Click on "Make a Difference" to discuss how your family can live your faith and share it with others.

The Church: The Age of the Spirit

We Pray

[LORD,] teach me to do
  your will,
  for you are my God.
May your kind spirit
  guide me.   PSALM 143:10

God our Father, may your Church always be a sign of your holiness for all the world.   Amen.

What are some of the signs of a school or a team that has spirit?

Spirit days at school are filled with enthusiasm. Excitement and energy fill the school. The Holy Spirit energizes the Church with the gift of enthusiasm. At Baptism you received the gift of the Holy Spirit.

If you were asked to talk to younger students about what it means to belong to a Spirit-filled Church, what would you tell them?

Pope Benedict XVI at vigil on the eve of World Youth Day Mass, Cologne, Germany, August 20, 2005

85

The Work of the Spirit in the World

Faith Focus

Why is Pentecost called the birthday of the Church?

Faith Vocabulary

Church. The Body of Christ, the Temple of the Holy Spirit, the Bride of Christ, the new People of God the Father has called together in Jesus Christ by the power of the Holy Spirit.

Pentecost. The liturgical feast and holy day when the Church celebrates the coming of the Holy Spirit on the disciples and the birth of the Church; a word meaning "fiftieth day."

The Holy Spirit

The **Church** is the "temple of the Holy Spirit." The Holy Spirit dwells within the Church and within each member of the Church. The Church, the Body of Christ and the new People of God, is a Spirit-filled people.

When Christians think of the Holy Spirit, we might think that the Holy Spirit waited until **Pentecost** to begin his work among us. The truth is that the Holy Spirit has always been at work in the world.

We read about the Holy Spirit in the story of creation and the Holy Spirit's work with the Old Testament prophets. We read about the work of the Holy Spirit in the life of Mary in the Gospel story of the Annunciation.

When Jesus began his public ministry, he announced in the synagogue in Nazareth:

"The Spirit of the Lord is upon me." LUKE 4:18

The work, or mission, of Jesus, the Son of God, and the Holy Spirit always go together and cannot be separated one from the other.

Pentecost

Fifty days after Jesus was raised from the dead the disciples were suddenly filled with enthusiasm. The word *enthusiasm* means "filled with spirit" or "filled with God."

Mary and the Disciples, Pentecost

This is how the New Testament describes that day.

When the time for Pentecost was fulfilled, they were all in one place together. And suddenly there came from the sky a noise like a strong driving wind, and it filled the entire house in which they were. Then there appeared to them tongues as of fire, which parted and came to rest on each one of them. And they were all filled with the holy Spirit and began to speak in different tongues, as the Spirit enabled them to proclaim.

ACTS OF THE APOSTLES 2:1–4

The Holy Spirit came upon the disciples as Jesus had promised. From every nation under heaven people listened to Peter, were moved by the Holy Spirit, and were baptized. The work of the **Church** began.

On this first **Pentecost**, the Holy Spirit brought very different people together. Through faith and Baptism they were joined with Christ and one another. The promise made to Abraham had come true in Christ. The Holy Spirit began the work of gathering people of all races and cultures into the one People of God.

The Church is a sign and instrument of God's communion with all humanity. It is a sign in the world of the unity of the whole human race. That mission, which began on that first Pentecost, continues today and will continue until Christ comes in glory at the end of time.

 What can you do or say to show your belief that the whole human race is one family?

One People of God

Read Acts of the Apostles 2:5–11. Circle the places the Jewish pilgrims came from to celebrate Pentecost.

- • **Philippi**
- PONTUS
- ← MACEDONIA
- GALATIA
- • **Athens**
- • **Corinth**
- • **Ephesus**
- CAPPADOCIA
- • **Pamphylia**
- MESOPOTAMIA PARTHIA → MEDIA
- CYPRUS
- CRETE
- MEDITERRANEAN SEA
- JUDEA
- • **Cyrene**
- **Jerusalem** •
- LIBYA
- EGYPT
- RED SEA

Faith Focus

What do the four Marks of the Church tell us about the Church?

Faith Vocabulary

Marks of the Church.
One, holy, catholic, and apostolic; the four signs and essential qualities of the Church and her mission founded by Jesus Christ.

We live in a world in which people travel freely and quickly. Images of people of all races fill our television screens on daily news reports and "Special Reports." We are becoming more and more familiar with the unique characteristics of a diversity of peoples.

The Marks of the Church

The Church has unique and essential characteristics. At Mass we profess that the Church is "one, holy, catholic, and apostolic." These four characteristics identify the Church founded by Christ. They are called the four **Marks of the Church**.

One

The night before he died Jesus prayed to his Father:

"I pray . . . that they may all be one, as you, Father, are in me and I in you."

JOHN 17:20–21

The Church of Jesus Christ is one Church. There is "one Lord, one faith, one baptism; one God and Father of all, who is over all and through all and in all." (EPHESIANS 4:5–6).

What we see in the world today is the one Church founded by Jesus separated into many parts. The whole Church must work to be one, as Jesus and the Father are one.

Holy

The Church is holy because we are joined to Christ, the Holy One of God, through Baptism. We are:

"[A] holy nation, a people of his own."   1 PETER 2:9

We are adopted sons and daughters of God. We have received the gift of the Holy Spirit. We live in communion with the Holy Trinity—one God who is Father, Son, and Holy Spirit.

Catholic

The Church continuously carried out Jesus' command:

"Go, therefore, and make disciples of all nations, baptizing them in the name of the Father, and of the Son, and of the holy Spirit, teaching them to observe all that I have commanded you."
MATTHEW 28:19–20

The Church invites all people to become disciples of Jesus. All over the world the Church gathers and, in many diverse ways, celebrates one faith in Christ.

Apostolic

The fourth mark of the Church, apostolic, tells us that the faith of the Church is rooted in what the Apostles preached and taught in Jesus' name. Saint Paul reminded the early Church in Corinth:

I handed on to you . . . what I also received.
1 CORINTHIANS 15:3

There is an unbroken connection, or apostolic succession, between the Apostles and their successors, the pope and the other bishops.

 What does each Mark of the Church mean?

Faith-Filled People

The Popes of the 20th–21st Centuries

Leo XIII	1878–1903
Saint Pius X	1903–1914
Benedict XV	1914–1922
Pius XI	1922–1939
Pius XII	1939–1958
Blessed John XXIII	1958–1963
Paul VI	1963–1978
John Paul I	Aug. 26–Sept. 28, 1978
John Paul II	1978–2005
Benedict XVI	2005–

Signs of the Church for Others

Decorate this banner with symbols that show that the Church is one, holy, catholic, and apostolic.

Faith Focus

Why do we use images
to help us understand
what the Church is?

Come All Ye Faithful, Julie
Lonneman, contemporary
American artist

Look at the image on this page. What does it tell you about the Church? We often use images to help us understand and explain things. Images give us insight into the meaning of things. There are many images in the New Testament for the Church. These images, like the Marks of the Church, help us understand the mystery of the Church.

Images for the Church

The new People of God, Body of Christ, and Temple of the Holy Spirit are three images for the Church that you have heard many times. What do these images tell you about the Church?

Bride of Christ

Another image the New Testament uses for the Church is the Bride of Christ. In the New Testament we read:

Husbands, love your wives, even as Christ loved the church and handed himself over for her to sanctify her, cleansing her by the bath of water with the word, that he might present to himself the church in splendor, . . . that she might be holy and without blemish. . . . This is a great mystery, but I speak in reference to Christ and the church. EPHESIANS 5:25–27, 32

Jesus himself described his love for us this way:

"No one has greater love than this, to lay down one's life for one's friends."

JOHN 15:13

Christ loves the Church with a love that has no limits. His love for his Church will never end.

Mother

We also use the image of a mother for the Church. This image helps us understand that we receive the gift of our life in Christ through the Church.

As a mother nourishes and teaches the children to whom she has given life, the Church nourishes and teaches us. She nourishes us with the gift of her Son, the Bread of Life, as we gather around the table of the Eucharist. She shares with us Jesus, the Word of God. She teaches us the language of our faith and how to live as a child of God and follower of Christ. Through the gift of the Holy Spirit, the Church faithfully passes on to us and teaches us what God has revealed to us.

 What does the image of a mother help us understand about the Church?

Our Catholic Identity

Church Documents

The Church issues several types of documents to teach and guide the members of the Church in living the faith of the Church. Among these documents, in order of importance, are apostolic constitutions, issued by the pope or by a council of the Church with the approval of the pope; encyclical letters; apostolic exhortations; apostolic letters; and letters.

Picturing the Church

Create an image or symbol that helps you understand the Church. Draw and explain that image in this space.

Our Church Makes a Difference

IOANNIS PAULI PP. II
SUMMI PONTIFICIS

LITTERAE ENCYCLICAE

« EVANGELIUM VITAE »

EPISCOPIS
PRESBYTERIS ET DIACONIS
RELIGIOSIS VIRIS ET MULIERIBUS
CHRISTIFIDELIBUS LAICIS
UNIVERSISQUE BONAE VOLUNTATIS HOMINIBUS

DE VITAE HUMANAE INVIOLABILI BONO

LIBRERIA EDITRICE VATICANA
MCMXCV

Letters from the Church

Beginning with Saint Paul the Apostle and the other writers of the New Testament letters, the Church has a long tradition of letter writing. These letters help the Church and all people understand the meaning of the faith of the Church and the difference living that faith each day will make to bring about peace and unity among all peoples. This tradition continues in the Church today.

Encyclical letters are one of the most important types of letters in the Church. An encyclical letter is a formal letter written by or authorized by the pope. The use of encyclicals as we know them today was begun in 1740 by Pope Benedict XIV.

Encyclicals are official letters of the Church. They spotlight issues on doctrine, morality, or discipline, such as the meaning of the truths of our faith, the Eucharist and the sacraments, war and peace, social and economic justice, moral behavior, and living the Ten Commandments.

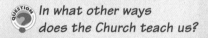 In what other ways does the Church teach us?

What Difference Does Faith Make in My Life?

You are a sign, or image, of the Church. The Holy Spirit is always with you, helping you send a clear message to others about the Church.

Use symbols, pictures, and words to create a bulletin board announcement that tells others about the Church.

The People of God

My Faith Choice

This week I will try to be a clear image of what the Church is. I will

_____

_____ .

"Father, May They All Be One"

Leader: At the Last Supper, Jesus prayed for his followers. Let us listen to the prayer of Jesus in John's Gospel.

Reader: A reading from the holy Gospel according to John.
All: **Glory to you, O Lord.**

Reader: [Jesus said:] "I pray not only for them,
but also for those who will believe in me
through their word, so that they may all be one,
as you, Father, are in me and I in you,
that they also may be in us, that the world
may believe that you sent me."   JOHN 17:20–21
The Gospel of the Lord.
All: **Praise to you, Lord Jesus Christ.**

Leader: Let us reflect on what it means to be a member of the Church.

Leader: Lord God, Father of all,
fill us with the love of the Holy Spirit.
Make us one in the fullness of faith and fellowship of love.
We ask this through Jesus Christ, your Son,
who lives and reigns with you and the Holy Spirit,
one God, for ever and ever.
All: **Amen.**

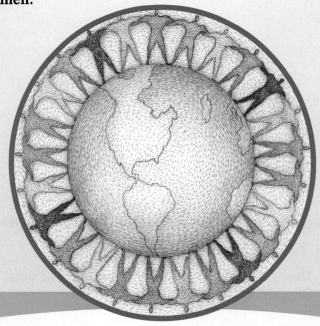

We Remember

What I Have Learned

Use the clues to describe the identity and mission of the Church.

Down

1. Image of Church focusing on the love of Christ for the Church

3. Mark of the Church meaning "living in communion with God"

Across

2. Mark of the Church that tells us Jesus is the Savior of all people

4. Mark of the Church meaning "linked to the Apostles"

5. Image of Church focusing on the Church as the source of our life in Christ

Answer the following.

6. Describe the Church as the sign and instrument of God's communion with all humanity.

_____

_____

7. Explain the meaning of apostolic succession.

_____

_____

8. Describe what the image of a mother tells us about the mystery of the Church.

_____

_____

_____

To Help You Remember

1. The Holy Spirit is at work bringing about the divine plan.

2. The Holy Spirit strengthens the Church to be one, holy, catholic, and apostolic.

3. The Holy Spirit strengthens the Church to be a sign of Christ's love for the Church.

Growing in Faith

One important thing I learned this week is

_____

_____

_____.

This is important because

_____

_____

_____.

What will people see me doing as I live my faith choice this week?

_____

_____

_____

This Week . . .

In chapter 7, "The Church: The Age of the Spirit," your child learned more about the mystery of the Church. In this first of two lessons on the Church, your child learned more about the role of the Holy Spirit in the life of the Church. A closer look was taken at the meaning of the words "We believe in one holy catholic and apostolic church," which we profess in the creed. Finally, the traditional images of Bride of Christ and Mother, which are used for the Church, were explored.

For more on the teachings of the Catholic Church on the Holy Spirit and the mystery of the Church, see *Catechism of the Catholic Church* paragraph numbers 687–741, 748–801, and 811–865.

Sharing God's Word

Read together Acts 2:1–13. Emphasize that the Holy Spirit came to the disciples on Pentecost and is at work in the whole Church and in the life of each member of the Church today.

Praying

In this chapter your child prayed a prayer for unity among all the believers in Christ. Read and pray together this prayer on page 94.

Making a Difference

Choose one of the following activities to do as a family or design a similar activity of your own.

- Discuss the four Marks of the Church: one, holy, catholic, and apostolic. Talk about the meaning of each and the ways each Mark of the Church is a characteristic of your family.

- One way the pope teaches about the faith is through encyclicals. Discuss other ways that your family can learn more about what the Catholic Church teaches.

- Choose one thing your family can do this week to tell others about the work and teachings of the Catholic Church.

For more ideas on ways your family can live your faith, visit the "Faith First for Families" page at **www.FaithFirst.com**. Click on "Family Prayer" to find a special prayer to pray together this week.

The People of God

8

We Pray

LORD, you are the strength
   of your people. . . .
Save your people, bless your
   inheritance;
   feed and sustain them
   forever!   PSALM 28:8, 9

**God our Father, may your
Church be a leaven in the
world, transforming us
into your family.   Amen.**

*What images do you know that
people use to help us understand
what they are saying?*

When we talk about something
that is difficult to understand,
we sometimes use images and
symbols to help people
understand what we mean.
We use images and symbols to
help us understand the mystery
of the Church.

*What images do you know that
are used to describe the Church?*

The Church

Faith Focus

Why do we call the
Church the People
of God?

Faith Vocabulary

People of God. Biblical
image for the Church;
the people God has
gathered and chosen
to be his own; the
people through whom
God has revealed
himself most fully
and has invited all
nations to live as the
one family of God.

Remember how God promised Abraham that his descendants would be as numerous as the stars? Well, each one of us is one of those stars.

The New People of God

At Mass we name Abraham as our father in faith. The Church is the new People of God.

Everything in the Old Testament points to Jesus Christ. In him and through him God the Father calls all peoples to be brought into the People of God. This is how the Church teaches us this truth of our faith:

> "Christ instituted . . . the new covenant in his blood . . . he called a race made up of Jews and Gentiles which would be one . . . in the Spirit, and this race would be the new People of God . . . That messianic people has as its head Christ."
>
> DOGMATIC CONSTITUTION
> ON THE CHURCH 9

The image of the **People of God** helps us understand what the Church is. The Church is the new People of God, whom God has chosen in Jesus Christ. Like Abraham who left his homeland and like Moses and the Hebrews who journeyed from slavery in Egypt to freedom, the Church is a people on a journey of faith. Our destination is the kingdom that will be brought to completion at the end of time when Christ will appear in glory.

After the Risen Jesus returned to his Father, the Holy Spirit helped the early Church understand what Jesus taught and did. This included helping them understand what the Church is. In his writing Saint Paul the Apostle teaches that the Church is a community of saints and the Temple of the Holy Spirit.

The Communion of Saints

The Church, the new People of God, is the Communion of Saints. The word *communion* comes from a Latin word meaning "sharing something in common." The word *community* also comes from the same Latin word. The Church is the community of the new People of God. We are a communion of "holy people" and "holy things."

Holy People

The Communion of Saints includes all the faithful members of the Church on earth and those who have died. It includes both the saints living with God in heaven and those faithful in purgatory who are being prepared to receive the gift of eternal life in heaven.

Holy Things

The Church shares in the one faith revealed in Sacred Scripture and passed on in Sacred Tradition from the times of the Apostles. We share in the sacraments, above all the Eucharist. We share in the charisms, or gifts, of the Holy Spirit. We share with all people the goods, the blessings, that God shares with us.

 What do the terms People of God and Communion of Saints mean?

The Church

Describe three ways the Church shows she is the new People of God, the Communion of Saints.

Faith Focus

Why do we call the
Church the Body of
Christ?

Faith Vocabulary

charisms. Graces, or
gifts, given by the
Holy Spirit to build
up the Church on
earth for the good
of all people and the
needs of the world.

Body of Christ. An
image for the Church
used by Saint Paul
the Apostle that
teaches that all the
members of the
Church are one in
Christ, the Head of
the Church, and that
all members have a
unique and important
role in the work of
the Church.

The images of a temple
and human body also help us
understand the mystery of the
Church. In his First Letter to the
Corinthians, Saint Paul the Apostle
asks the early Church in Corinth:

Do you not know that your
body is a temple of the holy
Spirit within you, whom you
have from God?
1 CORINTHIANS 6:19

The Temple of the Holy Spirit

A temple is a sacred place.
Both the Jewish and Gentile
disciples of Jesus in Saint Paul's
time believed that the Temple of
Jerusalem was the dwelling place
of God. The Jewish disciples of
Jesus who heard Saint Paul use
this image believed that the
Temple in Jerusalem was the
center of God's presence among
his people.

The Church is the Temple of
the Holy Spirit. He dwells within
each of the baptized and within
the whole Church. The Holy Spirit
is the source of the Church's life
and of its unity as the one People
of God.

The Holy Spirit is also the
one source of the richness of the
Church's many gifts and charisms.
Charisms are graces of the Holy
Spirit that are given to build up the
Church and to help the Church
fulfill her work in the world.

The Body of Christ

Saint Paul also uses the image
of the human body to help us
understand the mystery of the
Church. He teaches that the
Church is the **Body of Christ:**

Now you are Christ's body,
and individually parts of it.
1 CORINTHIANS 12:27

The Church is both visible and spiritual, human and divine. Christ is the Head of the Body, and we are its members. All the members of the Church—the ordained, members of religious communities, and laypeople—make up the one Body of Christ. Each member of the Church has different gifts and responsibilities to build up the Church.

Jesus gave Saint Peter a unique responsibility in the Church. He said to Peter the Apostle:

"[Y]ou are Peter, and upon this rock I will build my church, and the gates of the netherworld shall not prevail against it." MATTHEW 16:18

This unique responsibility is known as the Petrine ministry. The Petrine ministry is continued today in the Church by the pope, the bishop of Rome and the successor of Saint Peter. The pope is the immediate and universal pastor, or shepherd, of the whole Church on earth. His ministry includes the responsibility to:

- keep the Church together as one,
- keep the Church faithful to the truth of Jesus, and
- strengthen and encourage all the members of the Church.

 What are the three groups of baptized faithful who make up the Body of Christ?

Different Gifts, Different Responsibilities

Name three members of the Catholic Church. Tell what they do to build up the Church.

_____
(Name)

_____

_____

_____
(Name)

_____

_____

_____
(Name)

_____

_____

Faith Focus

Why is the Kingdom of God so important to the teaching of Jesus?

Faith Vocabulary

Kingdom of God. The fulfillment of God's plan for all creation in Christ at the end of time when Christ will come again in glory.

What other images do you know that Jesus used to help people understand the work the Father sent him to do?

The Kingdom of God

All throughout his work on earth Jesus proclaimed the **Kingdom of God,** or Reign of God.

Jesus came to Galilee proclaiming the gospel of God: "This is the time of fulfillment. The kingdom of God is at hand. Repent, and believe in the gospel."

MARK 1:14–15

At its core, the Kingdom of God is:

- a kingdom of truth, mercy, and eternal life;
- a kingdom where holiness and grace will prevail; and
- a kingdom where justice, love, and peace triumph over injustice, hatred, and war.

All the people of the Church join together in this work of Christ. We continue the work of Christ in our world and prepare for the coming of the Kingdom of God. Here are three ways that we fulfill this responsibility.

We Pray

We pray for the coming of the Kingdom of God. Each time we pray the Lord's Prayer, we pray, "Thy kingdom come." Every time we celebrate the Eucharist, we pray for the coming of the Lord Jesus to fulfill his work and to bring about the Kingdom of God.

We Prepare the Way

We prepare the way for the coming of the kingdom. We do not make the Kingdom of God happen. It is God's work. We do, however, prepare the way for the coming of the kingdom. We bring the truth of God to those who have not heard it. We are forgiving, just, merciful, and compassionate as Jesus was.

We Live the Beatitudes

We live the Beatitudes to seek the Kingdom of God first in all we do. The Beatitudes help us be lights in the world directing others to the Kingdom of God. The Beatitudes are:

"Blessed are the poor in
    spirit,
  for theirs is the kingdom
    of heaven.
Blessed are they who
    mourn,
  for they will be comforted.
Blessed are the meek,
  for they will inherit the
    land.
Blessed are they who
    hunger and thirst for
    righteousness,
  for they will be satisfied.
Blessed are the merciful,
  for they will be shown
    mercy.

Blessed are the clean of
    heart,
  for they will see God.
Blessed are the
    peacemakers,
  for they will be called
    children of God.
Blessed are they who are
    persecuted for the
    sake of righteousness,
  for theirs is the kingdom
    of heaven."

MATTHEW 5:3–10

Living the Beatitudes will help us do the work of leading others to the kingdom. It will lead us to the happiness God created us to have. We will discover and help others discover happiness here on earth and eternal life and happiness with God the Holy Trinity.

 What is the Kingdom of God announced by Jesus?

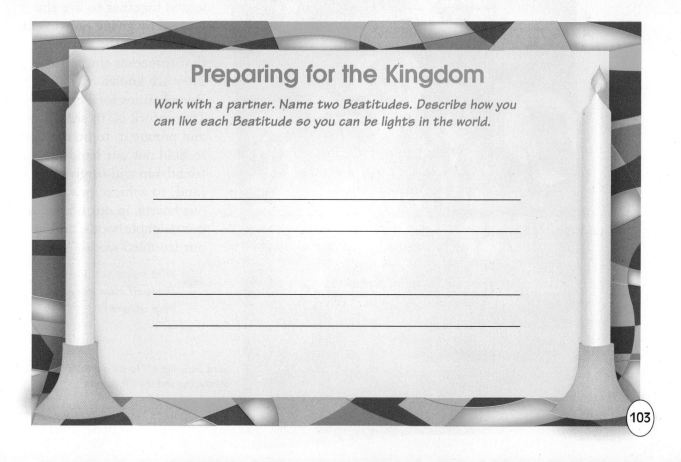

Preparing for the Kingdom

Work with a partner. Name two Beatitudes. Describe how you can live each Beatitude so you can be lights in the world.

_____

_____

_____

_____

Our Church Makes a Difference

Benedictines for Peace

Christians look to one another and need one another to live the Gospel. Saint Benedict of Nursia (480–547) wrote a rule of life that spelled out a clear way to live the Gospel. His rule of life was so helpful that people came from all over to live together to follow it. Saint Scholastica (480–543), Benedict's twin sister, was the first woman to choose to follow his rule of life.

Soon other women came to live together to follow the same rule.

The followers of Saint Benedict and Saint Scholastica are consecrated religious and are known as Benedictines. Many Benedictines today have joined together to live the Gospel by giving nonviolent responses to the violence that threatens the world. They are known as Benedictines for Peace. There work is "to seek peace and pursue it, to be the first to hold out our hands in friendship and forgiveness [and] to achieve peace in our hearts, in our homes, in our neighborhoods, and in our troubled world."

 Who helps you live the Gospel? How do you help others?

Saint Benedict of Nursia and Saint Scholastica and their followers

What Difference Does Faith Make in My Life?

You are a member of the Body of Christ, the People of God, the Church. The Holy Spirit dwells within you, giving you the grace to live the Gospel and continue the work Jesus began while he lived on earth.

Think about all the things your parish does. Name at least three things you can do with other members of your parish to live the Gospel.

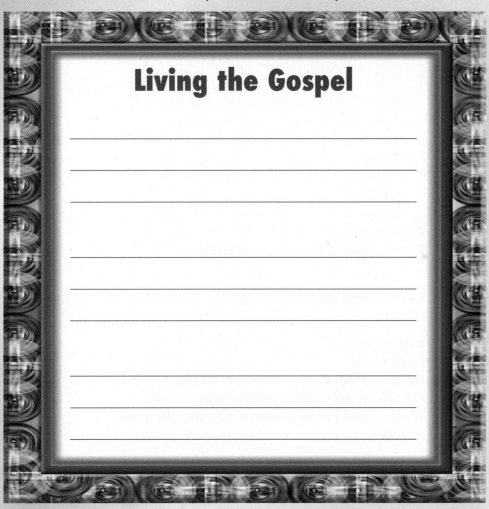

Living the Gospel

_____

_____

_____

_____

_____

_____

_____

_____

My Faith Choice

This week I will use the gifts the Holy Spirit has given me to work with other members of the Church to continue Christ's work in the world. I will

_____

_____.

Prayer for Vocations

Leader: God calls each member of the Church to share in the work of Christ. All the baptized have the responsibility to prepare the way for the coming of the Kingdom of God.

Let us pray that we hear and respond to God's invitation to spread the Gospel.

Reader: A reading from the holy Gospel according to Matthew.
All: **Glory to you, O Lord.**

Reader: Jesus went around to all the towns and villages, teaching in their synagogues, proclaiming the gospel of the kingdom, and curing every disease and illness. At the sight of the crowds, his heart was moved with pity for them because they were troubled and abandoned, like sheep without a shepherd. Then he said to his disciples, "The harvest is abundant but the laborers are few; so ask the master of the harvest to send out laborers for his harvest." MATTHEW 9:35–38
The Gospel of the Lord.
All: **Praise to you, Lord Jesus Christ.**

Leader: Let us take a moment so we can respond to Jesus' invitation. *(Pause.)*

Let us pray.
All: **Lord God,**
we pray that all the members of the Church
may hear your call to serve your people.
We ask this in the name of Christ, our Lord.
Amen.

We Remember

What I Have Learned

Use the words in the word box to complete each sentence. Not all words will be used.

> ordained ministers   Kingdom of God
> blessings   Petrine ministry
> Charisms   Communion of Saints

1. Bishops, priests, and deacons are the
_____.

2. _____ are
graces of the Holy Spirit given to help the Church
fulfill her work in the world.

3. The _____ is the
unique ministry of the pope, the bishop of Rome.

4. The _____ includes
all the faithful members of the Church, those on
earth and those in heaven and in purgatory.

5. The _____ is all
people and creation living in communion with God.

Answer the following.

6. Describe the Church as the new People of God.

_____

_____

7. Describe the Church as the Body of Christ.

_____

_____

_____

8. Compare the work in the Church of the lay faithful,
consecrated religious, and the ordained.

_____

_____

_____

To Help You Remember

1. The Church is the new People of God, the Temple of the Holy Spirit, and the Communion of Saints.
2. Jesus Christ is the Head of the Church, the Body of Christ. The lay faithful, the ordained, and consecrated religious are her members.
3. The Kingdom of God begun by the Father and announced in the Gospel is mysteriously present in the Church and will come about in its fullness at the end of time.

Growing in Faith

One important thing I learned this week is

_____

_____

_____.

This is important because

_____

_____

_____.

What will people see me doing as I live my faith choice this week?

_____

_____

_____

This Week . . .

In chapter 8, "The People of God," your child continued to deepen his or her understanding of the mystery of the Church. The Church is the new People of God, the Temple of the Holy Spirit, and the Communion of Saints. Called by the Father, all the baptized are joined to Christ through the power of the Holy Spirit. The whole Church, Christ the Head and all the members (the lay faithful, the ordained, and consecrated religious), is the Body of Christ. Together the entire Body of Christ continues the work of Christ on earth with the help and guidance of the Holy Spirit until the kingdom announced by Christ comes about in its fullness at the end of time.

For more on the teachings of the Catholic Church on the mystery of the Church as the People of God, the Temple of the Holy Spirit, the Body of Christ, and the Communion of Saints, see *Catechism of the Catholic Church* paragraph numbers 770–801, 871–933, 946–959, and 1020–1150.

Sharing God's Word

Read together 1 Corinthians 6:19. Emphasize that the Holy Spirit is the source of the Church's life and its unity as the holy People of God.

Praying

In this chapter your child prayed a prayer for vocations. Read and pray together this prayer on page 106.

Making a Difference

Choose one of the following activities to do as a family or design a similar activity of your own.

- Invite all family members to share three things they are doing to fulfill their responsibilities to live as faithful members of the Church. Discuss ways that you can support one another.

- Talk about the work of the Benedictines of Peace. Share ideas about ways your family might grow as a family of peace. Create a banner using the words "Peace Be with Us," or similar words. Display it in your home as a reminder that you made the commitment to be a family of peace.

- Talk about the people who help you live the Gospel. Then name ways your family can help others live the Gospel.

For more ideas on ways your family can live your faith, visit the "Faith First for Families" page at **www.FaithFirst.com**. Check out this week's "Current Events" page and discuss it as a family.

Mary, Mother of the Church

We Pray

I lift up my soul to my God.
In you I trust.   PSALM 25:1–2

Father, may Mary's prayer
be your people's joy
through all ages.   Amen.

*Why could someone call you a
person of faith?*

People of faith are at the
center of the story of God's
people. Mary's faith in God is
unequaled among all the
People of God. She is a model
of faith for all Christians.

*How did Mary show her faith
in God?*

Mary, the New Eve, Queen of
Heaven and Earth, wood sculpture   109

Mary, Woman of Faith

Faith Focus

Why does the Church look to Mary as a model of faith?

Faith Vocabulary

Annunciation.
The announcement to the Virgin Mary by the angel Gabriel that God had chosen her to be the Mother of Jesus, the Son of God, by the power of the Holy Spirit; a word meaning "announcement."

Deborah   Ester   Judith   Ruth

We all know people of faith. Their faith in God seems so strong and unwavering that they hang in there when many other people would throw in the towel. In the Bible, many women stand out as models of faith for us to follow.

Women of Faith in the Bible

The Bible opens with the story of Eve. At first you might ask, How is Eve a woman of faith? Didn't she disobey God? While that is true, Eve first heard God's promise of a savior. She first heard and trusted in the promise that her descendants would eventually be victorious over the Evil One.

After Eve comes a long line of our ancestors in faith. Among these people are Sarah, Hannah, Deborah, Ruth, Judith, and Esther. All these women believed in God and trusted in his word and promises to them.

The Faith of the Blessed Virgin Mary

Looking back over the faith story of the People of God, we have come to see that all of these women of faith in the Old Testament prepared the way for Mary. It is through Mary's great act of faith in God's word to her that God's promise of the Savior would be fulfilled.

The Gospel of Luke tells us that the archangel Gabriel spoke to Mary, a virgin who lived in the town of Nazareth in Galilee. The angel said to her:

"The holy Spirit will come upon you, and the power of the Most High will overshadow you. Therefore the child to be born will be called holy, the Son of God." Mary said, "Behold, I am the handmaid of the Lord. May it be done to me according to your word." LUKE 1:35, 38

We call this event the **Annunciation.** Mary says, "May it be done to me according to your word." She does not understand how this will happen. Yet she does not hesitate to believe in God's word. Mary gives her trust to God completely. Wherever he leads her, she will go. Her *yes* changes the course of human history.

Mary is our model of faith. She listened, she freely believed, and she generously gave her assent, her yes, to God. There will be times in our lives when we too will face situations in which what God is asking of us seems impossible. If you want to know how to respond, look to Mary's example to guide you.

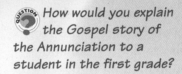 How would you explain the Gospel story of the Annunciation to a student in the first grade?

Annunciation, woodcarving

Walking With Mary

Take a moment. Be still and:

1. Think of a situation in which you might require a faith as strong as Mary's.
2. Place yourself in the Gospel story as you read Luke 1:31–38.
3. Have a conversation with Mary.
4. Write words or draw a picture to remind you of your conversation with Mary.

Faith Focus

Why do we honor Mary as the Mother of God and the Mother of the Church?

Faith Vocabulary

Immaculate Conception. Mary's freedom from all sin, both original sin and all personal sin, from the first moment of her existence, or conception, and throughout her entire life.

People of faith seem to overcome odds and do the impossible. They have the strength and courage to live in ways that change lives. We honor them and share their stories with others. God has honored Mary more than any other human person. God chose the Blessed Virgin Mary to be the Mother of his Son. She is the handmaid of the Lord.

Mother of God

Jesus, the child whom the Virgin Mary conceived by the power of the Holy Spirit and gave birth to, is the Son of God. Jesus is the second Person of the Holy Trinity who took on flesh and became human in all things

Our Lady of Siluva, statue of Mary in Great Upper Church at Basilica of the National Shrine of the Immaculate Conception, Washington, DC

except sin. Jesus is the Son of God and the Son of Mary. He is true God and true man. That is why the Virgin Mary, the Mother of Jesus, is the Mother of God.

Because of this special honor given to Mary, God's grace kept Mary free from sin. Mary was free from original sin from the very first moment of her existence, or conception. We call this the **Immaculate Conception** of Mary. She remained pure of all personal sin her whole life.

When her life on earth ended, the Most Blessed Virgin Mary was taken up, or assumed, body and soul, into the glory of heaven. There she already shares in the glory of her Son's Resurrection. We call this the Assumption of Mary.

Basilica of the National Shrine of the Immaculate Conception, Washington, DC

Mother of the Church

Mary is also the Mother of the Church, the Mother of the followers of her Son. The Gospel of John tells us:

Standing by the cross of Jesus were his mother and his mother's sister, Mary the wife of Clopas, and Mary of Magdala. When Jesus saw his mother and the disciple there whom he loved, he said to his mother, "Woman, behold, your son." Then he said to the disciple, "Behold, your mother." And from that hour the disciple took her into his home.   JOHN 19:25–27

The "beloved disciple" who is at the foot of the cross stands for all of us who are Jesus' disciples. Mary, the Mother of Jesus, is the mother of all who follow her Son, Jesus. Mary is the Mother of Jesus and the Mother of the Church, the Body of Christ.

 Why would you turn to Mary in your life?

Honoring Mary

Write and decorate a prayer to your Mother Mary. Take a few moments to pray your prayer. Learn it by heart and pray it often.

_____

_____

_____

_____

_____

_____

_____

_____

Faith Vocabulary

Rosary. A prayer of meditation on the life of Mary and Jesus and the mystery of Salvation.

Devotion to Mary

Mary is the most faith-filled person who ever lived. She is the greatest of all the saints. All the women of faith in the Bible give a glimpse of the faith of Mary.

Mary is her Son's first disciple. She listened to his word and kept it. She learned from him who is the way to God. She says to us as she did to the servers at the wedding feast in Cana, "Do whatever he tells you" (John 2:5).

Mary teaches and guides us to live as faithful followers of her Son.

We remember and celebrate the life of Mary and her Son when we pray the **Rosary**. The Rosary is a prayer of meditation on the life of Mary and Jesus and the mystery of Salvation. While praying the Rosary, we place ourselves in the main event of the mystery of Salvation. We remember Mary's unique place in God's plan of Salvation. We honor her as God honors her.

Joyful Mysteries

1. The Annunciation
2. The Visitation
3. The Nativity
4. The Presentation in the Temple
5. The Finding of the Child Jesus After Three Days in the Temple

Luminous Mysteries

1. The Baptism at the Jordan
2. The Miracle at Cana
3. The Proclamation of the Kingdom and the Call to Conversion
4. The Transfiguration
5. The Institution of the Eucharist

Glorious Mysteries

1. The Resurrection
2. The Ascension
3. The Descent of the Holy Spirit
4. The Assumption of Mary
5. The Crowning of the Blessed Virgin as Queen of Heaven and Earth

Sorrowful Mysteries

1. The Agony in the Garden
2. The Scourging at the Pillar
3. The Crowning with Thorns
4. The Carrying of the Cross
5. The Crucifixion and Death

Catholics honor Mary and express our devotion to her throughout the year. We pray to her and ask her help to live as loyal and true followers of Jesus.

During Advent we remember Mary as the handmaid of the Lord who prepared her heart for the coming of the Savior. During Christmas we remember Mary as the mother who gave birth to the Savior and brought Jesus into the world. During Lent and Holy Week we remember Mary, the Mother of Sorrows. Through the season of Easter we join with Mary, Queen of Heaven and Earth, and praise God with joyful hearts and await his coming in glory at the end of time.

At Mass we recognize Mary's presence with us and honor her.

During the Eucharist we pray to the Father, asking that we join our Mother Mary in heaven. We pray:

> To all of us, your children, grant, O merciful Father, that we may enter into a heavenly inheritance with the Blessed Virgin Mary, Mother of God, . . .
> EUCHARISTIC PRAYER IV

Mary joins with us and her Son in giving God the Father our praise and thanksgiving through the power of the Holy Spirit. We look forward to joining the angels, and Mary and all the saints in giving honor and glory to God forever and ever.

 Why and how do Catholics honor Mary?

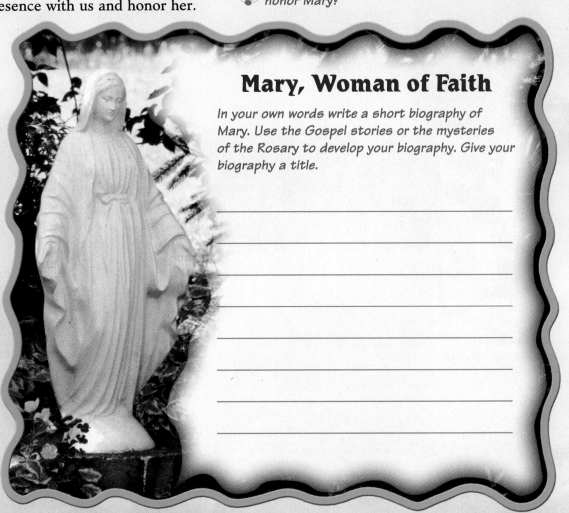

Mary, Woman of Faith

In your own words write a short biography of Mary. Use the Gospel stories or the mysteries of the Rosary to develop your biography. Give your biography a title.

_____

_____

_____

_____

_____

_____

_____

_____

Celebrating Mary

The Church around the world remembers and honors Mary, our mother, throughout the year by celebrating feast days in her honor. The Church in the United States joins with the Church in other countries in celebrating these feasts.

- January 1 brings us the Solemnity of Mary, the Mother of God.
- On May 31 we celebrate the feast of the Visitation, or the visit of Mary to Elizabeth.
- August 15 is the feast of Mary's Assumption, when Mary was taken, body and soul, into heaven.
- December 8 is the feast of the Immaculate Conception, which celebrates that Mary was free from original and personal sin throughout her entire life.

Hispanic pilgrims praying at shrine of the Virgin of Guadalupe, Los Angeles, California

- On December 12, the feast of Our Lady of Guadalupe, we celebrate Mary's appearance to Saint Juan Diego in Mexico in 1531.

Throughout the year, we think about Mary's great faith and how her yes to God changed the world. As we celebrate our love for Mary, we ask God for the grace to listen to his word and say yes to his invitation to bring about his plan for all people.

QUESTION *In what ways does your parish honor Mary?*

Junior high girl dressed as Mary standing on float during a procession honoring Mary

Pilgrims carrying statue of Our Lady of Lourdes during procession, Lourdes, France

What Difference Does Faith Make in My Life?

Mary was a woman of strong faith. Mary, the Mother of God, is your mother too. Mary cares about you. She wants to be a very important person in your life.

Think about some of the things that are part of your life or the lives of other people that you would like to share with Mary. Take the time to share your thoughts with her.

Mary, My Mother

Queen of All Saints ✱ Mother of Our Savior

Mother of the Church ✱ Queen of Peace

✱ Holy Mary ✱ Holy Mother of God ✱ Mother of Christ ✱

My Faith Choice

This week I will spend time with Mary in prayer.
I will

_____

_____ .

The Canticle of Mary

*The Magnificat is Mary's canticle, or song, of praise of God.
Divide into two groups and pray it antiphonally.*

All: "My soul proclaims the greatness of the Lord;
my spirit rejoices in God my savior."

Group 1: "For he has looked upon his handmaid's lowliness;
Group 2: behold, from now on will all ages call me blessed.

Group 1: The Mighty One has done great things for me,
Group 2: and holy is his name.

Group 1: His mercy is from age to age
Group 2: to those who fear him.

Group 1: He has shown might with his arm,
Group 2: dispersed the arrogant of mind and heart.

Group 1: He has thrown down the rulers
from their thrones
Group 2: but lifted up the lowly.

Group 1: The hungry he has filled with
good things;
Group 2: the rich he has sent away empty.

Group 1: He has helped Israel his servant,
remembering his mercy,
Group 2: according to his promise to our
fathers,
to Abraham and to his descendants
forever."

All: "My soul proclaims the greatness
of the Lord;
my spirit rejoices in God
my Savior." LUKE 1:46–55

We Remember

What I Have Learned

Circle the choice in the parentheses that best completes each statement.

1. (Sarah, Clopas, Mary of Magdala) was the wife of Abraham and a woman of great faith.

2. The angel (Michael, Gabriel, Raphael) announced to the Virgin Mary that she would be the Mother of the Son of God and name him Jesus.

3. The (Annunciation, Immaculate Conception, Incarnation) names Mary's unique privilege of being free from sin from the very moment of her existence.

4. The (Annunciation, Nativity, Assumption) names Mary being taken to heaven, body and soul.

Answer the following.

5. Why is Mary a model of faith for all believers?

_____

_____

_____

6. What do we mean when we say that Mary is the Mother of the Church?

_____

_____

_____

7. Why are Catholics so devoted to Mary?

_____

_____

_____

_____

To Help You Remember

1. Mary is a model of faith for all Christians.

2. The Blessed Virgin Mary is the Mother of God who was free from sin from the first moment of her existence and who was assumed, body and soul, into heaven at the end of her life on earth.

3. Mary is the Mother of the Church, who we honor throughout the year.

Growing in Faith

One important thing I learned this week is

_____

_____

_____.

This is important because

_____

_____

_____.

What will people see me doing as I live my faith choice this week?

_____

_____

_____

This Week . . .

In chapter 9, "Mary, Mother of the Church," your child learned more about the Church's devotion to Mary. Mary, the Mother of Jesus, is the Mother of God and the Mother of the Church. God's love for Mary is unique. From the first moment of her existence Mary received the unique grace of being free from all sin, both original and personal, and remained free from sin her entire life. At the end of her life on earth, she was assumed, body and soul, into heaven. We look to Mary, as she expects us to, for prayerful guidance.

For more on the teachings of the Catholic Church on Mary, see *Catechism of the Catholic Church* paragraph numbers 484–507 and 963–972.

Sharing God's Word

Read together Luke 1:26–38. Emphasize that Mary, the Mother of Jesus, the Incarnate Son of God, is the Mother of God and the Mother of the Church.

Praying

In this chapter your child prayed the Magnificat, Mary's canticle, or song, of praise. Read and pray together this prayer on page 118.

Making a Difference

Choose one of the following activities to do as a family or design a similar activity of your own.

- Use "The Canticle of Mary" on page 118 as part of your family mealtime prayer this week.

- Take time this week to pray and talk about the meaning of the mysteries of the Rosary. Talk about how Mary is a model of faith for your family. Share ideas on ways Mary inspires you to live as followers of Jesus.

- Talk about how your family honors Mary. Choose to do one thing this week to honor her and to show your love for her.

For more ideas on ways your family can live your faith, visit the "Faith First for Families" page at **www.FaithFirst.com**. Click on "Games" and make learning fun for your child.

"Come, You Who Are Blessed"
A Scripture Story

We Pray

I announced your deed
   to a great assembly. . . .
Your deed I did not hide
   within my heart. . . .
I made no secret of your
   enduring kindness.

PSALM 40:10–11

God our loving Father,
prepare us for the day of
the coming of your Son,
Jesus Christ, in glory.

Amen.

*What good news have you shared
lately?*

We all share good news with
excitement and enthusiasm.
The better the news, the more
excited and enthusiastic we
feel. The Gospel is the best
news the world has ever heard.

*Why should the good news of the
Gospel fill us with excitement
and enthusiasm today?*

Bible Background

Faith Focus

How did the accounts of the Gospel come to be written?

Faith Vocabulary

Gospels. The first four books of the New Testament, which pass on the faith of the Church in Jesus Christ and in the saving events of his life, Passion, death, Resurrection, and Ascension.

Evangelists. Matthew, Mark, Luke, and John, the writers of the four inspired accounts of the Gospel in the New Testament; a word meaning "announcer of the good news."

Traditional symbols for the Evangelists: Matthew is symbolized by a winged man; Mark, by a lion; Luke, by an ox; and John, by an eagle.

How do you remember what is important to you? Perhaps you memorize what is important or write it in a diary or journal. There are so many ways to share what is important to us. First of all, we just might tell others about it. We might call them on the phone or e-mail them. We might share our good news during lunch or pull our friends aside to tell them our good news.

Sharing the Good News of Jesus

The early Christians had important news to share. It was the good news about Jesus. After Jesus' Resurrection the once-fearful Apostles and other disciples quickly spread Christ's message far and wide by word of mouth. Then they wrote it down so they would not forget it.

In the New Testament there are four written accounts of the **Gospel** according to Matthew, Mark, Luke, and John.

The word *gospel* is from an old English word *God-spell*. The Gospels of Matthew, Mark, Luke, and John announce the good news of our Salvation in Jesus who is our Lord and Savior. Each of the four written accounts of the Gospel tells about Jesus. But each does so in a slightly different way:

- Mark emphasizes what it means to be a disciple of Jesus and to walk with him toward the cross.
- Matthew pays special attention to the needs of the Church.
- Luke shows how Jesus' Salvation embraces all people.
- John tries to understand the inner meaning of Jesus' words and deeds.

The Writing of the Gospel

The four written accounts of the Gospel were formed in three different stages. The first stage, of course, belongs to the very words and deeds of Jesus. When he walked the earth, he went about teaching and healing the sick. Eventually, he was put to death and was raised from the dead on the third day.

The second stage belongs to the time of the Apostles. After the Holy Spirit descended on the disciples at Pentecost, the Apostles and others preached about Jesus. In this preaching they used their memories of Jesus' words and actions as teaching tools.

The third stage belongs to the **Evangelists**, Matthew, Mark, Luke, and John. These four were inspired by the Holy Spirit to write what the Apostles had passed on to them and the community of believers about Jesus.

 Why is it important to read the Gospel?

Same Story . . . Different Words

Read Matthew 26:6–13, Mark 14:3–9, Luke 7:36–50, and John 12:1–8. See how the same event is reported in different ways. What are some of the similarities and differences?

Similarities:_____

_____

_____

_____

Differences: _____

_____

_____

_____

What does Matthew tell us about how we are to live as followers of Jesus?

Good Shepherd Separating the Sheep from the Goats, sixth-century Byzantine mosaic

When have you waited and waited for something really good to happen? You knew it would happen but you did not know when. In Jesus' time the People of God were waiting for the coming of the Kingdom of God.

The Kingdom of God

All four Gospels teach the good news of the Kingdom of God, or the Kingdom of heaven. They teach that those who faithfully follow Jesus will be invited to join with him in the kingdom that God has prepared for them since the beginning of creation.

Read how Matthew passes on to us that teaching of Jesus.

"When the Son of Man comes in his glory, and all the angels with him, he will sit upon his glorious throne, and all the nations will be assembled before him. And he will separate them one from another, as a shepherd separates the sheep from the goats. He will place the sheep on his right and the goats on his left. Then the king will say to those on his right, 'Come, you who are blessed by my Father. Inherit the kingdom prepared for you from the foundation of the world. For I was hungry and you gave me food, I was thirsty and you gave me drink, a stranger and you welcomed me, naked and you clothed me, ill and you cared for me, in prison and you visited me.' Then the righteous will answer him and say, 'Lord, when did we see you hungry and feed you, or thirsty and give you drink? When did we see you a stranger and welcome you, or naked and clothe you? When did we see you ill or in prison, and visit you?' And the king will say to them in reply, 'Amen, I say to you, whatever you did for one of these least brothers of mine, you did for me.' Then he will say to those on his left, 'Depart from me, you accursed, into the eternal fire prepared for the devil and his angels. For I was hungry and you gave me no food, I was thirsty and you gave me no drink, a stranger and you gave me no welcome, naked and you gave me no clothing, ill and in prison, and you did not care for me.' Then they will answer and say, 'Lord, when did we see you hungry or thirsty or a stranger or naked or ill or in prison, and not minister to your needs?' He will answer them, 'Amen, I say to you, what you did not do for one of these least ones, you did not do for me.' And these will go off to eternal punishment, but the righteous to eternal life." MATTHEW 25:31–46

Jesus clearly teaches us that we are to do the things that he did while he was on earth. We are to love one another as he did. We are to reach out and help people in need.

 Who does Jesus say will be invited to live in the Kingdom of God?

Living the Gospel

What are some of the ways you can be like the people blessed by God in the story Jesus told?

Understanding the Word of God

Faith Focus

What does the Gospel tell us about how we are to live and what happens to us after death?

Faith Vocabulary

heaven. Everlasting life in communion with God the Holy Trinity, and with Mary, the angels, and all the holy people who live in eternal happiness.

What do you remember about the meaning of the Gospel term *Kingdom of heaven*? How does it help you understand what Jesus taught about the Kingdom of God?

Life After Death

The good news proclaimed in Matthew 25:31–46 is that God invites all people to live with him forever. When we die, life is not ended but changed. When we die, God will judge the way each of us has lived our life on earth.

We call this our particular judgment. At our particular judgment we will be assigned to heaven, hell, or purgatory.

Heaven. Those who have been faithful on earth will be invited into the Kingdom of heaven. **Heaven** is everlasting life in communion with God the Holy Trinity, and with the Virgin Mary, the angels, and all the holy men and women who live in eternal happiness.

Purgatory. Some people who die are not ready to receive the gift of eternal life in heaven. After death, they are purified of their weakness and given the opportunity to grow in their love for God. This opportunity is called purgatory.

Hell. Sadly, some people choose to turn themselves completely away from God's love. They do this by sinning seriously and not asking God for forgiveness. When people do this and die, they choose to stay separated from God forever. We call this eternal separation from God hell.

On the last day, at the end of time, the lives of everyone will be judged. We call this the Last Judgment. On this day, God will invite all the saints to eternal life in the kingdom. Our bodies will be reunited with our immortal souls. We will rise from the dead just as Christ was raised from the dead and lives forever.

Preparing for the Kingdom

The Holy Spirit guides us and helps us while we are on earth to prepare for the Kingdom of heaven. The Gospel gives us clear advice to help us do this. We are to prepare for the coming of the kingdom by living the Great Commandment. We are to love God with all our heart, with all our soul, and with all our mind and all our strength. And we are to love our neighbors as we love ourselves. When we act with compassion toward others, we love our neighbors as ourself.

Compassion is the virtue that helps us reach out to those who are suffering as Jesus taught by his life and summarized in Matthew 25:31–46. We are to treat others as God treats us.

The Gospel also gives us a warning. It is the kind of advice we sometimes do not want to hear. He tells us that we can also choose to live separated from Christ forever. We can neglect the needy, turn our backs on society's outcasts, and simply look out for ourselves. By such neglect and selfishness, we effectively separate ourselves from Christ.

 What is the connection between our life on earth and our life after we die?

Those Blessed by God

Jesus talked about the hungry, thirsty, naked, ill, imprisoned, and the stranger. What other people can you add to that list? What is something that you can and will do to act with compassion toward these people?

Our Church Makes a Difference

ministry the Love Truck. They put into practice exactly what Saint Matthew wrote about. No one in need is left out.

You all know how important it is to be comfortable and nicely dressed for school. When the people of Saint Elizabeth's heard about the children in another parish who needed shoes for the start of school, they saw to it that every child who needed shoes received them. This is certainly the work of the "Blessed" that Saint Matthew wrote about. You might say that they put new shoes on Jesus' feet each and every time they put new shoes on a child.

 How can you help your parish follow the teaching of Jesus that Saint Matthew shares with us?

"Blessed Are the Merciful"

Since the first days of the Church, Christians have continued to help one another as Jesus asked us to do. We reach out to the hungry and thirsty, to those without shelter and in need of clothes, to those who are ill and those in prison.

The people of Saint Elizabeth Parish take this work very seriously. They have named their

What Difference Does Faith Make in My Life?

Each day the Holy Spirit is helping you see the many opportunities you have to share mercy with others as Jesus did. Every time you help someone, Jesus says that you are helping him.

Describe some of the ways you see others reaching out to people who are poor and vulnerable. Name some of the ways you might do the same.

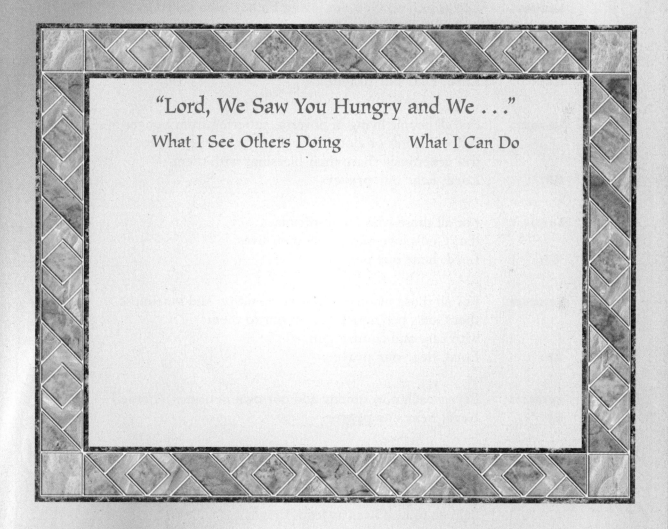

"Lord, We Saw You Hungry and We . . ."

What I See Others Doing   What I Can Do

My Faith Choice

I know that when I try to help someone in need, I am also treating Christ with kindness. This week I will

_____

_____ .

Prayer of Intercession

One way we can help others is by praying for them. In a prayer of intercession, we pray for others. Pray this prayer of intercession together.

Leader: Let us pray to God our loving Father, who called us to be his Church.
For all the members of the Church on earth that they may share God's mercy and compassion with people,

All: **Lord, hear our prayer.**

Leader: For all people living in poverty, suffering from hunger or lack of shelter or clothing or illness, that God's people will generously share their blessings with them,

All: **Lord, hear our prayer.**

Leader: For all those who are in prison, that God's love may touch their lives,

All: **Lord, hear our prayer.**

Leader: For all those who suffer from alienation and loneliness, that God's people may reach out to them with care and compassion,

All: **Lord, hear our prayer.**

Leader: Let us each now quietly add our own petitions. *(Pause.)*

All: **Lord, hear our prayer.**

Leader: God, our loving Father,
help us to see Jesus in everyone.
Through the grace of the Holy Spirit,
help us to lead lives as Jesus taught
so that we may live forever in communion with you,
your Son, and the Holy Spirit.

All: **Amen.**

We Remember

What I Have Learned

1. Use the code to discover this important message about the Gospel.

A	B	C	D	E	F	G	H	I	J	K	L	M
1	2	3	4	5	6	7	8	9	10	11	12	13

N	O	P	Q	R	S	T	U	V	W	X	Y	Z
14	15	16	17	18	19	20	21	22	23	24	25	26

4x5   12-4   10÷2   12-5   3x5   24-5   4x4   10÷2   6+6
___   ___   ___   ___   ___   ___   ___   ___   ___

6-5   2x7   12+2   3x5   22-1   9+5   3+0   10÷2   24-5
___   ___   ___   ___   ___   ___   ___   ___   ___

4x5   12-4   10÷2   21-10   3x3   28÷2   19-12   2x2   5x3   26÷2
___   ___   ___   ___   ___   ___   ___   ___   ___   ___

3+12   18-12   13-6   8+7   19-15 .
___   ___   ___   ___   ___

Answer the following.

2. Name and explain the three stages during which the forming of the Gospel took place.

_____

_____

_____

3. Compare the people Jesus says will be invited and will not be invited to enter the Kingdom of God.

_____

_____

_____

4. Describe what it means to prepare for the coming of the Kingdom of God.

_____

_____

_____

To Help You Remember

1. The Gospels are the inspired Word of God announcing Salvation in Jesus Christ.

2. The Gospels teach that we need to live the faith we profess in Jesus.

3. The death of our body is our entrance into life everlasting.

Growing in Faith

One important thing I learned this week is

_____

_____

_____ .

This is important because

_____

_____ .

What will people see me doing as I live my faith choice this week?

_____

_____

This Week . . .

In chapter 10, "'Come, You Who Are Blessed': A Scripture Story," your child learned that the Gospel is the announcement of the good news of Salvation in Jesus Christ. The four Evangelists—Matthew, Mark, Luke, and John—wrote their accounts of the Gospel under the inspiration of the Holy Spirit, who assisted them to write faithfully and without error the saving truth that God revealed in Jesus Christ. Among those truths that Saint Matthew taught is that all those who have faithfully lived as children of God will be invited to enter the Kingdom of God, which he has prepared since the beginning of the world.

For more on the teachings of the Catholic Church on the Gospel and life everlasting, see *Catechism of the Catholic Church* paragraph numbers 124–127, 946–959, 1172–1173, and 1402–1405.

Sharing God's Word

Read together Matthew 25:31–46. Emphasize that Jesus clearly teaches us that those who faithfully follow him will be invited to join him in the Kingdom of God.

Praying

In this chapter your child prayed a prayer of intercession. Read and pray together this prayer on page 130.

Making a Difference

Choose one of the following activities to do as a family or design a similar activity of your own.

- Jesus taught his disciples to reach out and help people in need. Name some of the people in need in the world today and talk about what you can do to reach out to them.

- Read and discuss some of the other Bible stories about the Kingdom of God. See Matthew 13:24–48, Matthew 20:1–16, Matthew 22:1–14, Luke 13:18–21, and Luke 14:15–24.

- Identify some of the ways that your parish follows what Jesus teaches in Matthew 25:31–46. Decide as a family how your family can join with other members of your parish to follow the teachings of Jesus.

For more ideas on ways your family can live your faith, visit the "Faith First for Families" page at **www.FaithFirst.com**. Click on "Make a Difference" to discover how your family can continue the work of Christ.

Catholic Social Teaching

Caring for Future Generations

Rodrigo is a farmer in Quichua, Ecuador. He grows food for his family to eat, but now he also grows food to sell at the market. He uses this income to buy meat and other foods for his family. His family also needs the money for clothing, school supplies, and to build an out-house.

Now timber and cattle companies want to lease his land. They would clear it completely to use it for lumbering or for cattle grazing. This would mean money for Rodrigo's family. But the land is also important to his culture, and there are sustainable and renewable resources in the rain forest that can bring in money.

Rodrigo is trying to balance his family's need for more money with the need to conserve the rain forest and pass on the land to his children.

We Care for God's Creation

God commands us to be good stewards of his creation. We have a responsibility to preserve God's creation for future generations.

Harvesting palm fronds, El Aromo, Manabi, Ecuador

VENEZUELA
GUYANA
COLUMBIA
FRENCH GUIANA
ECUADOR
SURINAME
PERU
BRAZIL
BOLIVIA
PARAGUAY
CHILE
URUGUAY
ARGENTINA
CAPE HORN

Making Connections . . .

God entrusts us with the responsibility of protecting his creation. This includes making choices that will protect the fragile ecosystem. Rather than destroying the rain forests, using them wisely and responsibly is an example of how people can use renewable and sustainable resources.

with Language Arts

Write different types of letters, such as persuasive, business, and informal, regarding the rain forests. For example, write a letter to the president of a corporation responsible for destructive logging in the Amazon. Persuade him to consider sustainable forms of logging or to use fibers not made from trees in his production of materials. Or write a letter to your government representative asking that he or she support legislation that will help reduce global warming.

with Math and Science

Rodrigo owns forty acres of land. If he leases the land to the timber company, he will make approximately $400.00 per acre. Since the land would be worthless after it is cleared, this amount is a one-time payment. If he leases to the cattle company, he will make $60.00 per acre. Yet what Rodrigo does not know is that by using the renewable and sustainable resources of his rain forest to harvest plants for medicines, the land will yield $2,400.00 per acre.

Rodrigo is facing pressure from the representatives of the timber and cattle corporations. He would receive money from them immediately. It would take longer to set up an operation to harvest plants for medicine. Create a chart to show Rodrigo what his options are. Include your own ideas, such as suggesting that Rodrigo clear a little more of his land so that he can grow more crops to sell while he preserves his other acreage to set up the harvesting venture. What do you recommend?

with Social Studies

Decorate your classroom as a rain forest. Consider the many species of animals and plants, the layers of the rain forest—floor, understory, canopy, emergent layer—and the climate. Include posters that tell facts about the rain forests and ways we can protect them.

⮕ **Faith Action** *Become a conscious steward of God's creation. Name five things you can do to help preserve the rain forests of the world.*

Name _____

A. Best Response

Read each statement and circle the best answer.

1. What is faith?
   - a. a belief of the Church
   - b. a way to pray
   - c. a supernatural gift from God
   - d. a commandment

2. What are summaries of the principal beliefs of the Church?
   - a. Gospels
   - b. proverbs
   - c. psalms
   - d. creeds

3. Where in the Bible do you find stories about the early Church?
   - a. wisdom books
   - b. New Testament
   - c. Old Testament
   - d. historical books

4. The message of the prophets centered on _____.
   - a. wisdom and sacrifice
   - b. fidelity and hope
   - c. faith and love
   - d. understanding and courage

5. We call the mystery of one God in three divine Persons _____.
   - a. Divine Revelation
   - b. the Incarnation
   - c. the Holy Trinity
   - d. Divine Providence

6. Which of the following is a result of the fall of Adam and Eve?
   - a. original sin
   - b. justice
   - c. happiness
   - d. trust

7. Who is the center of God's plan of Salvation?
   - a. Moses
   - b. Abraham
   - c. John the Baptist
   - d. Jesus Christ

8. The events of Jesus' life that make up the Paschal Mystery are his _____.
   - a. public ministry
   - b. arrest, Passion, and Crucifixion
   - c. Passion, death, Resurrection, and glorious Ascension
   - d. Baptism

9. Which feast does the Catholic Church not celebrate in honor of Mary?
   - a. Immaculate Conception
   - b. Assumption
   - c. Visitation
   - d. Pentecost

10. Which of the following is not an image of the Church?
    - a. Body of Christ
    - b. Communion of Saints
    - c. Temple of the Holy Spirit
    - d. Breath of God

B. Completing the Paragraph

Use the terms in the word bank to complete the paragraph.

> **Covenant**   **faith**   **YHWH**   **revealed**
>
> **desire**   **fidelity**   **creeds**

God has _____ himself in many ways. He places both

his word and a _____ for him within us. God calls us to

respond by accepting his gift of _____. The Pentateuch tells

the story of God revealing his name, _____. The prophets

often spoke about _____ to the promises they made to God.

In the New Testament Jesus reveals that he is the new and everlasting

_____. The Church proclaims her belief in God in the

_____ of the Church.

C. What I Have Learned

Write three things you learned in this unit. Share them with the group.

_____

_____

_____

Look at the list of faith terms in "Words to Know" on page 12.
Circle the terms you know now.

D. From a Scripture Story

*In the story of the Kingdom of God told by Matthew, Jesus names some
of the ways we are to live as his faithful disciples. In column A list two
ways that his disciples were to live. In column B describe how a faithful
disciple might put those teachings into practice today.*

Column A	Column B
_____	_____
_____	_____
_____	_____
_____	_____

Unit 2 • We Worship

What do we celebrate when we celebrate the Eucharist?

Getting Ready

What I Have Learned

What is something you already know about these faith terms?

Sacraments of Christian Initiation

_____

_____

Sacraments at the Service of Communion

_____

_____

Sacraments of Healing

_____

_____

Words to Know

Put an X next to the faith terms you know. Put a ? next to the faith terms you need to know more about.

Faith Vocabulary

_____ liturgy

_____ Passover

_____ Sabbath

_____ Confirmation

_____ Eucharist

_____ parables

_____ Liturgy of the Word

_____ Holy Communion

Questions I Have

What questions would you like to ask about the meaning of the words and actions of the sacraments that the Church uses in celebration?

_____

_____

_____

_____

A Scripture Story

Studying the Scriptures

What does Sacred Scripture teach about living a holy life?

Celebrating the Liturgy

We Pray

[L]et us bow down in worship;
let us kneel before the LORD
who made us.   PSALM 95:6

Father, all life,
all holiness comes from
you through your Son,
Jesus Christ our Lord,
by the working
of the Holy Spirit.   Amen.

*What rituals are a part of
your life?*

We all have daily rituals—
things we do pretty much the
same way each time. We may
have the same way of getting
ready for school or celebrating
a birthday or playing a sport.
The Church has rituals too.
All over the world, the Church
celebrates certain rituals day
after day, year after year.

*What rituals of the Church do
you know?*

Blessing of baptismal water
at the Easter Vigil

The Liturgy and the Body of Christ

Faith Vocabulary

liturgy. The Church's work of worshiping God.

sacraments. The seven main liturgical signs of the Church, given to us by Jesus Christ, that make his saving work present to us and make us sharers in the life of God, the Holy Trinity.

One Monday morning you are walking by a Catholic church. You decide to stop and go in. Once inside, you notice a priest, an altar server, and a group of people taking part in the celebration of Mass. It is something you have seen over and over again. But what are you seeing? Are you seeing what is really taking place?

The Liturgy

What you have witnessed is the celebration of the **liturgy**. What you are seeing is the Body of Christ, alive with the Holy Spirit, giving praise and thanksgiving to God the Father.

The mystery of Salvation in Christ is made present by the power of the Holy Spirit. The work of the Holy Spirit is to prepare the assembly to meet Christ and to recall and make him known to the assembly.

In every celebration of the liturgy and **sacraments**, the story of God's loving plan of creation and salvation is proclaimed in our midst. God speaks and we listen attentively. That is why the Liturgy of the Word is always part of our celebration of the sacraments and liturgy.

At the center of the liturgy is the Eucharist and the other sacraments. The sacraments are signs given to us by Christ. They are signs of God's grace through which we share in his life.

Just as road signs guide us in a direction, sacramental signs also point to something beyond what we see. Christ's saving work is being made present to us by the power of the Holy Spirit. We are sharing in the life of the Holy Trinity. Christ touches our lives and we are changed. This is a great mystery of our faith.

BAPTISM

CONFIRMATION

EUCHARIST

RECONCILIATION

Celebrations of the Whole Church

Every celebration of the liturgy and sacraments is a celebration of the whole Body of Christ, the Church. It is a celebration of Christ, the Head of his Body, and all the members of the Body of Christ. We join with Christ who himself leads the Church in her celebration. It is Christ himself who presides over, or leads, the Church in her celebration.

- At Baptism, for example, when the priest says, "*I baptize you*," he speaks in the name of Jesus, who baptizes.

- In the Eucharist when the priest says, "FOR THIS IS MY BODY," he speaks in the name of Jesus, who gives us his Body and Blood in the forms of bread and wine.

Because Jesus acts in the sacraments, the sacraments really do what they say they do. They unfailingly allow us to share in Christ's saving work and make us sharers in the life of God. The sacraments anticipate the coming of the Kingdom of God and give us grace to get there.

 What does the liturgy of the Church celebrate?

The Sacraments

Look at the stained-glass images of the sacraments on these two pages. Write what each of the images tells about the sacrament it portrays.

ANOINTING OF THE SICK

_____

_____

_____

HOLY ORDERS

_____

_____

_____

MATRIMONY

_____

_____

_____

Faith Focus

What are some of the
signs and symbolic
actions used in the
sacraments?

We experience many signs. Some signs are word signs, such as "Room 102," and indicate places. Other signs are action signs, such as billowing smoke, that points to a blazing fire. Still other signs combine pictures and words, such as road signs, and guide us to drive safely.

Sacramental Signs

Jesus used a variety of signs and symbolic actions during his life on earth. He anointed people and placed his hands on them. He talked about the ordinary signs of water, darkness, and light to point to the mystery of God and our life with God. He gave deeper meaning to such ordinary human activities as eating and drinking, washing and anointing.

Eucharist

Holy Orders

Sacramental celebrations combine words and signs with symbolic actions such as immersing in water, breaking bread, anointing with oil, and imposing of hands. It makes sense that the Church would use words, signs, and symbolic actions—things that we can see, touch, and hear—in the celebration of the sacraments. Through these signs, Jesus brings us into the mysteries of his life and into the very life of God, who is Father, Son, and Holy Spirit.

Celtic cross

Paschal Mystery

What is the work of Jesus when his Church, the Body of Christ, gathers with him for the celebration of the sacraments? He makes his Paschal Mystery, his Passion, death, Resurrection, and Ascension, present to us so that we can share in it and let it move us toward God's kingdom.

The celebration of the sacraments helps us take part in Jesus' passing from life to death and reminds us that we have been promised eternal life. Christ died once and was raised once. So how do we share, here and now, in the Paschal Mystery? Through the sacraments, until the end of time when Christ will come again in glory, the Holy Spirit brings Christ's Paschal Mystery to all his believing people.

The sacraments give us a glimpse at the fullness of life that God has prepared for all his faithful ones. In Jesus, the Father prepared the way for all to receive the great gift of new and resurrected life. Jesus said:

"I am the resurrection and the life; whoever believes in me, even if he dies, will live, and everyone who lives and believes in me will never die."

JOHN 11:25–26

On the last day, we will rise bodily and see God face-to-face. Beloved, we are God's children now; what we shall be has not yet been revealed. We do know that when it is revealed we shall be like him, for we shall see him as he is. 1 JOHN 3:2

❓ Why do Christ and his Body, the Church, use signs and symbolic actions to celebrate the sacraments?

Understanding Jesus Through the Liturgy

What are some of the things that you see and hear during the Eucharist and other sacraments? How do these things help you better understand what is really happening?

Faith Focus

How can we use the seasons of the liturgical year to celebrate Christ's life and grow closer to him?

Faith Vocabulary

liturgical year. The Church's yearly cycle of seasons and feasts that celebrate the mysteries of Jesus' birth, life, death, and Resurrection.

The calendar year is filled with signs and actions that let us know what time of the year we are in. Each season of the calendar year invites us to take part in it in unique ways. The Church year is called the **liturgical year**. It too is filled with signs and actions that invite us to participate in it in ways unique to each of its seasons.

The Liturgical Year

The liturgical year is not simply the passing of time. Each year is a time of grace. Each year is a celebration, a yearlong celebration of our life in Christ.

Deacon carrying lighted Easter candle, leading procession into church during the Service of Light at the beginning of the Easter Vigil

Advent

The liturgical year begins with the Advent season. Advent begins on the last Sunday in November or the first Sunday in December and lasts about four weeks. Advent is a time of preparation for Christ's coming among us.

Christmas

The Christmas season celebrates that the Son of God took on flesh and became one of us without giving up his divinity. Jesus is true God and true man. Christmas is not a one-day celebration but includes the celebration of Mary, the Mother of God, Epiphany, and the Baptism of the Lord. The word *epiphany* means "manifestation or making something known for all to see." Epiphany manifests that Jesus is the Savior of the whole world.

Lent

The Lenten season begins on Ash Wednesday, which is about forty days before Easter, not counting Sundays. Lent calls us to change our hearts, seek God's forgiveness, add new members for initiation into the Church, and renew our commitment to live our Baptism.

Easter Triduum

The center of the whole liturgical year is the Easter Triduum, or "the three days" of celebration beginning on Holy Thursday evening, continuing on Good Friday, and ending with the celebrations of the Easter Vigil and Easter Sunday.

Easter

The fifty days of the Easter season are a time of joyfully proclaiming and celebrating the Resurrection and the mystery of the new life that we have in the Risen and Glorified Christ. On the fortieth day after Easter, the Church celebrates the Ascension of the Lord. Ten days later we celebrate the great feast of Pentecost, which concludes the Easter season.

Ordinary Time

Ordinary Time is the longest time of the liturgical year. There are two parts that make up Ordinary Time. During Ordinary Time we hear stories from Jesus' public ministry from one of the four accounts of the Gospel—Matthew, Mark, Luke, or John. We learn about and work at growing as disciples of Jesus.

Sundays

Every Sunday is really a celebration of Easter. It is the Lord's Day, the day of the Lord's Resurrection. We gather around the Risen Lord, who is truly present with us, drawing us into new life with God.

Solemnities and Feasts

Throughout the liturgical year the Church celebrates solemnities and feasts of the Lord and of Mary, the Apostles, martyrs, and other holy men and women. We praise and thank God for what he has done for us through them and is doing for us through the holy men and women in our world today.

 What is your favorite season of the liturgical year? How do you celebrate it?

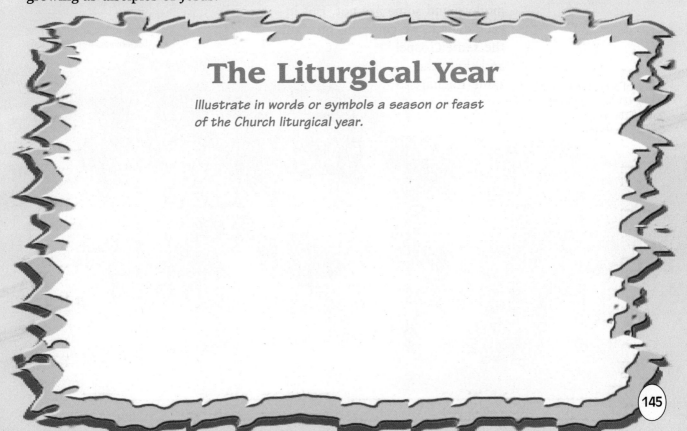

The Liturgical Year

Illustrate in words or symbols a season or feast of the Church liturgical year.

Our Church Makes a Difference

Indian dancers during liturgy celebrated by Pope John Paul II

One Faith, One Lord

No matter where you go throughout the world, the Catholic Church celebrates the sacraments. The look of the churches may be different. Some churches are massive cathedrals filled with statues and stained-glass windows. Others are simple huts. Some are modern and some are not. But in each church, we gather to proclaim the same Gospel and share the same Eucharist.

The language may be different. The music may be different. The people may even dress differently, but what is essential to our liturgy is always the same: Christ is with us as we celebrate and share in his death and Resurrection.

When the Church gathers to celebrate the sacraments, we proclaim for all to see and hear that Jesus is the Savior of the whole world and of all people. All people are invited to be joined to Christ in Baptism. There is one faith and one Lord, one God who is the Father of all. All people are invited to share in the new life of Christ. All people have the promise of eternal life.

Look at these photos of the celebration of Mass. What do they say to you about the Church and her work in the world?

Nigerian music accompanying celebration of Mass (left)

Liturgical procession during celebration of the feast of the Virgin of Guadalupe (below)

What Difference Does Faith Make in My Life?

The Holy Spirit prepares you to celebrate the sacraments. Jesus is always there, leading the Church in the celebration.

What are some of the things the Church does at the celebration of the Eucharist? How do these things help you and others take part in the celebration?

Celebrating the Eucharist

What the Church Does	How These Help Me Participate
_____	_____
_____	_____
_____	_____
_____	_____
_____	_____
_____	_____
_____	_____
_____	_____

My Faith Choice

Before Mass this week I will try to spend a few moments remembering that we are joining with Jesus in our celebration. I will

_____

_____ .

Give Praise and Thanks to God

A doxology is a prayer of praise to God the Father in the name of Jesus through the power of the Holy Spirit. Conclude this prayer by reciting the Doxology from the conclusion of the Eucharistic Prayer of the Mass.

Leader: Lord God, Father of all,
you are the source of all goodness and blessings.
Your Son is your greatest gift to us.
Send us the Holy Spirit to open our hearts
to give you praise and thanksgiving.

Reader 1: For the gift of Jesus Christ, in whose image the world was created,
All: **we praise you and give you thanks.**

Reader 2: For the gift of Jesus Christ who suffered, died, and was raised from the dead so we might enjoy the promise of eternal life,
All: **we praise you and give you thanks.**

Reader 3: For Mary, the Mother of God, the Mother of Jesus, and the Mother of the Church, whose yes to you gave us Jesus,
All: **we praise you and give you thanks.**

Reader 4: For all the saints whose faith, hope, and love model for us ways to say yes to your invitation to know, love, and serve you,
All: **we praise you and give you thanks.**

Reader 5: For the Church, the Body of Christ, our Mother and Teacher, who guides us on our earthly journey to the heavenly home Jesus has prepared for us,
All: **we praise you and give you thanks.**

Leader: Let us join with Christ and give glory to the Father.
All: **Through him, and with him, and in him,
O God, almighty Father,
in the unity of the Holy Spirit,
all honor and glory is yours,
for ever and ever. Amen.**

We Remember

What I Have Learned

Match the terms in column A with their meanings in column B.

Column A

____ **1.** liturgy

____ **2.** Paschal Mystery

____ **3.** sacraments

____ **4.** liturgical year

____ **5.** Easter Triduum

Column B

a. The Church's yearly cycle of seasons and feasts that make up the Church year of worship

b. Christ's Passion, death, Resurrection, and glorious Ascension

c. The three-day celebration that is at the center of the liturgical year of the Church

d. The seven main celebrations of the Church's liturgy given to us by Christ that make us sharers in the life of God

e. The Church's work of worshiping God

Answer the following.

6. Describe the liturgy of the Church.

_____

_____

7. Explain how the Church uses words and symbolic actions to celebrate the sacraments.

_____

_____

_____

8. Name ways the Church remembers and takes part in God's saving plan of love for us throughout the whole year.

_____

_____

_____

To Help You Remember

1. The celebration of the liturgy and sacraments is the Church's work of worshiping God.

2. The sacraments make us sharers in the life of God through the power of the Holy Spirit.

3. Throughout the year the Church praises God for what he has done and continues to do for us.

Growing in Faith

One important thing I learned this week is

_____

_____

_____.

This is important because

_____

_____

_____.

What will people see me doing as I live my faith choice this week?

_____

_____

_____

This Week . . .

In chapter 11, "Celebrating the Liturgy," your child learned more about the liturgy. The liturgy is the Church's work of worshiping God. The liturgy of the Church centers around the Eucharist and the other sacraments. In the liturgy the members of the Church gather with Christ, the Head of the Church. Through the power of the Holy Spirit, we remember and share in the Paschal Mystery of Christ's saving Passion, death, Resurrection, and glorious Ascension. The whole Church gathers to share in the life of God the Holy Trinity and to bless, praise, and give thanks to the Father with Christ. What Jesus did while he was on earth is made present here and now. We join with Christ all year long and share in the divine work of Salvation. We call the Church year of worship the liturgical year.

For more on the teachings of the Catholic Church on the liturgy, see *Catechism of the Catholic Church* paragraph numbers 1076–1109, 1136–1186, and 1206.

Sharing God's Word

Read together Psalm 95:1–7. Emphasize that the sacraments are signs and sources of God's grace through which we share the life and work of Jesus Christ, the Good Shepherd.

Praying

In this chapter your child prayed a doxology. Read and pray together this prayer on page 148.

Making a Difference

Choose one of the following activities to do as a family or design a similar activity of your own.

- When you take part in the celebration of Mass this week, notice the liturgical decorations and the priest's vestments. Talk about what they tell you about what liturgical season it is.

- Invite each family member to share their favorite liturgical season. Ask each person to explain their choice.

- Create a doorknob hanger for the front door of your home. Decorate it so that it is a reminder of the current liturgical season.

For more ideas on ways your family can live your faith, visit the "Faith First for Families" page at **www.FaithFirst.com**. Click on "Family Prayer." This week pray the special prayer as a family.

Passover and the Sabbath
A Scripture Story

We Pray

One thing I ask of the LORD;
  this I seek:
To dwell in the LORD's house
  all the days of my life.
                    PSALM 27:4

Father, all-powerful
and ever-living God,
we do well always
and everywhere
to give you thanks.   Amen.

What are some customs our nation has for remembering the important events of our history?

Families, communities, and even nations have special customs for celebrating events that are important to them. Many of these customs are passed down from generation to generation. The Church also has customs and rituals for celebrating religious feasts.

What customs do your family and parish use to celebrate the faith of the Church?

People praying at Wailing Wall in Jerusalem during Passover. The West Wall is what is left of the Temple in Jerusalem after its destruction in A.D. 70. This is the holiest shrine of the Jewish people.

151

Bible Background

Faith Focus

Why is the Book of Leviticus important?

Faith Vocabulary

rituals. The combination of words and actions used in the celebration of the liturgy.

The tribes of Israel encamped around the Ark of the Covenant during the Exodus, illuminated page from a 16th-century Latin Bible

Would you think of celebrating Christmas in August? Having a birthday pizza with candles? Easter eggs for Thanksgiving? At first you might think it would be fun. If you really did do one or two of those things, it would probably feel very strange to you.

Rituals

Why? Because special days and celebrations are kept special by observing certain rules and customs. Usually, these rules and customs have been set up for years and years before you were born, and people have practiced them for generations.

Over the years the People of God have developed **rituals**. The rituals of the Church are a combination of the words and actions used to celebrate both our faith and hope in God and our love for him. Some of the rituals have developed from the traditions and laws of God's people who lived in Old Testament times. That is why reading the Old Testament can help us learn about the liturgy of the Church.

The Book of Leviticus

One of those Old Testament books that can help us learn about the liturgy of the Church is Leviticus, the third book of the Pentateuch. Leviticus served as a liturgical handbook for the Levites, or the priests of the Israelites, who were descendants of Levi.

Levi is the name of one of the sons of Jacob and Leah. It is also the name of one of the twelve tribes of Israel, which served as a priestly tribe for God's people. The name *Levi* also appears two times in the genealogy of Jesus in Luke's Gospel.

When Jesus began his ministry he was about thirty years of age. He was the son, as was thought, of Joseph, the son of Heli, the son of Matthat, the son of Levi, . . . the son of Joshua, the son of Eliezer, the son of Jorim, the son of Matthat, the son of Levi. . . .
LUKE 3:23–24, 29

Leviticus centers on the call of God's people to holiness and the laws and rituals of worship used by the Israelites. Following rituals in the celebration of their liturgy and feasts taught the Israelites the necessity of holiness in every aspect of their lives. It made them aware that observing the laws of the Lord God provided a way of life that leads to holiness.

The LORD said to Moses, "Speak to the whole Israelite community and tell them: Be holy, for I, the LORD, your God, am holy." LEVITICUS 19:1–2

 What is the purpose of a ritual?

Special Celebration

Name your favorite celebrations of the Church. Circle one and describe how you and your family celebrate it. What things do you do over and over again each year?

Celebrations	How We Celebrate It
_____	_____
_____	_____
_____	_____

Things We Do the Same Each Year When We Celebrate It

_____

_____

_____

Reading the Word of God

Faith Focus

What does the Book of Leviticus tell us about celebrating the Sabbath and Passover?

Faith Vocabulary

Sabbath. The day of rest, the seventh day of the week, that the Israelites dedicated to God and that the Jewish people today dedicate to God as a day of rest and a holy day.

Passover. The Jewish feast that celebrates the sparing of the Hebrew children from death and God's saving his people from slavery in Egypt and leading them to freedom in the land he promised them.

Observing rules, laws, and codes of conduct plays an important role in our lives. Rules, laws, and codes of conduct help us, both as individuals and as groups, achieve common goals. Holiness is a goal shared by all God's people.

Holiness Code

The Book of Leviticus contains the Holiness Code. In this section we learn about the rituals and rules for celebrating the Israelite year of worship, including the feast of Pentecost, or Unleavened Bread, the Day of Atonement, and the Feast of Booths. We also learn, in detail, about the celebrations of the Sabbath and Passover.

Sabbath

The Holiness Code begins with the **Sabbath**. The Sabbath is the seventh day of the week. It is the day that the Israelites dedicated to God as a holy day and a day of rest. We read:

The LORD said to Moses, . . . "For six days work may be done; but the seventh day is the sabbath rest, a day for sacred assembly, on which you shall do no work. The sabbath shall belong to the LORD wherever you dwell."

LEVITICUS 23:1, 3

Passover

We next read about the feasts of **Passover** and Unleavened Bread, which are joined together in Leviticus. Passover is the Jewish feast that celebrates the sparing of the Hebrew children from death and God's saving his people from slavery in Egypt and leading them to freedom in the land he promised them. We read:

"The Passover of the LORD falls on the fourteenth day of the first month, at the evening twilight. The fifteenth day of this month is the LORD's feast of Unleavened Bread. For seven days you shall eat unleavened bread. On the first of these days you shall hold a sacred assembly and do no sort of work. On each of the seven days you shall offer an oblation to the LORD. Then on the seventh day you shall again hold a sacred assembly and do no sort of work."

LEVITICUS 23:5–8

Celebrating the Sabbath and Passover rituals helped the Israelites remember and celebrate their faith in God, hope in his promises, and share in his love. It helped them remember all that YHWH did for them, that they were his people, and to live the Covenant.

 What guidelines did the Israelites follow to celebrate the Sabbath and Passover?

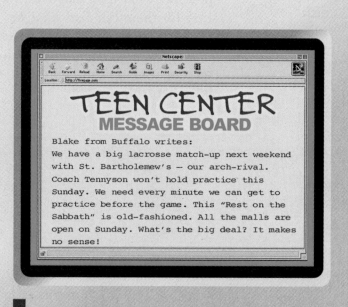

TEEN CENTER
MESSAGE BOARD

Blake from Buffalo writes:
We have a big lacrosse match-up next weekend with St. Bartholemew's — our arch-rival. Coach Tennyson won't hold practice this Sunday. We need every minute we can get to practice before the game. This "Rest on the Sabbath" is old-fashioned. All the malls are open on Sunday. What's the big deal? It makes no sense!

Observing Our Laws of Worship

Read this e-mail. How would you respond to it? Share your response with someone in your class.

Understanding the Word of God

How does observing special feasts help us live holy lives?

Holiness Is . . .

Why did the Jewish people need to have a particular kind of bread, an exact counting of days, a yearling, their first fruits? How would this make them holy? Put simply, it helped them focus on three things:

- faith in God,
- gratitude to God, and
- remembrance of God.

The painstaking time devoted to observing these feasts was time devoted to God and to living the Covenant.

Faith

The Passover feast celebrated the Israelites' faith in God who delivered them from slavery. The Sabbath expressed their belief in God who gave them all things.

Gratitude

By fasting and praying during the time of Passover, the people showed their gratitude to God, who was their true source of freedom and all blessings in the past, present, and future. By preparing meals in a special way and by sacrificing their best livestock, they gave thanks to God, who provided for them.

Remembrance

The use of unleavened bread at Passover reminded the Israelites that their ancestors had to flee Egypt so quickly that they were not able to bake bread made with yeast. By sacrificing lambs, rams, goats, and the fruit of the earth, the people paused to remember not only what God had done to care for them but also what he was doing now. God was still beside them, present with them, helping them journey through life's hardships.

The rituals for Sabbath and Passover set aside time for the Israelites to celebrate their faith, hope, and love for God. It was a time dedicated to helping them respond to God's invitation to center their lives on knowing, loving, and serving him. It was a time to respond to his invitation to be holy as he, the Lord God, is holy.

The Liturgy of the Church

The rituals and the feasts and seasons of the Church year help us celebrate and take part in the mysteries of our faith. Through the power of the Holy Spirit, we hear again and share in the Passover of Christ from his death to his entrance into new life in glory. We journey from slavery to sin to freedom as children of God. We renew our hope in God and journey toward the kingdom Jesus promised.

Each week Christians keep Sunday as the Lord's Day, a holy day and a day of rest. We remember in faith that Jesus died and was raised for us. He has truly redeemed us from sin and death and given us new life. Out of gratitude we recognize the wonders of his grace and lift up our hearts and voices and sing out God's praise. We rest from unnecessary work and acknowledge God— Father, Son, and Holy Spirit—to be both the source of our life and the end of our life.

 What is the importance of faith, gratitude, and remembrance in our life of worship?

Our Catholic Identity

Vigils

Some feasts of the Church have a vigil Mass. The celebration of the feast begins on the evening before the feast. This custom comes from the Jewish custom of beginning a day from sundown of one day to sundown of the next day. This is the reason the Catholic Church celebrates the Mass for Sunday on Saturday evening.

Give Glory to the Lord God

In this space write those things that help you celebrate your life in Christ. Then take a moment to thank God for all his gifts to you.

_____

_____

_____

_____

How great is your goodness, LORD. . . .
Blessed be the LORD,
who has shown me wondrous love.

PSALM 31:20, 22

Our Church Makes a Difference

The Lord's Day

Sunday is the Lord's Day for Christians. It is the day on which Jesus was raised from the dead. It is the day we celebrate the victory of Christ over sin and death.

At one time Christian workers were not always free to join with others in the celebration of the Eucharist on Sundays. Workers were forced to work seven days a week. The Church then made a law forbidding work on Sundays. Today this law is "On Sundays and other holy days of obligation the faithful are bound to participate in Mass; they are also to abstain from those labors and business concerns which impede the worship to be rendered to God, the joy which is proper to the Lord's Day, or the proper relaxation of mind and body" (*Code of Canon Law*, Canon 1247).

The purpose of this law of the Church is to free all workers to have time to celebrate Eucharist and rest on the Lord's Day. The law gives them the freedom to keep the Lord's Day holy and the time to be with their families and to relax. It guides workers from becoming slaves to their work and keeps employers from making workers slaves to their work.

QUESTION *What are some of the ways you see Christians keeping Sunday as the Lord's Day? How does keeping Sunday as the Lord's Day free people to live as children of God?*

What Difference Does Faith Make in My Life?

Each week you take part in the celebration of Mass. You give thanks to God and keep him at the center of your life.

It is one of those sunny, warm days at the beach—one of those days when the whole wide world seems to be in perfect harmony. Right overhead comes a plane trailing an advertisement. Everyone looks up. Within the banner write an invitation to people that best expresses how we all need to thank and celebrate God.

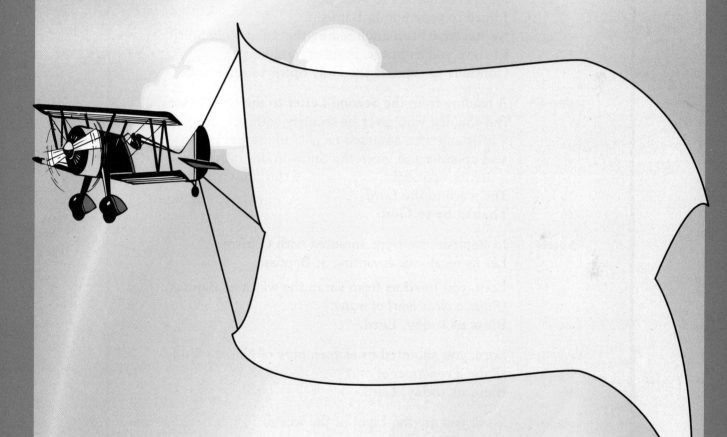

My Faith Choice

I will try to celebrate Sunday as a holy day. This week I will

_____

_____.

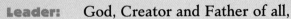

Bless Us Today

In the Old Testament, kings and priests were anointed with oil. This was a sign that they were chosen by God for a special service to God's people. It was also a sign that God would be with them to help them in their work.

Leader: God, Creator and Father of all,
You sent the Holy Spirit to anoint kings,
  prophets, and priests in the Old Covenant
for special service to your people.
Joined to your Son in Baptism,
we too have been anointed by the same Holy Spirit,
to serve you as priest, prophet, and king.
Continue to send us the Holy Spirit to serve you.

Reader: A reading from the Second Letter to the Corinthians.
But the one who gives us security with you in
Christ and who anointed us is God; he has put his
seal upon us and given the Spirit in our hearts as
a first installment.   2 CORINTHIANS 1:21–22
The word of the Lord.

All: **Thanks be to God.**

Leader: In Baptism, we were anointed with Chrism.
Let us recall our anointing at Baptism.

Lord, you freed us from sin in the water of Baptism.
(Raise a clear bowl of water.)

All: **Bless us today, Lord.**

Leader: Lord, you anointed us as members of Christ's Body.
(Raise a container of oil.)

All: **Bless us today, Lord.**

Leader: Lord, you are the Light of the world.
(Lift up a candle.)

All: **Bless us today, Lord.**

Leader: Let us now go forth to love and serve the Lord.

All: **Thanks be to God.**

What I Have Learned

1. Use the letters in the word RITUAL to describe what the Bible tells us about celebrating rituals.

R _____

I _____

T _____

U _____

A _____

L _____

Answer the following.

2. Describe the importance of the Holiness Code in the Book of Leviticus.

_____

_____

3. Compare codes of conduct in daily life with the rituals of the Church.

_____

_____

_____

4. Explain how Catholics celebrate Sunday as the Lord's Day.

_____

_____

_____

To Help You Remember

1. The Old Testament Book of Leviticus contains the liturgical rituals of the Israelites.

2. The rituals for Passover and the Sabbath and other liturgical rituals helped the Israelites celebrate their faith in God and grow in holiness.

3. Some of the rituals of the Catholic Church have their roots in the rituals of the Israelites, our ancestors in faith.

Growing in Faith

One important thing I learned this week is

_____

_____

_____.

This is important because

_____

_____

_____.

What will people see me doing as I live my faith choice this week?

_____

_____

This Week . . .

In chapter 12, "Passover and the Sabbath: A Scripture Story," your child learned more about the liturgy. They discovered that many of the liturgical rituals of the Church have their roots in the Old Testament. They became familiar with the Old Testament book of Leviticus, which was a liturgical handbook for the Israelites. Leviticus contains many of the liturgical laws and rituals of the Israelites and centers on the call of God's people to be "holy as the LORD God is holy" (Leviticus 19:2).

For more on the teachings of the Catholic Church on the use of rituals in the liturgy of the Church, see *Catechism of the Catholic Church* paragraph numbers 1136–1181.

Sharing God's Word

Read together Leviticus 23:1, 3, 5–8. Emphasize that taking part in the ritual celebrations of their religion helped the Israelites remember and celebrate their faith in God.

Praying

In this chapter your child recalled their Baptism and participated in a prayer asking for God's blessing. Read and pray together this prayer on page 160.

Making a Difference

Choose one of the following activities to do as a family or design a similar activity of your own.

• Talk about the rituals your family has for celebrating Thanksgiving, Christmas, and Easter. Discuss how these rituals began and why they are important to your family.

• Discuss the following questions: What are some of the ways you see people keeping Sunday as the Lord's Day? How does keeping Sunday as the Lord's Day help people live as children of God?

• Choose one thing your family does or will do together to keep Sunday as the Lord's Day.

For more ideas on ways your family can live your faith, visit the "Faith First for Families" page at **www.FaithFirst.com**. This week share some of the ideas on the "Gospel Reflections" page as a family.

Baptism and Confirmation

13

We Pray

I will live for the LORD.
PSALM 22:31

Lord God,
send your Holy Spirit
to make us witnesses
to Jesus Christ.   Amen.

Describe the way you formally became a member of a group to which you now belong.

Think of a time that you joined with friends to become members of a group. Baptism, Confirmation, and Eucharist initiate us, or bring us, into new life with Jesus Christ and his Body, the Church.

What happens when a person is baptized?

Newly baptized clothed
with white baptismal garments

163

We Belong to Christ

Faith Vocabulary

Baptism. The Sacrament of Christian Initiation in which we are joined to Jesus Christ, become members of the Church, are reborn as God's adopted children, receive the gift of the Holy Spirit, and original sin and our personal sins are forgiven.

Baptism, Confirmation, and Eucharist are the Sacraments of Christian Initiation. Through the celebration of these three sacraments a person becomes joined to Christ and his Body, the Church. What do you remember about your celebration of Baptism? Why was it an important event in your life and in the life of your family?

Baptism

Baptism is the first sacrament we receive. In the rite of Baptism the Church uses certain objects, words, and actions that all point to what is happening in this sacrament. The proper use of these objects, words, and actions makes us sharers in the life of Christ.

Rite of Baptism

The Church uses water in the celebration of Baptism. Jesus told Nicodemus:

"Amen, Amen, I say to you, no one can enter the kingdom of God without being born of water and Spirit." JOHN 3:5

In different ways the sign of water in the Old Testament prepared for its use in the Sacrament of Baptism. The bishop, priest, or deacon who is the ordinary minister of this sacrament blesses the water to be used in Baptism. He prays in part:

Father,
you give us grace through
   sacramental signs,
which tell us of the wonders of
   your unseen power. . . .
At the very dawn of creation
your Spirit breathed on the
   waters,
making them the wellspring
   of all holiness. . . .
Through the waters of the
   Red Sea
you led Israel out of slavery
to be an image of God's holy
   people
set free from sin by baptism.

The minister of Baptism then immerses the person to be baptized into the water three times or pours water over the person's head three times, saying,

(Name), I baptize you in the
   name of the Father,
   and of the Son,
   and of the Holy Spirit.

The immersing of the person in water or the pouring of water on the person's head while saying the words is essential to Baptism.

Sacramental Graces

What happens to us when we are baptized? What happens is called the sacramental graces of Baptism. They are the effects of celebrating this sacrament. The sacramental graces of Baptism are:

- We are joined to Christ in his dying and rising.
- We receive new birth in Christ and become adopted daughters and sons of God the Father.
- We receive the gift of the Holy Spirit.
- We become members of the Church, the Body of Christ, and are made sharers in the priesthood of Christ.
- We are freed from all sin—original sin and personal sins.
- We are spiritually marked as belonging to Christ forever. This mark, or sacramental character, which no sin can erase, is indelible. This mark means that Baptism is given once and for all and cannot be repeated.

Since the early days of the Church, both adults and children have been baptized. Baptism is the gateway, or doorway, to new life in the Holy Spirit and to Salvation in Christ.

 How does the image of water in the Old Testament help us understand Baptism?

"It Changed My Life!"

Imagine that a person who recently became a member of the Catholic Church is coming to visit your class. What questions would you ask this person?

Q

Q

Q

Faith Vocabulary

Confirmation. The Sacrament of Christian Initiation that strengthens the grace of Baptism and in which our life in Christ is sealed by the gift of the Holy Spirit.

Anointing with Chrism

Think about the groups to which you belong. Becoming a full member of a group often involves a long process that includes many steps. The Sacrament of **Confirmation** is the second of the three Sacraments of Christian Initiation.

Confirmation

Receiving all three Sacraments of Christian Initiation makes a baptized person a full member of the Church. Most Catholics today are baptized as infants and receive the Sacrament of Confirmation many years later.

The Rite of Confirmation

The anointing with oil in the Old Testament prepared for its use in the Sacrament of Confirmation. For example, after God chose Saul to be the first king of his people, he sent Samuel to anoint Saul:

> When Samuel caught sight of Saul, the LORD assured him, "This is the man of whom I told you; he is to govern my people." . . . Then, from a flask he had with him, Samuel poured oil on Saul's head; he also kissed him, saying: "The LORD anoints you commander over his heritage. You are to govern the LORD's people Israel."   1 SAMUEL 9:17, 10:1

In this passage and in other Old Testament passages, anointing with oil was a sign that the Holy Spirit lived within a person. The Holy Spirit helped the person do the work God had chosen them to do.

In Confirmation the bishop or priest-delegate rests his hand on the top of each candidate's head as he anoints the candidate's forehead with Chrism, saying:

(Name), be sealed with the gift of the Holy Spirit.

The bishop then says to the newly confirmed, "Peace be with you." The newly confirmed replies, "And with your spirit."

Sacramental Graces, or Effects, of Confirmation

Confirmation, as does Baptism, has special sacramental graces. At Confirmation we receive and accept important responsibilities and the graces to fulfill them. The sacramental graces of Confirmation are:

- We receive the grace of the Holy Spirit in our lives.
- We accept that grace and commit to join Christ in his mission to prepare for the coming of the Kingdom of God.

- We cooperate with the grace of the Holy Spirit and bring healing and reconciliation to the world.
- The grace of the Holy Spirit strengthens our bond with the Church and her mission to defend the faith.
- The grace of the Holy Spirit guides us to live as signs of the Covenant as the prophets did.

Confirmation, like Baptism, may be received only once. We receive the grace to remain witnesses for Christ, even in the face of misunderstanding, ridicule, and suffering. The Gifts of the Holy Spirit, namely, wisdom, understanding, right judgment (counsel), courage (fortitude), knowledge, reverence (piety), and wonder and awe (fear of the Lord) help us live as followers of Jesus Christ.

 QUESTION *What does the Church celebrate at Confirmation?*

Our Catholic Identity

Laying On of Hands

The laying on of hands is an important ritual of the Church. This ancient ritual is found in both the Old Testament and the New Testament. Its use signifies a bestowal of an office or a responsibility, of God's blessing, or of God's healing through the invocation of the Holy Spirit. The laying on of hands is an essential part of the rite of Confirmation. Strengthened by the Holy Spirit, we receive the grace to be witnesses for Christ.

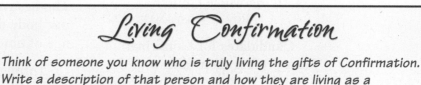

Living Confirmation

Think of someone you know who is truly living the gifts of Confirmation. Write a description of that person and how they are living as a "confirmed" Catholic.

_____

_____

_____

_____

_____

_____

_____

Think of the groups of which you are a member. What were the requirements you had to meet to become a member of those groups?

Candidates' Requirements for Confirmation

Who can receive the Sacrament of Confirmation? The Catholic Church in her wisdom asks that a person meet these requirements before being confirmed.

Faith

The person who is to be confirmed must be baptized. Baptism is the doorway to the other sacraments. During the rite of Confirmation the bishop asks the candidates:

> Now, before you receive the Spirit, I ask you to renew the profession of faith you made in baptism or your parents and godparents made in union with the whole Church.
> RITE OF CONFIRMATION 22

Candidates for Confirmation must profess their faith with the Church. Those who are confirmed take on the special responsibility of witnessing to their faith and even defending it when necessary. They must be willing to share what they believe.

Age

The grace of Confirmation is a gift of God. Receiving this grace does not depend on the age of the person being confirmed. As Saint Thomas Aquinas wrote, "Age of our body does not determine the age of our soul."

Throughout the history of the Church, infants, school-age children, and high school students, as well as adults, have received the Sacrament of Confirmation. Today, in the United States, young people who are Roman Catholics are confirmed at various ages. In Eastern Rite Catholic Churches, Confirmation is administered immediately after Baptism and is followed by participation in the Eucharist.

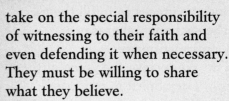

Grace

Candidates for Confirmation must be in a state of grace. Those who are confirmed receive a renewed gift of the Holy Spirit, a deeper unity with Jesus Christ, and a closer bond with the whole Body of Christ. Thus, their relationship with God must be close.

Will, or Choice

The candidates need to have a clear and deliberate intention to receive the sacrament. They must be open to accept the responsibilities of being witnesses for Christ.

Preparation for Confirmation

Confirmation marks our lifelong commitment to be witnesses for Christ. With the help of the Holy Spirit, we prepare ourselves for Confirmation. This preparation includes prayer, service, and reception of the Sacrament of Reconciliation. It also includes choosing a sponsor.

A sponsor is someone who gives spiritual help and encouragement to a person who is preparing to receive Confirmation. Because Confirmation continues and deepens the graces of Baptism, it is fitting that our Confirmation sponsor be one of our baptismal godparents.

QUESTION *What are the requirements for Confirmation?*

Sponsors

Name a quality you would look for in your sponsor for Confirmation. Describe why you named that quality.

Quality	Reasons
_____	_____
_____	_____
	_____
	_____

Our Church Makes a Difference

Saint of the Holocaust

Maximilian Kolbe was a living witness for Christ. Jesus' greatest sign of his love for God and for all people was his freely giving up his life on the cross. Maximilian Kolbe was a Franciscan priest who lived in Poland. During World War II Father Maximilian and his brother Franciscans gave shelter to more than three thousand people being sought by the Nazis. Because of his work, Father Kolbe was arrested and on May 28, 1941, was sent to Auschwitz and branded prisoner number 16670.

In July 1941 several prisoners tried to escape. As punishment, ten men prisoners were chosen to be put to death. Francis Gajowniczek, a young father, was among the prisoners chosen. Strengthened by the Gifts of the Holy Spirit, Father Maximilian stepped forward and volunteered to give up his life in place of the young father. And on August 14, 1941, he was put to death by fatal injection.

Father Maximilian became "a martyr of charity, out of love for Jesus and others" (Pope John Paul II). On October 10, 1982, Pope John Paul II named Father Maximilian a saint of the Church. The pope described him as a "martyr of charity" for us to imitate.

QUESTION *What people do you see living as witnesses for Christ?*

Pope John Paul II walking in the Auschwitz concentration camp, after visiting Saint Maximilian Kolbe's cell block

Saint Maximilian Kolbe (1894–1941), patron of journalists, families, and the pro-life movement

What Difference Does Faith Make in My Life?

You are called to be a living witness for Christ. Strengthened with the gift of the Holy Spirit, you continue the work of Christ in the world today.

Look at your life right now. Create a motto or brief statement describing what you can do right now to be a witness for Christ.

Sealed with the Gift of the Holy Spirit

My Faith Choice

This week I will put my witness motto into action. I will

_____

_____.

Come, Holy Spirit

We first receive the gift of the Holy Spirit at Baptism and are sealed with the gift of the Holy Spirit at Confirmation.

Leader: On the day of Pentecost tongues of fire parted and came to rest on the disciples. They were all filled with the Holy Spirit.

Let us listen to God's word to discover ways that show we are truly living as witnesses for Christ.

Reader: A reading from the letter of Paul to the Galatians.
. . . the fruit of the Spirit is love, joy, peace, patience, kindness, generosity, faithfulness, gentleness, self-control. Against such there is no law. Now those who belong to Christ [Jesus] have crucified their flesh with its passions and desires. If we live in the Spirit, let us also follow the Spirit. Let us not be conceited, provoking one another, envious of one another.   GALATIANS 5:22–26
The word of the Lord.

All: **Thanks be to God.**

Leader: Remember that the Holy Spirit dwells within us. Let us ask the Holy Spirit to give us the grace to be living witnesses for Christ.

All: **Come, Holy Spirit,**
fill the hearts of your faithful.
And kindle in them the fire of your love.
Send forth your Spirit
and they shall be created.
And you will renew the face of the earth.

We Remember

What I Have Learned

1. *Compare and contrast the Sacrament of Baptism and the Sacrament of Confirmation.*

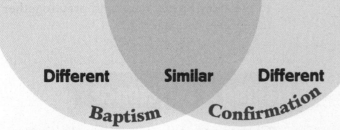

Different   **Similar**   **Different**

Baptism   **Confirmation**

Answer the following.

2. Describe what the use of water in Baptism tells us about Baptism.

_____

_____

_____

3. Describe what the anointing with Chrism in Confirmation tells us about Confirmation.

_____

_____

_____

4. Describe how someone might prepare for Confirmation.

_____

_____

_____

To Help You Remember

1. A person becomes fully initiated into the Church through the celebration of the three Sacraments of Christian Initiation—Baptism, Confirmation, and Eucharist.

2. Baptism is the first sacrament we receive. It is the doorway to new life in the Holy Spirit and Salvation in Christ.

3. Confirmation perfects the grace of Baptism.

Growing in Faith

One important thing I learned this week is

_____

_____

_____.

This is important because

_____

_____

_____.

What will people see me doing as I live my faith choice this week?

_____

_____

_____

This Week . . .

In chapter 13, "Baptism and Confirmation," your child learned more about Baptism and Confirmation. We are joined to Christ and made sharers in the life of the Holy Trinity through the Sacraments of Christian Initiation—Baptism, Confirmation, and Eucharist. Through Baptism we first receive new life and Salvation in Christ and become members of the Body of Christ, the Church. By God's gift, through water and the Holy Spirit, original sin and everything that separates us from God is washed away. Confirmation confirms, or seals, Baptism. The Holy Spirit strengthens us to be witnesses for Christ by empowering us to live the Gospel and proclaim Jesus Christ to others.

For more on the teachings of the Catholic Church on Baptism and Confirmation, see *Catechism of the Catholic Church* paragraph numbers 1210–1274 and 1285–1314.

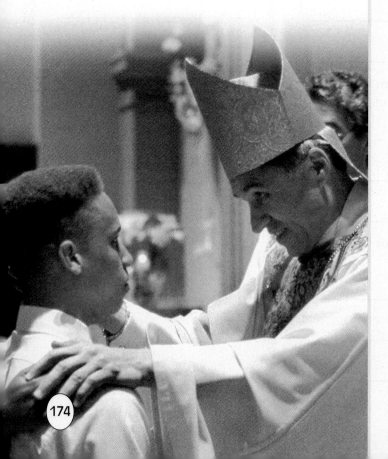

Sharing God's Word

Read together John 3:3–6. Emphasize that through the Sacrament of Baptism we are reborn of water and the Holy Spirit.

Praying

In this chapter your child prayed a prayer to the Holy Spirit. Read and pray together this prayer on page 172.

Making a Difference

Choose one of the following activities to do as a family or design a similar activity of your own.

- Water can symbolize many things. Talk about what water symbolizes for you. Share ideas about how water helps you understand what happens in Baptism.

- Place a dish of holy water in a convenient location in your home. Bless each other and yourself as you come and go during the day and before bedtime. As you bless yourself with the holy water, remember that in Baptism we become members of the Body of Christ.

- Invite family members to name someone who is living as a witness for Christ. Describe what this person does to live as a witness for Christ.

For more ideas on ways your family can live your faith, visit the "Faith First for Families" page at **www.FaithFirst.com**. This week click on "Just for Parents."

ff

David, King of Israel
A Scripture Story

14

We Pray

The LORD swore an oath
   to David,
 a pledge never to be broken:
 "Your own offspring I will
   set upon your throne."

PSALM 132:11

Father, send the Holy Spirit
to guide the ministers
of the Church to carry
out their ministry with
gentleness and concern
for others as Jesus did.

Amen.

*Name some types of writing that
you enjoy reading.*

There are many different types
of literature and other writings.
The writers of the Bible used
many types of writing to
communicate God's word.

*Name some of the types of
writing you know that the writers
of the Bible used.*

David, king of Israel (1040–970 B.C.)
and writer of psalms

Bible Background

Faith Focus

What do the historical books of the Old Testament tell about God and his Covenant?

Faith Vocabulary

judges of Israel. The leaders of Israel before they had kings—Othniel, Ehud, Deborah and Barak, Gideon, Abimelech, Jephthah, and Samson are among the judges of Israel whose stories are told in the Book of Judges.

Alexander the Great was king of Macedonia from 336–323 B.C. He became the ruler of the largest empire ever led by one ruler. Alexander's army entered Jerusalem in 332 B.C.

The Bible is a mini-library. As a library does, the Bible contains many different kinds of writings or books. In chapter 2 you learned that the forty-six books of the Old Testament are grouped into four types of writings, namely, the Pentateuch, or Torah; the historical writings; the wisdom writings; and the writings of the prophets.

The Historical Books

All together, the historical books cover about a thousand years of history. The historical books include:

- Joshua, Judges, and Ruth
- 1 and 2 Samuel
- 1 and 2 Kings
- 1 and 2 Chronicles
- Ezra, Nehemiah
- Tobit, Judith, and Esther
- 1 and 2 Maccabees

The historical books begin with the time of the **judges of Israel** (ca. 1200–1050 B.C.). Then the spotlight of history shines on the monarchy, or office of the king, in Israel.

Israelite pottery of the 10th–7th centuries B.C. (Iron II period), lamps, bowls, juglets, and larger water jugs

German archaeologists discovered and excavated ancient Babylon in the early 1900s. This painting shows the grandeur Babylon once had.

In this chapter you will learn more about the First Book of Samuel. This book of the Old Testament includes the anointing of Saul and David as kings of Israel.

This part of the story begins with Saul (ca.1020 B.C.), David (1000–962 B.C.), and Solomon (961–922 B.C.). The historical writings continue with the stories of other kings until the destruction of Jerusalem and the exile of God's people in Babylon in the year 587 B.C.

Eventually, God's people returned to their homeland, as the prophets promised, and they rebuilt their broken lives. The last historical books, 1 and 2 Maccabees, tell of the persecution of the Jewish people and their struggle to keep the faith.

The historical books are very important for Catholics. They help us understand how God is active and involved in our history. Sharing the story of God's people, the Israelites, the historical books show us that God is able to draw good things out of difficult and even sinful situations.

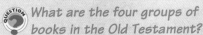 What are the four groups of books in the Old Testament?

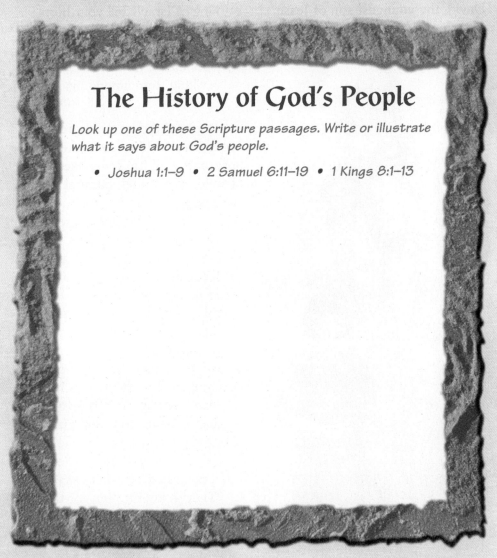

The History of God's People

Look up one of these Scripture passages. Write or illustrate what it says about God's people.

- Joshua 1:1–9
- 2 Samuel 6:11–19
- 1 Kings 8:1–13

Some Important Events in the History of God's People

ca. 2000–1700 B.C.
Covenant with Abraham

ca. 1300–1050 B.C.
Exodus and Covenant with Moses

ca. 1200–1050 B.C.
The Period of the Judges

ca. 1020–539 B.C.
The Period of the Kings and the Exile

333–323 B.C.
Alexander the Great defeats Persians and rules Israel and other countries in Asia Minor

175–135 B.C.
The Revolt of the Maccabees

Reading the Word of God

Who was David and how did he come to be anointed king?

When we read the historical books today, we can begin to understand more clearly how God continues to be with us. We discover that he guides and calls to us to live lives of faith, hope, and love.

The Anointing of David

In chapter 13 we read about Samuel's anointing of Saul as the first king of God's people in Israel. The First Book of Samuel also recounts Samuel the Prophet's anointing of David as king. The Hebrew name *David* means "beloved." Born in Bethlehem, David, the youngest son of Jesse, was chosen by God to be king of God's people.

After the failure of Saul to serve faithfully as king, God rejected Saul and said to Samuel:

"I regret having made Saul king, for he has turned from me and has not kept my command." 1 SAMUEL 15:11

Samuel, who became tremendously upset, went off to tell Saul that God had rejected him. Saul eventually became so angry that he and Samuel never spoke again.

God again came to Samuel and said:

"How long will you grieve for Saul, whom I have rejected as king of Israel? Fill your horn with oil, and be on your way. I am sending you to Jesse of Bethlehem, for I have chosen my king from among his sons." 1 SAMUEL 16:1

Samuel did as the Lord commanded him. And after Jesse presented all his sons, except for David, to Samuel, Samuel said to Jesse:

"The LORD has not chosen any one of these." Then Samuel asked Jesse, "Are these all the sons you have?" Jesse replied, "There is still the youngest, who is tending the sheep." Samuel said to Jesse, "Send for him; we will not begin the sacrificial banquet until he arrives here." Jesse sent and had the young man brought to them. He was ruddy, a youth handsome to behold and making a splendid appearance. The LORD said, "There—anoint him, for this is he!" Then Samuel, with the horn of oil in hand, anointed him in the midst of his brothers; and from that day on, the spirit of the LORD rushed upon David.

1 SAMUEL 16:10–13

Samuel did as God commanded him. He went to Bethlehem where he anointed David as king of Israel. David ruled as king for nearly forty years. He drew up the plans to build the Temple in Jerusalem and wrote many prayer poems, or psalms.

From the house of David would come the Messiah, the Anointed One of God, who would save his people. Both Saint Matthew and Saint Luke in their genealogies of Jesus name David as an ancestor of Jesus.

As Jesus entered the city of Jerusalem for the last time before his death and Resurrection, we read that:

the crowds preceding him and those following kept crying out and saying:

"Hosanna to the Son of David; blessed is he who comes in the name of the Lord; hosanna in the highest."

MATTHEW 21:9

Jesus is the Son of David. He is the Messiah and Savior promised by God.

 What qualities do you think are needed for someone to be a leader of God's people?

King David

Design this shield with symbols that tell about David, who was shepherd, king, psalm writer, and ancestor of Jesus, the Messiah.

Understanding the Word of God

Faith Focus

What is the meaning of the symbolic act of anointing someone with oil?

Faith Vocabulary

consecrate. Set aside and dedicate for a holy purpose.

In the Old Testament, kings, priests, and prophets were anointed for special service among God's people. This set them aside for the holy purpose of doing God's work among his people. The word consecrate means "to set aside for a holy purpose."

Set Aside to Serve God's People

From the time of the Apostles until the present, the Church continues this Old Testament ritual of consecrating people and things by anointing. In Baptism, Confirmation, and Holy Orders, people are anointed for the service of God and the People of God.

Baptism

During the rite of Baptism, the newly baptized person is anointed with Chrism. Chrism is the blessed oil used by the Church only for the consecration of people and things. The bishop, priest, or deacon anoints the crown of the head of the newly baptized, saying,

The God of power and Father
    of our Lord Jesus Christ
has freed you from sin
and brought you to new life
through water and the
    Holy Spirit.

He now anoints you with the
    chrism of salvation,
so that, united with his people,
you may remain for ever a
    member of Christ,
who is Priest, Prophet,
    and King.

RITE OF BAPTISM FOR CHILDREN 62

This shows that the baptized are to live by serving God and others as Jesus did.

Anointing
in Baptism

Anointing in Confirmation

Confirmation

Confirmation includes the anointing of our forehead with Chrism. Sealed with the gift of the Holy Spirit, we are to be witnesses for Christ, the Anointed One of God, who proclaimed:

"The Spirit of the Lord is
    upon me,
  because he has anointed me
    to bring glad tidings to
        the poor,
He has sent me to proclaim
    liberty to captives
  and recovery of sight to the
    blind,
    to let the oppressed go free,
  and to proclaim a year acceptable
    to the Lord."   LUKE 4:18

Holy Orders

In Holy Orders the hands of the newly ordained priests are anointed with Chrism. The bishop prays:

The Father anointed our Lord Jesus Christ through the power of the Holy Spirit. May Jesus preserve you to sanctify the Christian people and to offer sacrifice to God.

This signifies that priests have the ministry to sanctify the people and to offer sacrifices to God.

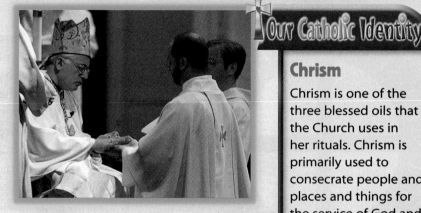
Anointing of hands of newly ordained priest

When we read the historical books of the Bible, we can appreciate the long tradition of anointing in the life of God's people. We can see more clearly that God strengthens his people for a life of faith, hope, and love in service to him, to the Church, and to all people.

 What is the meaning of the anointing of the baptized with Chrism in the sacraments?

Holy Oils

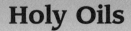

Design a label on this jar that is used to hold Chrism. Include on your label the meaning of the use of Chrism.

Our Church Makes a Difference

United States Conference of Catholic Bishops

The bishops are anointed to serve the People of God, the Church. They are anointed to lead the Church in worshiping God, living the Gospel, and proclaiming the Gospel to all people. In the United States of America the bishops work together to fulfill these responsibilities.

One way they work together is in the United States Conference of Catholic Bishops (USCCB). The USCCB proclaims the teachings of Jesus by writing pastoral letters. These letters often remind Catholics and all Americans of their responsibility to be faithful to the laws of God. They teach about working for justice and peace, for the equal sharing of food and health care by all people, for the protection of all human life and the environment, and other issues that proclaim the dignity of all people.

In a meeting in Rome in 2001, bishops from the United States and other parts of the world discussed this important work. At the end of the meeting, the pope reminded all the bishops that they are "servants of the Gospel for the hope of the world." Just as the anointed leaders in the Old Testament led the people to live the Covenant with God, the bishops of the Church bring hope to the world by courageously leading the Church to live the Gospel.

QUESTION *How do you see Catholics working together to serve others?*

Bishops process in the Basilica of the National Shrine of the Immaculate Conception, Washington, DC, during evening Mass on first day of a general meeting of the United States Conference of Catholic Bishops

What Difference Does Faith Make in My Life?

When you were baptized, you were anointed on the crown of your head with Chrism. This was a sign that God was now anointing you to serve others as Jesus did.

In the circle write one thing you can do to serve others as Jesus did. On the lines coming from the circle, write how that action helps others.

Anointed to Serve

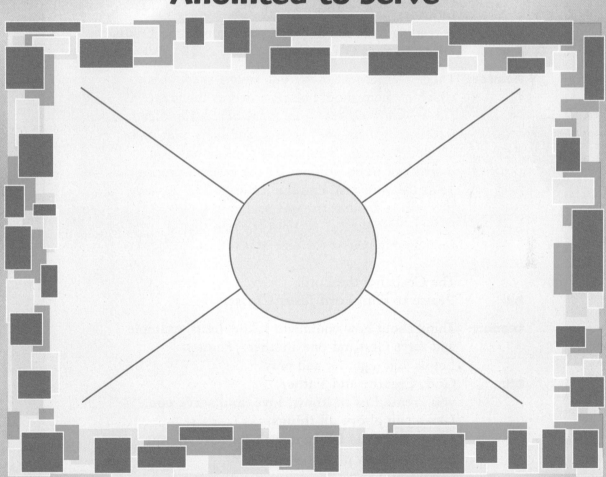

My Faith Choice

This week I will remember that I have been anointed to serve God and others. I will

_____

_____.

Serve as Jesus Did

We serve as Jesus did when we love God and others as Jesus did. Pray this act of love asking God the Father to help you respond to his call to you to serve others.

Leader: Jesus told us to serve others out of love for God and for them. Close your eyes; imagine you are among the disciples at the Last Supper listening to Jesus.

Reader: A reading from the holy Gospel according to Luke.

All: **Glory to you, O Lord.**

Reader: Then an argument broke out among them about which of them should be regarded as the greatest. [Jesus] said to them, "The kings of the Gentiles lord it over them and those in authority over them are addressed as 'Benefactors'; but among you it shall not be so. Rather, let the greatest among you be as the youngest, and the leader as the servant. For who is greater: the one seated at table or the one who serves? Is it not the one seated at table? I am among you as the one who serves."

LUKE 22:24–27

The Gospel of the Lord.

All: **Praise to you, Lord Jesus Christ.**

Leader: Think about how you might follow Jesus' example and serve God and one another. *(Pause.)* Let us join together and pray.

All: **God, Creator and Father,
you created us to know, love, and serve you.
I love you above all things.
I love others as I love myself for love of you.
Send the Holy Spirit to guide me
to love and serve as Jesus did. Amen.**

We Remember

What I Have Learned

Write the letter of the name of the person in the word box on the line next to the phrase that describes that person.

> **a.** Samuel   **b.** Saul   **c.** David

_____ **1.** Anointed David as king of Israel

_____ **2.** Wrote some of the Psalms in the Book of Psalms

_____ **3.** Made plans to build the Temple in Jerusalem

_____ **4.** Ancestor of Jesus

_____ **5.** Told by Samuel that he would no longer be king of the Israelites

Answer the following.

6. Describe the role of anointing in the Old Testament.

_____

_____

_____

7. Explain the meaning of Samuel's anointing of David.

_____

_____

_____

8. Compare the ritual of anointing in the Old Testament with anointing in the Church.

_____

_____

_____

_____

To Help You Remember

1. The historical books of the Old Testament pass on the story of the Israelites from the time they entered the Promised Land to the persecution of the Jewish people just before the birth of Jesus.

2. The historical books tell us about the anointing of David as king of Israel.

3. The historical books help Christians discover that God is active in the history of the Church.

Growing in Faith

One important thing I learned this week is

_____

_____

_____ .

This is important because

_____

_____

_____ .

What will people see me doing as I live my faith choice this week?

_____

_____

_____

This Week . . .

In chapter 14, "David, King of Israel: A Scripture Story," your child learned more about the Old Testament and its integral connection with the New Testament. Christians often divide the writings of the Old Testament into the Pentateuch (or Torah), historical writings, the writings of the Prophets, and wisdom writings. In this chapter your child took a deeper look at the historical books. In particular, they learned about David and his anointing as the king of Israel. The historical books of the Old Testament help Christians come to know that God is active and involved in the Church today.

For more on the teachings of the Catholic Church on the unity of Sacred Scriptures see *Catechism of the Catholic Church* paragraph numbers 54–64, 101–133, and 839.

Sharing God's Word

Read together 1 Samuel 16:1–13. Emphasize that God chose David to serve his people as king.

Praying

In this chapter your child prayed an act of love. Read and pray together this prayer on page 184.

Making a Difference

Choose one of the following activities to do as a family or design a similar activity of your own.

• David was chosen as the leader of God's people. Discuss the following questions: What makes a good leader? In what ways are you a leader? Why do leaders love what they do? How does God help leaders accomplish good things?

• In this chapter is a time line of important events in the history of the Israelites. Make a family time line. Include all the significant dates for your family. Be sure to include the events and people that have had great influence on your family.

• When you take part in Mass this week, find the ambry in your church. The ambry is where the blessed oils are kept. These oils are used in the sacraments. Talk about how you are living out your baptismal anointing.

For more ideas on ways your family can live your faith, visit the "Faith First for Families" page at **www.FaithFirst.com**. Click on "Current Events" and discuss it as a family.

The Eucharist

15

We Pray

They asked and . . .
   with bread from heaven
   [the LORD] filled them.
                    PSALM 105:40

Lord Jesus Christ,
we worship you among us
in the sacrament of your
Body and Blood.   Amen.

*Name some symbols you
sometimes see or hear and tell
what they point to.*

Symbols point to something
beyond themselves. For
example, when you see smoke
you look for fire. The Church
uses symbols in the celebration
of the sacraments.

*What symbols or symbolic
actions do you see used
at Mass?*

The Bread of Life

Faith Focus

How does the Old Testament help us understand the meaning of the Eucharist?

Faith Vocabulary

manna. White bread-like flakes or grains with a taste like flour and honey.

Shrub producing manna

Table setting at Passover meal

The Church uses many symbols to help us understand the mysteries of the faith of the Church. Symbols have a deeper meaning than we might at first suspect. There are many Old Testament events involving bread that point to, or prefigure, and help us understand the mystery of the Eucharist. These include the stories of Melchizedek, the Passover, and the feeding of the Hebrews with manna in the desert.

Melchizedek

When Abram returned from his victory over Chedorlamor and the kings who were allied with him, Melchizedek, the king of Salem, brought out bread and wine.

Being a priest of God Most High, he blessed Abram with these words:

"Blessed be Abram by God
Most High,
the creator of heaven and
earth."   GENESIS 14:19

The three elements in the story prefigure Christ's giving of himself to us in the Eucharist. The elements are (1) bread and wine, (2) the offering of bread and wine as gifts to God, and (3) grateful remembrance of what God has done for his people.

Passover

The Israelites did not have time to put yeast into their bread dough when they fled Egypt. They made unleavened bread and then ran for their lives. God commanded his people to celebrate Passover each year with unleavened bread, the Passover lamb, bitter herbs, and wine. (Read Exodus 12:1–20.) When Jesus gave us the Eucharist, he gave new meaning to the blessing of the bread and wine at Passover.

Manna

During the Exodus while the Israelites were in the desert, God promised and gave them manna to eat.

Then the LORD said to Moses, "I will now rain down bread from heaven for you. Each day the people are to go out and gather their daily portion." . . . In the evening quail came up and covered the camp. In the morning a dew lay all about the camp, and when the dew evaporated, there on the surface of the desert were fine flakes like hoarfrost on the ground. On seeing it, the Israelites asked one another, "What is this?" for they did not know what it was. But Moses told them, "This is the bread which the LORD has given you to eat." EXODUS 16:4, 13–15

These "fine flakes" on the ground were **manna**. This "bread from heaven" was more than food for the body. Receiving the manna reminded the Israelites that they lived by the bread of the Word of God.

The Eucharist, prefigured by the manna, the offering of Melchizedek, and the Passover meal, is the great sacrament of God's love for us. Celebrating the Eucharist recalls and makes present the sacrifice of Christ, who said:

"This is my commandment: love one another as I love you. No one has greater love than this, to lay down one's life for one's friends." JOHN 15:12–13

QUESTION How do the stories of Melchizedek, Passover, and manna help you understand the mystery of the Eucharist?

Melchizedek

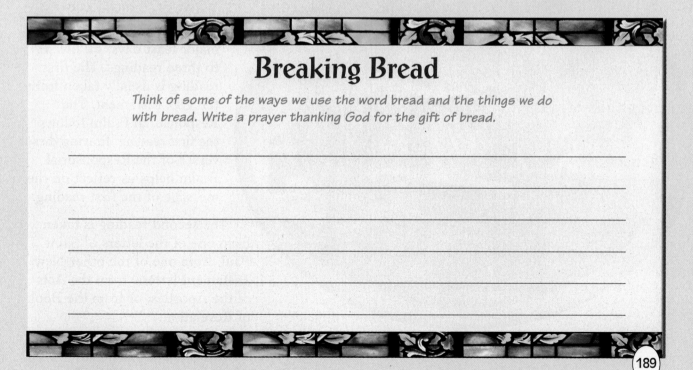

Breaking Bread

Think of some of the ways we use the word bread and the things we do with bread. Write a prayer thanking God for the gift of bread.

_____

_____

_____

_____

_____

_____

Faith Vocabulary

Mass. The main sacramental celebration of the Church at which we gather to listen to God's word and through which we share in the saving death of Christ and give praise and glory to the Father.

Saying thank-you to others for their generosity is natural. The Eucharist is the Church's great prayer of thanksgiving. The Church celebrates the Eucharist during the celebration of the **Mass.**

The Mass

The Mass is the main sacramental celebration of the Church. At Mass we give God honor and glory. We gather to listen to God's word. We are made sharers in the saving death of Christ. The celebration of Mass includes:

- The Introductory Rites
- The Liturgy of the Word
- The Liturgy of the Eucharist
- The Concluding Rites

The two main parts of the Mass are the Liturgy of the Word and the Liturgy of the Eucharist.

Liturgy of the Word

The proclamation of God's very own word in the Scriptures is the center of the Liturgy of the Word. The Word of God:

- *feeds* us, nourishing our minds and hearts;
- *reminds* us of God's involvement in our lives;
- *inspires* us to praise and thank God; and
- *shows* us a path for living.

The Scripture Readings

At Mass on Sundays and major feast days, we listen to three readings. The first reading is usually taken from the Old Testament. The Responsorial Psalm follows the first reading. Praying these verses of the Responsorial Psalm helps us reflect on the message of the first reading.

The second reading is taken from one of the letters of Saint Paul, from one of the other New Testament letters, from the Acts of the Apostles, or from the Book of Revelation.

After the second reading and before the Gospel is proclaimed, we stand and sing the Gospel acclamation or another chant. This acclamation, except during Lent, includes the Alleluia, a Hebrew word that means "Praise the Lord." During the Gospel acclamation the worshiping assembly stands to greet and honor the Lord who is present with us in the Scriptures.

The proclamation of the Gospel is the last of the three readings. The Gospel reading, as well as the other Sunday readings, are on a three-year cycle—Year A (Matthew), Year B (Mark and John), and Year C (Luke). This enables us to hear readings from all four Gospels over a three-year period.

Homily

The homily follows the Gospel reading. In the homily the priest or deacon explains the readings. This helps us listen to God's word and connect it to our lives.

Profession of Faith and Prayer of the Faithful

We stand and profess our faith by praying the creed together. We then offer the petitions of the Prayer of the Faithful. We pray for the needs of the Church, the world, other people, and ourselves.

 What is one of your favorite Gospel stories? What do you think God is saying to you?

Speak, Lord. We Are Listening.

Read Acts 10:34, 37–43; Colossians, 3:1–4; and John 20:1–9. These are the readings for Easter Sunday. Work with a partner to discover the meaning of God's word to us. Then write a brief summary of that meaning.

Faith Vocabulary

Eucharist. The sacrament of the Body and Blood of Christ; the Sacrament of Christian Initiation in which we receive the Body and Blood of Christ, who is truly and really present under the appearances of bread and wine, and in which we are most fully joined to Christ and to the Church, the Body of Christ.

Liturgy of the Eucharist

The Liturgy of the Eucharist is the second main part of the Mass. The word *eucharist* comes from a Greek word meaning "to give thanks" or "to show gratitude." The **Eucharist** is the Church's great prayer of blessing and thanksgiving to God the Father. We make our prayer with Jesus Christ through the power of the Holy Spirit. The work of Christ by the one sacrifice of Christ is made present, and we are made sharers in it.

Preparation of the Gifts

The Liturgy of the Eucharist begins with the preparation of the gifts. Often there is a procession with the gifts of bread and wine. Bread made from wheat and wine made from grapes are necessary for the celebration of the Eucharist. The priest prays a prayer of blessing that is a form of grace before meals in the Jewish tradition. The Preparation of the Gifts concludes with the Prayer Over the Offerings, which is also called the Prayer Over the Gifts.

Eucharistic Prayer

The priest next invites us to prepare for the Church's great prayer of thanksgiving, the Eucharistic Prayer. We join in singing or praying aloud the Preface. In this prayer we name the reasons we are gathered to give God thanks and praise. The Preface concludes with the whole worshiping assembly singing or praying aloud the Holy, Holy, Holy Lord acclamation.

During the Eucharistic Prayer the priest pronounces the words of consecration. Through the words of the priest and the power of the Holy Spirit, the bread and wine truly become the Body and Blood of Christ. Holding the bread, the priest says:

> TAKE THIS, ALL OF YOU, AND EAT OF IT, FOR THIS IS MY BODY, WHICH WILL BE GIVEN UP FOR YOU.

Holding the cup of wine, he says:

> TAKE THIS, ALL OF YOU, AND DRINK FROM IT, FOR THIS IS THE CHALICE OF MY BLOOD, THE BLOOD OF THE NEW AND ETERNAL COVENANT, WHICH WILL BE POURED OUT FOR YOU AND FOR MANY FOR THE FORGIVENESS OF SINS. DO THIS IN MEMORY OF ME.

Communion Rite

This great Amen concludes the Eucharistic Prayer and leads into the communion rite. The faithful in the state of grace are invited to process forward to receive the Body and Blood of Christ. We become one with the Lord and with one another.

The Mass is the prayer of Christ and his Church. Together with the priest who leads us in the name of Jesus, we listen to God's word and are made sharers in the Paschal Mystery of Christ. Together we give praise to the Father through Jesus, his Son, in the unity of the Holy Spirit.

QUESTION *Why is the Eucharistic Prayer considered the heart of the Mass?*

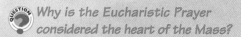

Our Catholic Identity

The Altar

The altar is the table of the Lord. From this table we are fed with the Body and Blood of the Lord Jesus. The altar is also a symbol of Christ. It reminds us that Jesus sacrificed his life for us on the cross. That is why at the beginning of the Mass and at the end of the Mass, the priest venerates, or honors, the altar by kissing and bowing before it.

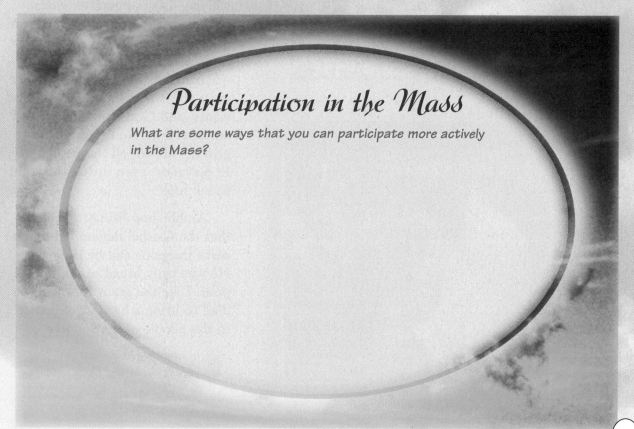

Participation in the Mass

What are some ways that you can participate more actively in the Mass?

Our Church Makes a Difference

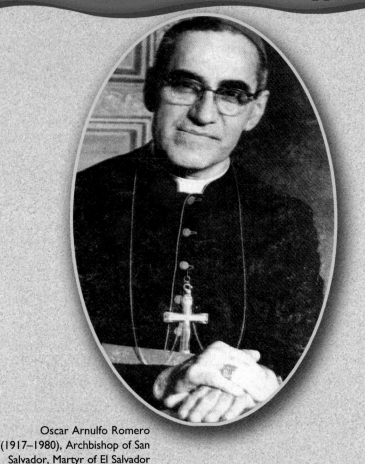

Oscar Arnulfo Romero
(1917–1980), Archbishop of San
Salvador, Martyr of El Salvador

*"...Every effort to improve society...
is an effort that God blesses."*

Archbishop Oscar Romero

Archbishop
Romero
greeting people
after Mass, 1979

Archbishop Oscar Romero

Christians since the early days of the Church have given their lives out of love for God and others. Oscar Romero, the Archbishop of San Salvador, gave up his life serving Christ and the people of San Salvador. On March 24, 1980, as he began to raise the consecrated bread, the Body of Christ, in his hands, he was shot through his heart and killed. He was assassinated because he truly lived the command we all receive during the concluding rite of the Mass, "Go in peace, glorifying the Lord by your life."

During his homily at that Mass, Archbishop Romero said, "Those who give their lives to the service of the poor through love will live like the grain of wheat that dies. The harvest comes from the grains that die. We know that every effort to improve society, when society is so full of injustice, is an effort that God blesses, God wants, and God demands of us. I am bound by God's command to give my life for all the people of El Salvador, even those who want to kill me."

Archbishop Romero believed that the Gospel demanded that he serve the poor and be their voice. He was truly bread of life for the poor. Like the grain of wheat, he died to bring a harvest of justice to the people of his country.

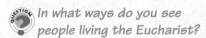 *In what ways do you see people living the Eucharist?*

What Difference Does Faith Make in My Life?

Each time you participate in Mass you receive the call and the grace of the Holy Spirit to love and serve the Lord.

Reflect on Jesus' words, "I am the bread of life" (John 6:35). What do Jesus' words tell you about being a follower of Christ?

The Bread of Life

My Faith Choice

This week I will continue to apply Jesus' words "I am the bread of life" to my life. I will

_____

_____.

Bread for the World

Leader: Sharing in the Eucharist strengthens us to live the Gospel. It unites us more closely to Christ and to one another. Let us celebrate this service of the word, asking God to strengthen us to be bread for the word. *(Pause.)*

God, giver of all blessings,
thank you for the gift of Jesus, your Son, the Bread of Life.
Send the Holy Spirit to help us serve others as your Son did.

Reader: A reading from the holy Gospel according to John.
All: **Glory to you, O Lord.**

Reader: So Jesus said to them, "Amen, amen, I say to you, it was not Moses who gave the bread from heaven; my Father gives you the true bread from heaven. For the bread of God is that which comes down from heaven and gives life to the world."

So they said to him, "Sir, give us this bread always." Jesus said to them, "I am the bread of life; whoever comes to me will never hunger, and whoever believes in me will never thirst."   JOHN 6:32–35

The Gospel of the Lord.
All: **Praise to you, Lord Jesus Christ.**

Leader: *Briefly apply the Gospel message to the life of Christians today.* Let us now pray to God the Father as Jesus taught.
All: **Our Father . . .**

Leader: Let us offer one another a sign of peace. *(Pause.)* Go in the peace of Christ.
All: **Thanks be to God.**

We Remember

What I Have Learned

Unscramble the words to complete the sentences.

1. The _____ is the sacrament
   shaucErit
   of the Body and Blood of Christ.

2. The _____ meal prefigures
   sPaersov
   the Last Supper and the Eucharist.

3. During the Eucharistic Prayer the priest pronounces
   the words of _____. These are
   crcontionsea
   the words Jesus spoke at the Last Supper.

4. The _____ is the main
   saMs
   sacramental celebration of the Church.

5. _____ is a breadlike
   naMan
   substance that prefigured the Eucharist.

Answer the following.

6. How does the Passover help us understand our
   celebration of the Eucharist?

   _____

   _____

7. Describe the parts of the Liturgy of the Word.

   _____

   _____

   _____

8. Describe what takes place during the Liturgy of the
   Eucharist.

   _____

   _____

   _____

To Help You Remember

1. Many events in the Old
   Testament prefigure, or
   point to, the mystery of
   the Eucharist.

2. The proclamation of the
   Word of God is at the center
   of the Liturgy of the Word.

3. The Eucharistic Prayer is
   the heart of the Liturgy of
   the Eucharist.

Growing in Faith

One important thing I learned
this week is

_____

_____

_____ .

This is important because

_____

_____

_____ .

What will people see me doing
as I live my faith choice this
week?

_____

_____

_____

This Week . . .

In chapter 15, "The Eucharist," your child learned more about the Mass and the Sacrament of the Eucharist. Several events in the Old Testament point to, or prefigure, the Eucharist. Understanding the meaning of the Old Testament stories of the manna, Melchizedek, and the Passover can enrich our understanding of the mystery of the Eucharist. The Eucharist is the sacrament of the Body and Blood of the Lord Jesus, the Bread of Life. At the Eucharist, the bread and wine truly become the Body and Blood of Christ through the power of the Holy Spirit and the words of the priest. When we celebrate the Eucharist, the sacrifice of Jesus is made present.

For more on the teachings of the Catholic Church on the Sacrament of the Eucharist, see *Catechism of the Catholic Church* paragraph numbers 1322–1405.

Sharing God's Word

Read together 1 Corinthians 11:17–34. Emphasize that the Eucharist is the Sacrament of the Body and Blood of Christ. Sharing in the Eucharist nourishes us and strengthens us to love and serve God and one another.

Praying

In this chapter your child participated in a service of the word. Read and celebrate this service of the word on page 196 as a family.

Making a Difference

Choose one of the following activities to do as a family or design a similar activity of your own.

- Find a favorite bread recipe and make homemade bread. Gather together and eat the bread for a snack or eat it as part of a special meal. You might even like to make some bread for special neighbors or friends.

- When you take part in Mass this week, think carefully about the readings. After Mass, gather together and share your ideas about the readings. Make a family decision about how you might put into practice what you heard.

- Talk about some ways you can participate in Mass more actively. Invite each family member to choose one thing they will do.

For more ideas on ways your family can live your faith, visit the "Faith First for Families" page at **www.FaithFirst.com**. Check out "Bible Stories." Read and discuss the Bible story as a family.

16

The Parable of the Great Feast

A Scripture Story

✛ THE FEAST IS READY ✛

We Pray

Sing joyfully to God our
  strength;
  shout in triumph to the
  God of Jacob!

PSALM 81:2

Lord God, you feed your
people with the Eucharist
and strengthen them
in holiness. Amen.

*When have you attended
a meal that honored someone?*

Banquets, or large
gatherings of people for
special meals, celebrate
people and achievements.
The writers of the Bible
used the image of a banquet
to help us understand what
it means to belong to the
People of God.

*What meal stories do you
remember from the Bible?*

199

Bible Background

Faith Vocabulary

parable. A form of story that compares one thing to another to help listeners understand the main point of the story.

Have you ever been to a wedding banquet or a sports banquet, or to some other large meal that celebrated something special? Banquets, such as weddings or scouting or sports banquets, are special meals that celebrate a special event or an achievement of a person or a group of people. Usually, only invited guests attend. People dress up, the hall and tables are decorated, and there is special seating at the tables.

Feast at the House of Levi, Paolo Veronese, (1528–1588), Italian painter

Meals

The people in Jesus' time celebrated special meals just as we do today. The most famous and important meal in the Gospel is the Last Supper. It is so important that all four of the Evangelists—Matthew, Mark, Luke, and John—wrote about it.

Parables of Jesus

The Gospel according to Luke includes many other stories that center around meals. These begin with a banquet at the house of Levi (5:27–39) and end with a meal in Jerusalem just before Jesus' Ascension.

Saint Luke and Saint Matthew both include a special meal story. It is the **parable** that Jesus told of a great banquet. It is called the parable of the Great Feast. A parable is a form of story that compares one thing to another to help listeners or readers understand the main point of the story.

When Jesus taught using parables, he used one thing his listeners knew well to help them understand something else, such as faith or the Kingdom of God, that he was teaching them about.

In parables storytellers compare two things. They use the words *like* and *as* to make their point. For example, in the parable of the Mustard Seed, Jesus said:

"What is the kingdom of God like? To what can I compare it? It is like a mustard seed that a person took and planted in the garden."

LUKE 13:18–19

In the parable of the Mustard Seed, Jesus compared something his listeners knew about, the planting of the mustard seed, to help them understand something he was trying to teach them about, the Kingdom of God.

After Jesus told the parable of the Sower, his disciples asked him why he taught in parables, and Jesus replied:

"Because knowledge of the mysteries of the kingdom of heaven has been granted to you, but to them it has not been granted. To anyone who has, more will be given and he will grow rich; from anyone who has not, even what he has will be taken away. This is why I speak to them in parables, because 'they look and do not see and hear but do not listen or understand.' . . .

But blessed are your eyes, because they see, and your ears, because they hear."

MATTHEW 13:11–13, 16

Then Jesus proceeded to explain to them the meaning of the parable of the Sower.

 Explain why Jesus used parables when he taught about the Kingdom of God.

Parable of the Sower, James J. Tissot, (1836–1902), French painter

Listening to Jesus

Much of Jesus' teaching was done when he was at a meal. Choose and read one of these stories in Saint Luke's account of the Gospel. Tell who was invited and what Jesus was teaching.

Luke 5:27–35   Luke 7:36–50   Luke 10:38–42   Luke 14:7–14

Who was invited?

_____

What was Jesus' message?

_____

_____

_____

Reading the Word of God

Faith Focus

What does Jesus say about those people who were first invited to the feast?

The Parable of the Great Feast

Jesus used his listeners' experiences of meals and banquets to help them understand his teaching on the Kingdom of God. In Saint Luke's account of the Gospel, we often read about Jesus teaching at a meal at which the Pharisees were present. Pharisees were a lay sect within Judaism whose members dedicated their lives to the strict keeping of the Law found in the Torah.

Some of the Pharisees criticized Jesus for sitting down at the same table "with certain people" whose behavior they did not approve of. Jesus responded by telling parables and other stories. These forced the Pharisees and his other listeners to think about their own behavior.

On one occasion Jesus was invited to the home of a leading Pharisee. The people were watching Jesus very carefully. Jesus also watched them as they tried to sit in places of honor at the table. Read this parable to discover what Jesus taught them.

One of his fellow guests on hearing this said to him, "Blessed is the one who will dine in the kingdom of God." He replied to him, "A man gave a great dinner to which he invited many. When the time for the dinner came, he dispatched his servant to say to those invited, 'Come, everything is now ready.' But one by one, they all began to excuse themselves. The first said to him, 'I have purchased a field and must go to examine it; I ask you, consider me excused.' And another said, 'I have purchased five yoke of oxen and am on my way to evaluate them; I ask you, consider me excused.' And another said, 'I have just married a woman, and therefore I cannot come.' The servant went and reported this to his master. Then the master of the house in a rage commanded his servant, 'Go

out quickly into the streets and alleys of the town and bring in here the poor and the crippled, the blind and the lame.' The servant reported, 'Sir, your orders have been carried out and still there is room.' The master then ordered the servant, 'Go out to the highways and hedgerows and make people come in that my home may be filled. For, I tell you, none of those men who were invited will taste my dinner.'"

LUKE 14:15–24

Jesus invited people who the Pharisees and their guests would have not usually invited. By doing this Jesus was teaching that God invites all people to the Kingdom of God and wants them to decide to come.

 What does this parable teach about God?

Banquet of Life

As a follower of Jesus, how would you respond to this invitation? Fill in your RSVP.

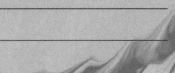

God the Father invites you to the great feast honoring his Son, Jesus Christ.

_____

_____

_____

Time Line

ca. 4 B.C.
Birth of Jesus

A.D. 30s
Passion, death, Resurrection, Ascension of Jesus; first Christian Pentecost

A.D. 45–60
Letters of Saint Paul, missionary journey of Saint Paul

A.D. 64
Rome burned, persecution of Nero

ca. A.D. 67
Saint Peter and Saint Paul martyred

A.D. 70
Temple in Jerusalem destroyed

ca. A.D. 70
Gospel of Mark written

ca. A.D. 80
Gospel of Matthew written

ca. A.D. 90–100
Gospel of Luke written, Gospel of John written

Understanding the Word of God

Faith Focus

What does the parable of the Great Feast tell us?

The Feast of the Kingdom

It is important to look at how and when Jesus told the parable of the Great Feast. Jesus was invited to a meal on the Sabbath in the home of a leading Pharisee. It seems that people wanted to be with Jesus, and he used these times to make people think about God's love for them and for all people.

Jesus noticed how the guests were trying to sit in the places of honor at the table. This clearly showed how important they thought they were. Jesus, seeing this, asked them to think about what they were doing. He went on to talk about inviting the poor, the crippled, the lame, and the blind. These were people whom the Pharisees and their guests would not have usually invited—or even thought about inviting—into their homes. What might all this mean?

Jesus was not merely talking about an ordinary banquet to honor people for their earthly achievements. It was not a banquet to which only "honored" guests were given an invitation to attend. Jesus was teaching about the banquet in the Kingdom of God, the heavenly banquet. Unlike the meal in the Pharisee's home to which only certain guests were invited, everyone is invited by God to the great feast in the Kingdom of God. In fact, Jesus goes on in the parable to say that many of those who are invited will refuse to come. And those who others believe should not be invited will take their place at the table.

At the Last Supper Jesus promised his faithful followers:

"I tell you, from now on I shall not drink this fruit of the vine until the day when I drink it with you new in the kingdom of my Father."

MATTHEW 26:29

Christians have come to understand this parable as a parable about the Kingdom of God and the Eucharist. Christ has given the Church the banquet of the Eucharist as both a pledge and an anticipation of the heavenly banquet in the Kingdom of God.

We prepare for the coming of the kingdom and sharing in the heavenly banquet by treating all people—without exception—with respect and compassion, with mercy and justice. We act in such a way that others can see that God invites and desires that everyone share in the eternal heavenly banquet in the Kingdom of God.

 In this parable, to what was Jesus comparing the "great dinner" the man was giving?

The Kingdom of God

Look at the pictures on pages 204 and 205. Describe what they portray about living for the Kingdom of God.

_____

_____

_____

_____

_____

_____

_____

_____

_____

_____

Our Church Makes a Difference

Catholic Campaign for Human Development

From its beginning the Church has preached the Gospel message that God desires all people to share in the great banquet in the Kingdom of God. The Catholic Campaign for Human Development brings that message to people living in poverty.

Established in 1969, the Catholic Campaign for Human Development shares that Gospel message in practical ways. First, it raises funds to support "organized groups of white and minority poor to develop economic strength and political power." Second, it educates "the People of God to a new knowledge of today's problems . . . that can lead to some new approaches that promote a greater sense of solidarity."

Every parish in the United States is invited to take part in this work of the Church. One way Catholics do this is by contributing to a special collection at Mass on the Sunday before Thanksgiving. This and the other projects of the Catholic Campaign for Human Development have significantly changed the lives of people living in poverty in our country.

QUESTION How can you and your friends work with people in your parish to support the Catholic Campaign for Human Development?

What Difference Does Faith Make in My Life?

You share in the banquet of the Eucharist and look forward to sharing in the great feast in the Kingdom of God. The Eucharist strengthens you to live for the kingdom.

Describe how you and your friends might show others that God invites them and all people to share in the great feast in the Kingdom of God.

All Are Invited

What We Can Do

_____

_____

_____

_____

What Our Actions Tell Others

_____

_____

_____

_____

My Faith Choice

This week I will remember and live the message of Jesus' parable of the Great Feast. I will

_____

_____.

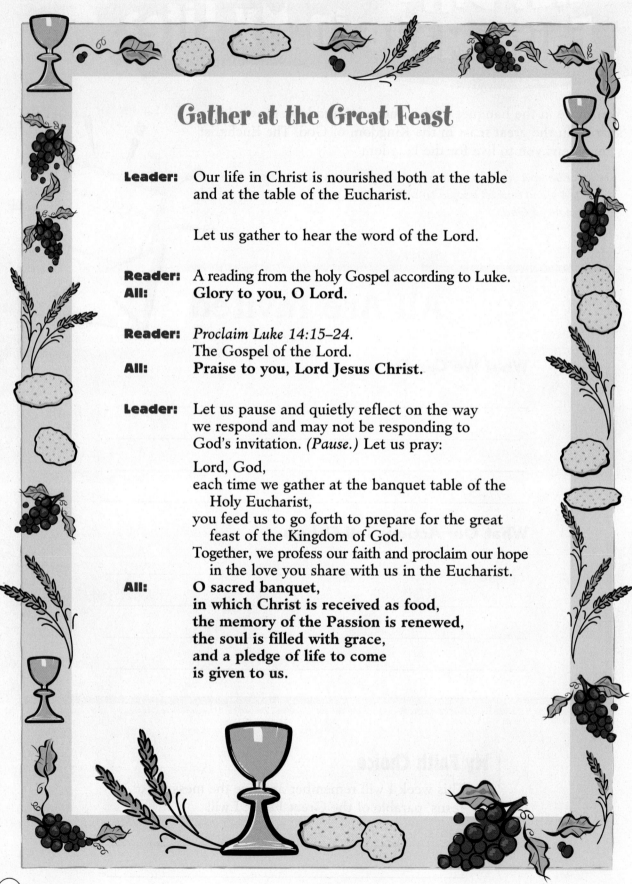

Gather at the Great Feast

Leader: Our life in Christ is nourished both at the table and at the table of the Eucharist.

Let us gather to hear the word of the Lord.

Reader: A reading from the holy Gospel according to Luke.
All: **Glory to you, O Lord.**

Reader: *Proclaim Luke 14:15–24.*
The Gospel of the Lord.
All: **Praise to you, Lord Jesus Christ.**

Leader: Let us pause and quietly reflect on the way
we respond and may not be responding to
God's invitation. *(Pause.)* Let us pray:

Lord, God,
each time we gather at the banquet table of the
  Holy Eucharist,
you feed us to go forth to prepare for the great
  feast of the Kingdom of God.
Together, we profess our faith and proclaim our hope
  in the love you share with us in the Eucharist.

All: **O sacred banquet,
in which Christ is received as food,
the memory of the Passion is renewed,
the soul is filled with grace,
and a pledge of life to come
is given to us.**

We Remember

What I Have Learned

1. Retell the parable of the Great Feast. Use words or pictures.

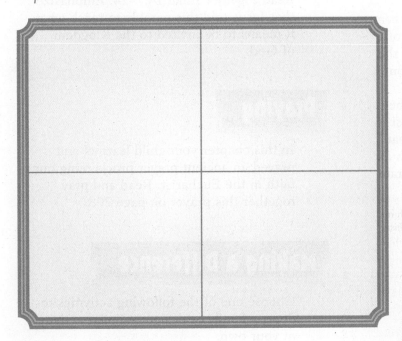

Answer the following.

2. Why did Jesus teach using parables?

_____

_____

_____

3. Compare the banquet in the parable of the Great Feast to the heavenly banquet.

_____

_____

_____

4. Describe how we show we are responding to God's invitation to come to the great feast in the Kingdom of God.

_____

_____

_____

To Help You Remember

1. Jesus used his listeners' experience of meals and banquets in a parable to teach them about the Kingdom of God.

2. The parable of the Great Feast teaches that God desires and invites all people to the great feast in the Kingdom of God.

3. Sharing in the Eucharist is a pledge of future glory and an anticipation of the great heavenly banquet.

Growing in Faith

One important thing I learned this week is

_____

_____

_____.

This is important because

_____

_____

_____.

What will people see me doing as I live my faith choice this week?

_____

_____

_____

This Week . . .

In chapter 16, "The Parable of the Great Feast: A Scripture Story," your child learned more about the connection between the Kingdom of God and the mystery of the Eucharist. Jesus told the parable of the Great Feast to teach about the Kingdom of God. This parable helps Christians today deepen their understanding of the mystery of the Eucharist. The Eucharist is a pledge and an anticipation of the great feast in the heavenly kingdom at which all the faithful will be united and will celebrate as the one family of God.

For more on the teachings of the Catholic Church on the Eucharist and the Kingdom of God, see *Catechism of the Catholic Church* paragraph numbers 541–554, 1402–1405, and 2816–2821.

Sharing God's Word

Read together Luke 14:7–24. Emphasize that Jesus told this parable to teach what it means to be invited to the Kingdom of God.

Praying

In this chapter your child learned and prayed an ancient prayer proclaiming our faith in the Eucharist. Read and pray together this prayer on page 208.

Making a Difference

Choose one of the following activities to do as a family or design a similar activity of your own.

- God invites all people to take their place in his kingdom. His invitation is always being offered to us. Discuss the following question: Are we reluctant to accept God's invitation? Why or why not?

- One way we show that we are living for the kingdom is by helping people who are in need. As a family choose one thing you can do this week to reach out to others.

- There are many parables in the Bible about the Kingdom of God. Read Matthew 13:24–33, 13:44–48, Mark 4:30–34, and Luke 13:18–21. Discuss what Jesus teaches us about God's kingdom in these parables.

For more ideas on ways your family can live your faith, visit the "Faith First for Families" page at **www.FaithFirst.com**. You will find it helpful to look at "Questions Kids Ask."

Sacraments of Healing

17

We Pray

LORD, have mercy on me;
   heal me, I have sinned
      against you.   PSALM 41:5

Lord God,
may all who suffer
know and trust that
they are joined to Christ
who suffered for the
salvation of the world.

Amen.

When have you or someone you love been in need of healing?

People can get hurt in many ways. Our bodies, our minds, and our feelings can get hurt. We can also get hurt spiritually when we sin. There are many stories in the Gospel that tell about Jesus healing people physically and spiritually.

What stories in the Gospel do you know that tell about Jesus healing people?

The Healing Ministry of the Church

Faith Focus

Why does the Church celebrate the Sacrament of Penance and Reconciliation?

Faith Vocabulary

sin. Freely choosing to say or do what we know is against God's will or freely choosing not to do something we know God wants us to do.

Penance and Reconciliation. The Sacrament of Healing through which we receive God's forgiveness through the ministry of a priest for sins that we have committed after Baptism.

The work of Jesus on earth was a ministry of healing. It was the work his Father sent him to do. There are many stories in the Old Testament that prefigure that work of Jesus.

The Healing Ministry of Jesus Christ

In the Book of Numbers we read that the people of Israel became ill in the desert during the Exodus. At God's direction Moses lifted up a bronze serpent, and all who looked upon it were healed. (Read Exodus 21:4–9.)

The Church has come to understand that the lifting up of the bronze serpent prefigured the lifting up of Jesus on the cross. Jesus would be the source of healing for the whole human family.

The Ministry of Forgiveness

Jesus continues his work today and until the end of time through the Church. He is especially present doing this work through the two Sacraments of Healing, Penance and Reconciliation and Anointing of the Sick.

When we **sin**, we turn away from the love of God and of other people. We hurt ourselves spiritually and we need healing. We need to heal our relationship with God and with the Church. We need the healing given by God who alone can forgive sins. In his mercy and goodness God shares his power to forgive sins with the Church, the Body of Christ. He shares this forgiveness through the celebration of the sacraments.

Baptism

Baptism is the first sacrament of forgiveness. In Baptism original sin and all personal sins are forgiven. Jesus also gave the Church the Sacrament of **Penance and Reconciliation** for the forgiveness of sins committed after Baptism. He said to his disciples,

"Receive the holy Spirit. Whose sins you forgive are forgiven them, and whose sins you retain are retained."

JOHN 20:22–23

This work of forgiveness is continued through the ministry of bishops and priests.

Eucharist

The Eucharist is also a sacrament of forgiveness. Sharing in the Eucharist joins us more closely to Christ and to others. Venial sins are forgiven. Mortal sins, however, must be confessed in the Sacrament of Reconciliation. Celebrating the Eucharist regularly helps us deepen our relationship with God and with others.

Reconciliation

The celebration of Reconciliation always includes these essential actions.

Contrition. We must be truly sorry, or contrite, for what we have done. We express this through an act of contrition. True sorrow includes making a firm purpose of amendment. This means we ask God's help and make a decision not to sin again in the future. It means deciding, with God's grace, to live in a new way.

Confession. We must ask for forgiveness by confessing our sins to a priest, who stands in the place of Christ. We must confess all mortal sins that we have not already confessed. The Church also encourages us to confess venial sins. This helps us strengthen our friendship with God.

Act of Penance. We offer satisfaction for our sins. We accept and agree to do a penance. This is usually a prayer or a good deed that helps heal the wound caused by our sin.

Absolution. We receive absolution, or forgiveness of our sins. The word *absolution* means "making free from." Absolution is the forgiveness of sins given by God through the ministry of the priest in the Sacrament of Reconciliation. Celebrating Reconciliation regularly helps us deepen our friendship with God.

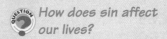 How does sin affect our lives?

PARABLE

Read Luke 18:9–14. Compare the Pharisee and the tax collector. What do we know about these two people? What insight about ourselves does Jesus give us in this parable?

Pharisee _____

_____

Tax Collector _____

_____

My Insight _____

_____

Faith Focus

What are the spiritual effects, or sacramental graces, of Penance and Reconciliation?

Reconciliation is one of the two Sacraments of Healing. Sacraments are efficacious signs, given to the Church by Christ, that make us sharers in God's life through the power of the Holy Spirit. Penance and Reconciliation, like the other sacraments, has special sacramental graces, or spiritual effects. Why is it important to celebrate Penance and Reconciliation regularly?

The Graces of Penance and Reconciliation

Celebrating Penance and Reconciliation heals us spiritually. Some of the effects of this sacrament are:

- Reconciliation restores and strengthens the life of grace with God, which mortal sin caused us to lose or venial sin has weakened.

- Reconciliation renews our relationship with the Body of Christ, the Church.
- Reconciliation helps us make reparation for our sins and repair the damage caused by our sin.
- Reconciliation frees us from eternal separation from God. We call that separation hell.
- Reconciliation gives us the grace to faithfully follow Jesus Christ—even in the face of temptation and other difficulties.
- Reconciliation makes us sharers in the gifts of peace and forgiveness and gives us a renewed awareness of the merciful loving presence of God with us.

Freedom from the Punishment of Sin

When we sin, we turn our hearts away from God and his love and toward something that, at the moment, we decide is more important than God. If we allow it, this attachment to sin might move us to turn further away from God's love. We must free ourselves from this weakness either here on earth or after we die.

In Matthew 25, Jesus teaches that there is punishment connected with sin. Punishment for sin is one of the consequences of our sinning. That punishment may be eternal or temporary. Through prayers, good works, and indulgences the faithful can obtain remission, or the release from, the temporal punishment resulting from sin. We can do this for ourselves and for the souls in purgatory.

 How does the Sacrament of Reconciliation affect you?

Faith-Filled People

David

King David is a model of a person who was truly sorry for his sin. King David wanted to marry Bathsheba, the wife of Uriah who was one of David's generals. David sent Uriah on a mission that he knew would result in Uriah being killed. Nathan the Prophet told David that he had sinned and that God was very displeased with him. David was truly sorry, admitted his sin, begged God for forgiveness, and was forgiven.

Words of Reconciliation

Design or illustrate several words that describe your feelings when you are forgiven.

Faith Focus

Why does the Church celebrate the Sacrament of Anointing of the Sick?

Faith Vocabulary

Anointing of the Sick.
The Sacrament of Healing that strengthens our faith, hope, and love for God when we are seriously ill, weakened by old age, or dying.

Ministry to the Sick

Healing of broken or weakened friendships through forgiveness is an important kind of healing. Jesus healed people spiritually and physically. He healed their bodies and their souls. Matthew's Gospel tells us:

Jesus went around to all the towns and villages, teaching in their synagogues, proclaiming the gospel of the kingdom, and curing every disease and illness.

MATTHEW 9:35

Jesus sent his disciples to do the same in his name. He told them:

"As you go, make this proclamation: 'The kingdom of heaven is at hand.' Cure the sick, raise the dead, cleanse lepers, drive out demons."

MATTHEW 10:7–8

From its very beginning the Church has ministered to the sick. The New Testament Letter of James states:

Is anyone among you sick? He should summon the presbyters of the church, and they should pray over him and anoint [him] with oil in the name of the Lord, and the prayer of faith will save the sick person, and the Lord

will raise him up. If he has committed any sins, he will be forgiven.   JAMES 5:14–15

Anointing of the Sick

Jesus continues his ministry to the sick through the Sacrament of the **Anointing of the Sick.** Anointing of the Sick is the second of the Church's two Sacraments of Healing.

Only a priest is the minister of this sacrament. Oil of the Sick blessed by the bishop, or, if necessary, blessed by the priest himself, is used in the sacrament.

Anointing of the Sick is celebrated by the faithful who are seriously ill or who are, in any way, in danger of death. This sacrament may be received more than one time. A person may receive Anointing of the Sick each time they are seriously ill, or more than once during the same illness if the sickness becomes worse. Elderly people who are weakened by the effects of aging may also receive this sacrament.

Effects of Anointing of the Sick

In this Sacrament of Healing, we receive many graces. Some of the important graces of this sacrament are:

- When we are suffering from illness, this sacrament unites us to the sufferings of Jesus. In this union we find strength and consolation because we believe and trust that the Lord is with us.
- We receive peace and courage to face our sufferings.
- We can receive the forgiveness of our sins through Anointing of the Sick, if we are not able to celebrate the Sacrament of Reconciliation.
- Our health may be restored.
- We are prepared for our final journey to eternal life when we are very ill and near death.

Through the celebration of Anointing of the Sick, Christ's work of healing continues in the world today. His healing presence helps the sick and dying find courage, strength, and hope.

 What does James 5:14–15 teach you about Anointing of the Sick?

Prayer of Faith

Think of someone you know who is sick and in need of the prayers of the Christian community. Write a prayer of faith for that person.

_____

_____

_____

_____

_____

_____

_____

End-of-Life Care

Hospice is a ministry of caring for the terminally ill and their families. It is a ministry of the Church throughout the world. "Catholic Hospice" is a ministry of the Archdiocese of Miami and Mercy Hospital. It offers end-of-life care to people of all faiths.

Hospice care is founded on such Gospel virtues and values as compassion, mercy, and respect for the dignity of every person. It gives witness to the faith of the Church that death is the doorway to new and glorified life with God.

Jesus continues his ministry with the dying through hospice care given by the Church. In Catholic Hospice a team of physicians, nurses, social workers, home health aides, chaplains, bereavement and other counselors, and specially trained volunteers care for the dying. The hospice team is available seven days a week, twenty-four hours a day.

What are some of the ways your parish works with people who are sick?

What Difference Does Faith Make in My Life?

At times you need to step back from your life and simply look at it. You need to examine your conscience. You need to ask the Holy Spirit to help you take an honest look at the ways you might need healing and how you could bring healing to others.

Take a few minutes to think about things you have done and said that brought the gift of healing to people. Create some symbols to recall those moments of healing.

Sharing in Jesus' Work of Healing

My Faith Choice

This week I will be more aware of people and situations that need healing and offer help when I can. I will

_____

_____.

Prayer for the Sick

Leader: The Letter of James tells us to pray for the sick. During the care for the sick and dying, the Church prays a brief form of the Litany of the Saints. Think of people you know or have heard about who are sick. After each response silently include their name or names.

Leader:	All:
Holy Mary, Mother of God,	**pray for _____.**
Saint Joseph,	**pray for _____.**
Saint Peter,	**pray for _____.**
Saint James,	**pray for _____.**
Saint Mary Magdalene,	**pray for _____.**
Saint Frances Cabrini,	**pray for _____.**
Saint Paul of the Cross,	**pray for _____.**
Saint Martin de Porres,	**pray for _____.**
Saint Terese of the Andes,	**pray for _____.**

Leader: All-powerful and ever-living God, we find security in your forgiveness. Give us serenity and peace of mind; may we rejoice in your gifts of kindness and use them always for your glory and our good. We ask this in the name of Jesus the Lord.

All: **Amen.**

PASTORAL CARE OF THE SICK 60C

We Remember

What I Have Learned

The words needed to complete the sentences are hidden in the puzzle. Find and circle the words. Then complete the sentences.

```
L A X W O G H A
T P Q M M F T H E
S G F O Q I X E A
C R R R R A N A
B A P T I S M L
S C L A G R E I
T E E L I L L N
A E S P A M I G
```

1. The first sacrament of forgiveness we receive is
   _____.

2. _____ sins must be confessed in Penance
   and Reconciliation.

3. In Anointing of the Sick, we receive the
   _____ to face our sufferings.

4. In Anointing of the Sick, Christ continues his
   work of _____ among us.

Answer the following.

5. Compare Jesus' ministry of healing with the
   Church's celebration of the Sacraments of Healing.

   _____

   _____

   _____

6. Name and describe the four essential elements of
   the rite of Reconciliation.

   _____

   _____

   _____

   _____

To Help You Remember

1. Jesus continues this work
   of healing through the two
   Sacraments of Healing,
   Penance and Reconciliation
   and Anointing of the Sick.

2. Penance and Reconciliation is
   the sacrament through which
   we receive God's forgiveness
   for the sins we commit after
   we have been baptized.

3. Anointing of the Sick is the
   sacrament that strengthens
   our faith and trust in God when
   we are seriously ill or dying.

Growing in Faith

One important thing I learned
this week is

_____

_____

_____.

This is important because

_____

_____

_____.

What will people see me doing
as I live my faith choice this
week?

_____

_____

_____

This Week . . .

In chapter 17, "Sacraments of Healing," your child learned more about the two Sacraments of Healing, Reconciliation and Anointing of the Sick. Through Reconciliation we receive forgiveness for sins committed after Baptism. Confession of sins, contrition (or sorrow), penance, and absolution are always a part of the celebration of this sacrament. Throughout his life on earth, Jesus not only healed people physically but also spiritually. Through Anointing of the Sick, Christ continues his healing ministry today with the seriously sick, those weak because of old age, and the dying.

For more on the teachings of the Catholic Church on the Sacraments of Healing, see *Catechism of the Catholic Church* paragraph numbers 1420–1484 and 1499–1525.

Sharing God's Word

Read together John 20:21–23. Emphasize that Jesus gave the Church the power to forgive sins.

Praying

In this chapter your child prayed for the sick, using a form of the Litany of the Saints. Read and pray together this prayer on page 220.

Making a Difference

Choose one of the following activities to do as a family or design a similar activity of your own.

- Talk about the ways your family cares for one another when you are sick. Include the ways you show your care for grandparents, aunts and uncles, and other relatives.

- Find out more about what your parish does to care for the sick and dying. Choose one thing your family can do to reach out to someone who is sick or dying.

- Read Matthew 22:34–40, Matthew 5:1–12, Isaiah 1:10–18, and Ephesians 5:1–14. Talk about what the passages teach about forgiveness.

For more ideas on ways your family can live your faith, visit the "Faith First for Families" page at **www.FaithFirst.com**. Click on "Family Prayer" and pray the prayer as a family this week.

Sacraments at the Service of Communion

Exchange of marriage promises

18

We Pray

Let your face shine on your
    servant;
    save me in your kindness.
        PSALM 31:17

God our Father,
may your Church
be for all the world
a sign of your unity
and holiness.   Amen.

What is one way you see married couples serving the people of your parish?

People very often measure success by power and wealth. Being successful in Jesus' eyes means being a servant just as he was. The Church celebrates the Sacrament of Holy Orders and the Sacrament of Matrimony to set aside some of her members to serve the whole Church.

What is one way you see priests serving the people of your parish?

Called to Serve the Whole Church

Faith Focus

What do we mean by service and communion?

Faith Vocabulary

Sacraments at the Service of Communion. The Sacrament of Holy Orders and the Sacrament of Matrimony.

communion. A word meaning "sharing with"; the unity in Christ of all the members of the Church, the Body of Christ.

Think about all the volunteers in your neighborhood and school, city and town, and nation who volunteer. All communities have people who generously give their time and talents for the good of the people who live in those communities. All of the baptized are called to deliberately choose to use their time and talents to serve God and others as Jesus did.

The Service of God and His People

Jesus set this standard for a successful life. He said to his disciples:

"[W]hoever wishes to be great among you will be your servant; whoever wishes to be first among you will be the slave of all. For the Son of Man did not come to be served but to serve and to give his life as a ransom for many."   MARK 10:43–45

To serve God and others as Jesus did means that we must be ready to make sacrifices. To serve as Jesus did means that we strive to serve others by giving ourselves as Jesus did.

Sacraments at the Service of Communion

Holy Orders and Matrimony set aside some members of the Church to work for the good of the whole Church, the **communion** of all believers in Christ. The word *communion* is used to name the unity in Christ of all the faithful. This is why Holy Orders and Matrimony are called the **Sacraments at the Service of Communion.**

We are joined to Christ through Baptism and become members of the one Body of Christ, the Church. We belong to the Lord, and we belong to each other in the Lord. We live our life in communion with Christ and one another. Saint Paul writes:

> As a body is one though it has many parts, and all the parts of the body, though many, are one body, so also Christ. For in one Spirit we were all baptized into one body, whether Jews or Greeks, slaves or free persons, and we were all given to drink of one Spirit.
>
> 1 Corinthians 12:12–13

This belonging and participating in the Body of Christ is our oneness, or communion, with Christ and one another. This is most evident when we celebrate the Eucharist:

> The cup of blessing that we bless, is it not a participation in the blood of Christ? The bread that we break, is it not a participation in the body of Christ? Because the loaf of bread is one, we, though many, are one body, for we all partake of the one loaf.
>
> 1 Corinthians 10:16–17

Christian married couples give themselves to each other and to the service of the Church. Bishops, priests, and deacons are consecrated to dedicate their lives for the benefit of the whole Church. Married and ordained Catholics serve God and the new People of God, the Church.

 How does Jesus measure success?

Wanted: Successful People

Write a job description for a successful Christian.

_____

_____

_____

_____

_____

_____

_____

Faith Focus

Why is Holy Orders
called a Sacrament
at the Service of
Communion?

Faith Vocabulary

Holy Orders. The
Sacrament at
the Service of
Communion through
which a baptized man
is consecrated to
serve the whole
Church as a bishop,
priest, or deacon.

Every Christian is joined to Christ in Baptism and is called to live a life of generous service to God and others as Jesus did. How do you serve God and others as Jesus did?

Holy Orders

Jesus Christ is the one true priest. Through his sacrifice on the cross, he has become our intercessor before God. Jesus Christ alone is our "go-between," linking God with humanity.

All the baptized share in the one priesthood of Christ in two ways. There is the common priesthood of all the faithful and the ordained priesthood. The ordained priesthood shares in the priesthood of Christ in a unique way.

Holy Orders is the sacrament of the Church in which a baptized man is consecrated to serve the Church as a bishop, priest, or deacon. An ordained man becomes a member of the order of bishop, priest, or deacon. All those who receive Holy Orders serve or aid all the baptized to live lives of priestly service.

Holy Orders is celebrated by the laying on of hands by a bishop on the head of the man to be ordained, which is followed by a prayer of consecration. At the prayer of consecration of a bishop the principal consecrator prays in part:

Father, you know all hearts.
You have chosen your servant for
the office of bishop.
May he be a shepherd to your
holy flock,
and a high priest blameless in
your sight,
ministering to you night and day.
ORDINATION OF A BISHOP 26

Later during the rite of ordination of a bishop, the newly ordained bishop is given the pastoral staff, or crozier. The ordaining bishop hands him the staff, saying:

Take this staff as a sign of your
pastoral office:
keep watch over the whole flock
in which the Holy Spirit has
appointed you to shepherd
the Church of God.
ORDINATION OF A BISHOP 32

Bishops continue the ministry of the Apostles. They work in communion with the pope, the successor of Saint Peter the Apostle. Helped by priests, their co-workers, and by deacons, bishops have the duty to authentically teach the faith; celebrate divine worship, above all the Eucharist; and guide their churches as true pastors. Together with the pope, the bishops share in the responsibility for Christ's Church throughout the world. Holy Orders, like Baptism and Confirmation, can be received only once and marks the man who is ordained with a spiritual character forever.

 How do you see a bishop, priest, or deacon serving the Church?

Pope Benedict XVI being greeted by bishops outside the cathedral in Cologne, Germany

Sharing in the Priesthood of Christ

Describe some of the ways you might live out your Baptism and serve the people of your parish. Choose one of the ways and plan how you will do it.

_____

_____

_____

_____

_____

Faith Focus

Why do we describe Matrimony as a Sacrament at the Service of Communion?

Faith Vocabulary

Matrimony. The Sacrament at the Service of Communion that unites a baptized man and a baptized woman in a lifelong bond, or covenant, of faithful love to serve the Church as a sign of Christ's love for the Church.

The home is the center of human life. It is the place where a Christian husband and wife and Christian parents and children learn to serve one another as Christ did. How do you help out in your family?

Matrimony

Matrimony is the second Sacrament at the Service of Communion. Through the Sacrament of Matrimony a Christian marriage becomes a sign of Christ's love for the Church. It is the sacrament of the Church that unites a baptized man and a baptized woman in a lifelong bond of faithful love. Joining hands the man and woman consent to the marriage, one at a time, promising:

I, *Name*, take you, *Name*, to be my wife (husband). I promise to be true to you in good times and in bad, in sickness and in health. I will love you and honor you all the days of my life.

Christian married love, like Christ's love for the Church, is a faithful and lifelong love. It is a sign of the faithful and unbreakable love of God for people. During the celebration of this sacrament, the priest asks God's blessing on the newly married couple, using these or similar words:

Father, to reveal the plan of your love,
you made the union of husband and wife
an image of the covenant between you and your people.
In fulfillment of this sacrament, the marriage of a Christian man and woman
is a sign of the marriage between Christ and the Church.

BASED ON NUPTIAL BLESSING, RITE OF MARRIAGE

The Christian Family, a Domestic Church

When husbands and wives nurture and cherish each other, they become a living sacrament. They become a living sign through which Christ works in the world.

Christian families form a domestic church, the "church of the home." They listen to God's word, pray together, and serve one another with generosity and compassion.

When Christian families serve one another, they are signs of God's loving presence with us. They become living signs that all the baptized are called to serve as Jesus did. They become living signs of God's saving presence among all people and invite everyone to love and serve God and one another as the one family of God.

QUESTION? What are some of the things your family does that show what it means to be a Christian family?

Family Album

Look at the pictures. Tell how each family is a sign of Christ's love.

Our Church Makes a Difference

Sacramentals

When Christians serve one another, they are signs of God's loving and caring presence with us. Celebrating Holy Orders and Matrimony consecrates and sets aside some members of the Church to serve the whole Church. They are living signs that all of the baptized are called to serve one another as Jesus did.

The Church also gives us sacramentals to remind us of God's caring presence with us. The Church dedicates certain objects and sets them aside for a holy purpose. For example, the Church dedicates church buildings, altars, and chalices, which are used for the celebration of the Eucharist.

During the prayer of dedication of an altar, the bishop, in part, prays:

Bless this altar built in the house
    of the Church. . . .
Make it a sign of Christ . . .
    a table
    of joy . . . a place of
    communion
    and peace . . . a source of unity
    and friendship . . . the center of
    our praise and thanksgiving.

He then anoints the altar with Chrism, praying:

We now anoint this altar.
May God in his power make
    it holy,
a visible sign of the mystery
    of Christ,
who offered himself for the
    life of the world.

The altar is the center of the church. The altar is the altar of sacrifice and the table of the Lord. The altar represents the altar of sacrifice on which Christ offers himself for our sins. It is the table of the Lord to which Christ invites us to receive his Body and Blood in Holy Communion.

Bishop using Chrism to consecrate altar

QUESTION *What other sacramentals of the Church do you know? How do they help you give praise to God and live a holy life?*

What Difference Does Faith Make in My Life?

Living your new life in Christ in service to others brings you closer to God and to other people.

Make a check next to those things you can do to be a sign of Christ's love.

I Make a Difference

☐ Read the Bible to a younger brother, sister, or student.

☐ Take part in a neighborhood clean-up project.

☐ Criticize my friends for helping out after school.

☐ Ask my parents how I can help them.

Write two more examples of your own.

☐ _____

☐ _____

My Faith Choice

This week I will live my baptismal call to serve others as Jesus did. I will

_____

_____ .

A Prayer for Married People

During the celebration of the Sacrament of Matrimony the Church prays for the newly married couple. Our prayers for married couples help them live their vocation to be signs of Christ's love in the world.

Leader: Let us pray for all who have been promised in the Sacrament of Matrimony to serve the Church.

Reader 1: May the peace of Christ live in their homes.
May they have true friends to help them.
May they be ready to help all who are in need.

All: **Bless them, O Lord.**

Reader 2: May they enjoy their work.
May they solve their daily problems.
May they not care too much about material things.

All: **Bless them, O Lord.**

Reader 3: May they find joy in God's gift of married life.
May they give witness to Jesus
by the goodness of their lives.

All: **Bless them, O Lord.**

Reader 4: May they praise God in the happy times
and rely on him in times of sadness.
May they take comfort in God's care and know
that he is with them every moment of their lives.

All: **Bless them, O Lord.**

Leader: May God reward them with a long life
and with eternal happiness.

All: **Amen.**

ADAPTED FROM THE RITE OF MARRIAGE

We Remember

What I Have Learned

Fill in the circle next to the word or phrase that completes each sentence correctly.

1. The word _____ is used to point out the sharing of Christians in the life of Christ.

   ○ sacrifice ○ communion ○ service ○ Gentiles

2. The priesthood of all the faithful refers to the Sacrament of _____.

   ○ Marriage ○ Eucharist ○ Baptism ○ Holy Orders

3. The ordained priesthood refers to the Sacrament of _____.

   ○ Marriage ○ Eucharist ○ Baptism ○ Holy Orders

4. Christian marriage, like _____ love for his Church, is a faithful and lifelong love.

   ○ the pope's ○ Christ's ○ the bishop's ○ the pastor's

Answer the following.

5. Describe the common vocation of service that all of the baptized are called to fulfill.

   _____

   _____

   _____

6. Describe the Christian family as a domestic Church.

   _____

   _____

   _____

   _____

To Help You Remember

1. Married and ordained Catholics are living signs that all the baptized are called to serve one another as Christ served his Father and others.

2. Holy Orders consecrates a baptized man to serve the whole Church as a bishop, priest, or deacon.

3. Matrimony unites a baptized man and a baptized woman to be a living sign of Christ's love for the Church.

Growing in Faith

One important thing I learned this week is

_____

_____

_____.

This is important because

_____

_____

_____.

What will people see me doing as I live my faith choice this week?

_____

_____

This Week . . .

In chapter 18, "Sacraments at the Service of Communion," your child learned about the vocation of all the baptized to serve others as Jesus did. While all the baptized are to live this vocation, or calling, God calls some members of the Church to serve the whole community of the Church. Holy Orders and Matrimony are called Sacraments at the Service of Communion. In Holy Orders a baptized man is ordained as a bishop, priest, or deacon to serve the whole Church by continuing the unique work Jesus entrusted to the Apostles. In Matrimony a baptized man and a baptized woman are united in a lifelong bond of faithful love as a sign of Christ's love for the Church.

For more on the teachings of the Catholic Church on the Sacraments at the Service of Communion, see *Catechism of the Catholic Church* paragraph numbers 1533–1589 and 1601–1658.

Sharing God's Word

Read together Mark 10:42–45. Emphasize that each of us receives a special call or vocation from God to serve God and the whole community of the new People of God, the Church.

Praying

In this chapter your child prayed a prayer from the rite of Marriage. Read and pray together the prayer on page 232.

Making a Difference

Choose one of the following activities to do as a family or design a similar activity of your own.

- Talk about the ways your family can or already does serve others as Jesus did. Choose one thing you will do together this week.

- Look in your parish bulletin to see all the ways your parish serves others. If there are ministries you do not know much about, take time to find out about them.

- The Christian family is called the church of the home. Identify some of the things your family does that the whole Church does. Discuss ways you learn about Jesus, ways you pray, and ways you live the Gospel.

For more ideas on ways your family can live your faith, visit the "Faith First for Families" page at **www.FaithFirst.com**. Click on "Make a Difference" for ideas on how your family can share God's love with others this week.

Catholic Social Teaching

Christians reach out to the vulnerable. Jesus calls us, as his disciples, to respond to the needs of all our brothers and sisters.

An Uncertain Future

On December 26, 2004, the most powerful earthquake in 40 years erupted under the Indian Ocean near Sumatra. Giant, deadly waves crashed ashore in nearly a dozen countries, killing more than 225,000 people.

Mu is an average eleven-year old Thai boy whose life was turned upside down on that December 26. Mu and his family lived on Platong Island in Phang Nga province of Thailand with three hundred others. His father was a fisherman.

The tsunami destroyed the island, and Mu lost his father and his home. Mu is luckier than many. He survived, as did his mother. She is a strong-willed woman who is a part of the women's group at the survivor camp where they live in a tent. She helps prepare food and take care of others.

Mu goes to a makeshift school, but the family has no livelihood and no means of support. Those children who were orphaned by the tsunami receive the most support. Mu's mother is afraid that people around the world will forget about the tsunami as time goes on. She and Mu are scared of what the future might bring.

Refugee camp for tsunami survivors, Takua Pa, Thailand

Making Connections . . .

Disasters, as we can see with Mu's family, can strike anywhere at anytime. Christians reach out to people who, for whatever reasons, need the loving assistance of others.

with Math and Science

Write a step-by-step description of what happens to the earth during an earthquake. Include information on the earth's surface and plate tectonics. Compare two different earthquakes, for example, the earthquake in the Indian Ocean in 2004 and the earthquake in Northridge, California, in 1994. Describe where the epicenter was for each of these quakes. Explain how factors, such as the size of the earthquake, its location, the distance of regions from the epicenter, local geology, type of land, construction, and population centers nearby, lessen or make greater the effects of the earthquake.

with Language Arts

Immediately after a natural disaster, such as the tsunami of 2004, organizations cooperate in rescue and relief efforts. These efforts take care of the immediate needs of survivors. After time passes, the cameras are gone, and the disaster no longer shows up in the headlines. Aid organizations stress the importance of continued assistance during the rehabilitation and reconstruction phase, which can, in some cases, take years.

Write an essay comparing and contrasting rescue and relief efforts with rehabilitation and reconstruction efforts. In your essay remind people of the importance of using their time and resources to continue to help people rebuild their lives in the months and even years after a disaster.

with Social Studies

Research the religions of the regions affected by the tsunami of 2004. Give a brief history of these religions.

⮑ **Faith Action** *Share with your peers some of the ways your family has worked together to help others. Decide on something you can do together as a class to reach out to people who need your assistance.*

Name _____

A. The Best Response

Read each question and statement and circle the best answer.

1. What are the seven sacraments?
   a. Beatitudes
   b. Corporal Works of Mercy
   c. main liturgical signs of the Church
   d. main liturgical seasons of the Church year

2. Which season of the Church year celebrates the Resurrection of Jesus?
   a. Advent
   b. Christmas
   c. Lent
   d. Easter

3. What are rituals?
   a. codes for happiness
   b. creeds of the Church
   c. words and actions used in the celebration of the liturgy
   d. ways of living the Commandments

4. Which sacrament is a Sacrament of Christian Initiation?
   a. Confirmation
   b. Penance and Reconciliation
   c. Matrimony
   d. Holy Orders

5. Which sacrament uses the rite of anointing?
   a. Eucharist
   b. Penance and Reconciliation
   c. Matrimony
   d. Holy Orders

6. What are the two main parts of the Mass?
   a. Introductory Rites and Liturgy of the Word
   b. Homily and Prayer of the Faithful
   c. Eucharistic Prayer and Communion Rite
   d. Liturgy of the Word and Liturgy of the Eucharist

7. The parable of the Great Feast is about the _____.
   a. Kingdom of God
   b. Beatitudes
   c. Ten Commandments
   d. seven sacraments

8. Which sacrament strengthens our faith and trust in God when we are ill?
   a. Holy Orders
   b. Anointing of the Sick
   c. Penance and Reconciliation
   d. Matrimony

9. What are the Sacraments at the Service of Communion?
   a. Baptism and Holy Orders
   b. Confirmation and Holy Orders
   c. Eucharist and Holy Orders
   d. Matrimony and Holy Orders

10. Which of these is a Sacrament of Healing?
    a. Holy Orders
    b. Penance and Reconciliation
    c. Confirmation
    d. all of the above

B. Completing the Paragraph

Fill in the blanks in the paragraph by using the terms in the word bank.

> **Last Supper**   salvation   **Holy Communion**
> **Word**   sacraments   **Paschal Mystery**

The story of God's loving plan of creation and _____

in Jesus Christ is proclaimed and celebrated by the Church in the

_____. Through rituals, the Church celebrates the

liturgy, and we are made sharers in the _____ of Jesus

Christ. The Sacrament of the Eucharist is celebrated at Mass. During the Liturgy

of the _____, we listen to readings from the Bible. During the

Liturgy of the Eucharist, we do what Jesus did at the _____.

The bread and wine become the Body and Blood of Christ, and we receive the gift

of the Body and Blood of Jesus in _____.

C. What I Have Learned

Write three things you learned in this unit. Share them with the group.

_____

_____

_____

Look at the faith terms in "Words to Know" on page 138. Circle the terms you know now.

D. From a Scripture Story

In the parable of the Great Feast, Jesus teaches what it means to be invited to the Kingdom of God. Describe what happens in the parable and who is invited.

What Happens	Who Is Invited
_____	_____
_____	_____
_____	_____

How do we show that we share in God's holiness?

239

Getting Ready

What I Have Learned

What is something you already know about these faith terms?

moral decisions

_____

_____

virtues

_____

_____

natural law

_____

_____

Words to Know

Put an X next to the faith terms you know. Put a ? next to the faith terms you need to know more about.

Faith Vocabulary

_____ holiness

_____ theological virtues

_____ morality

_____ capital sins

_____ natural law

_____ justice

_____ moral decisions

_____ venial sins

Questions I Have

What questions would you like to ask about making moral decisions?

_____

_____

_____

_____

A Scripture Story

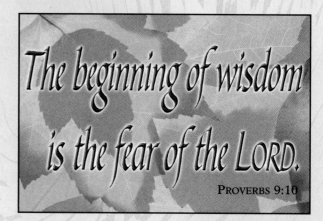

The beginning of wisdom is the fear of the LORD.

PROVERBS 9:10

A proverb from the Book of Proverbs

What does the Book of Proverbs in the Old Testament teach us about living as children of God?

Our Call to Holiness

We Pray

Exalt the LORD, our God; . . .
holy is the LORD, our God.

PSALM 99:9

God our Father,
you alone are holy.
You sent your Son, Jesus,
to restore us to holiness.
Send the Holy Spirit
to help us become
the holy people
you call us to be.   Amen.

What is something unique about yourself?

Every person is both different from every other person and the same in a unique way. Everyone is created in the image and likeness of God.

What does it mean to be created in the image and likeness of God?

241

Called to Be Saints

Faith Focus

What does it mean to say that everyone is called to live a holy life?

Faith Vocabulary

holiness. The quality, or condition, of a person who is living in communion with and in the right relationship with God, others, and with all of his creation; being in the state of grace.

theological virtues. The virtues of faith, hope, and love (charity); gifts of God that enable us to live a life of holiness, or a life in communion with the Holy Trinity.

Who would you describe as a very good person? What qualities would that person have? Why do you think that person comes to mind? More than likely, it is someone living a holy life.

Be Holy

God created us with a physical body and a spiritual soul, with an intellect and a free will. He created us to know him, to love him, to serve him, and to live with him forever in eternal happiness. Our life's job description is to share in God's holiness. **Holiness** is being in a state of grace. Grace is being in communion with God and sharing in his very life and love.

God's command to the Israelites is a command to all his people:

"For I, the LORD, am your God; and you shall make and keep yourselves holy, because I am holy. . . . Since I, the LORD, brought you up from the land of Egypt that I might be your God, you shall be holy, because I am holy."

LEVITICUS 11:44–45

When we were baptized, we received one overriding vocation: be holy. Sure, we have responsibilities, such as studying, cleaning our rooms, raising children, and going to work. We can excel at school and keep spotless rooms; we can raise brilliant children and have successful careers. But if we do all these things well and wind up leading lives that keep God far away or keep him out of the picture completely, we have missed the whole point about living—God created us to be holy as he is holy.

Living Holy Lives

The ability and freedom to live a holy life is a gift from God. He not only invites us to live a life in communion with him, but he also gives us the powers to live that life. He gives us the **theological virtues.**

The three theological virtues are faith, hope, and love.

- Faith is the theological virtue by which we believe in God and everything he has revealed to us.
- Hope is the theological virtue by which we desire and trust that God will fulfill all his promises, especially the promise of eternal happiness.

- Charity, or love, is the theological virtue by which we love God above all else for his own sake and love our neighbor as ourselves for the love of God.

Faith, hope, and charity connect us with God—Father, Son, and Holy Spirit—in a very direct way. The more we let these virtues take hold of our lives, the more we grow in holiness.

How do the theological virtues help us live a holy life?

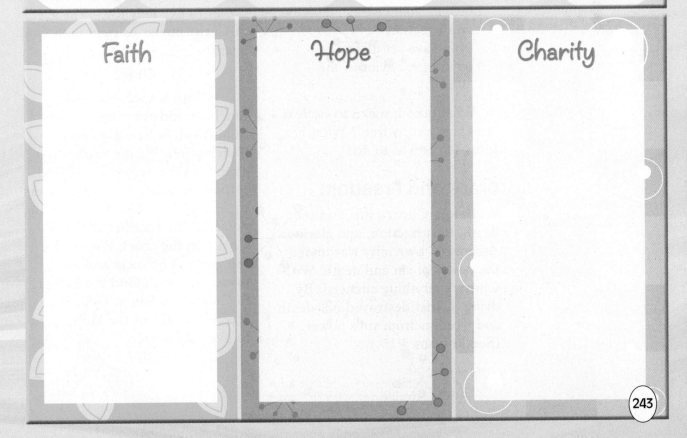

A Life of Faith, Hope, and Charity

What can you do to show that the theological virtues are at work in your life? Draw or describe an action for each virtue: faith, hope, and charity.

Faith	Hope	Charity

Faith Vocabulary

sanctifying grace. The gift of God's life and love that makes us holy and helps us live holy lives.

People seek freedom and defend their right to be free. What are some of the things you see people doing in the name of freedom? At Mass we profess:

Lord, by your cross and resurrection
you have set us free.
You are the Savior of the world.

What does it mean to profess "you have set us free"? What has Jesus set us free to do?

Grace and Freedom

Before Christ's life, Passion, death, Resurrection, and glorious Ascension, humanity was under the power of sin and death. With Christ, everything changed. By dying, Christ destroyed our death and freed us from sin's power. (See Romans 5:15.)

By rising from the dead, he restored our life of holiness. Through Christ we receive the grace of the Holy Spirit that makes us holy and gives us the power to live holy lives. The grace of Christ makes us right with God again.

Grace

At Baptism we are joined to Christ and are made sharers in his work of Salvation and Redemption. We are made sharers in the saving act of God setting humanity free from slavery to sin and from death through the power of the sacrifice of Jesus Christ on the cross. We receive the grace of holiness and are made right with God the Father in Christ, the Son of God. We receive the gift of the Holy Spirit to live holy lives.

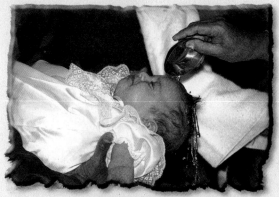

God freely gives us the gift of Salvation and Redemption in Christ. It is something we could never earn on our own. With the grace of God we are made holy again. We call this grace **sanctifying grace**. It is the grace of his own life and love that God freely shares with us.

Freedom of the Children of God

The grace of the Holy Spirit calls us to use the gift of freedom from sin's power responsibly and to grow in holiness. With the grace of the Holy Spirit, we grow in our ability to make the right choices and live as adopted children of God the Father. We turn toward God and away from sin. We accept forgiveness and the gift of having our communion and life with God restored.

 What has Christ freed us to do?

My Wish List

Describe some of the things that you and your friends "absolutely must have" in your life. Review the list and place a + next to those things that will really help you live a holy life.

Faith Vocabulary

Works of Mercy. Acts of loving kindness by which we come to the help of others in their bodily and spiritual needs.

We are not just people who live alone, separated from one another. We belong to families, communities, nations, and the world.

Growth in Holiness with Others

God's gift of holiness is not just for us as individuals. We live our life of holiness with others and, in a way, for others. Saint Paul taught:

Put on then, as God's chosen ones, holy and beloved, heartfelt compassion, kindness, humility, gentleness, and patience, bearing with one another and forgiving one another. . . . And over all these put on love, that is, the bond of perfection.

COLOSSIANS 3:12–14

Jesus taught us that we are to love others as we love ourselves. As God shares his life and love with us, we too share our life and love with others. Our growth in holiness involves the way that we live with other people. Holiness is about how we act with others.

Works of Mercy

The Church gives us the **Works of Mercy** to guide us in living the life of holiness that Saint Paul describes. The Works of Mercy are acts of loving kindness by which we come to the help of others in their bodily and spiritual needs.

The **Corporal Works of Mercy** are actions that help people in their bodily needs. They are:

- Feed people who are hungry.
- Give drink to people who are thirsty.
- Clothe people who need clothes.
- Visit prisoners.
- Shelter people who are homeless.
- Visit people who are sick.
- Bury people who have died.

The **Spiritual Works of Mercy** are actions that help people in their spiritual needs. They are:

- Help people who sin.
- Teach people who are ignorant.
- Give advice to people who have doubts.
- Comfort people who suffer.
- Be patient with other people.
- Forgive people who hurt you.
- Pray for people who are alive and for those who have died.

The Works of Mercy are concrete, practical things we are to do to live the Gospel. They clearly show that holiness is not just an idea. It is something that we must practice every day. It is a life of true courage, a life that requires God's grace.

 How do the Works of Mercy guide us in living a life of holiness?

The Beatitudes

The Beatitudes summarize the attitudes and actions of a person living a life of holiness. The Beatitudes are part of the Sermon on the Mount found in Matthew's Gospel. (See Matthew 5:3–12.) The Sermon on the Mount is a summary of Jesus' teachings on what it means to live as his disciples.

The Works of Mercy

List one Spiritual Work of Mercy and one Corporal Work of Mercy. Then write a practical way that a sixth grader can put them into practice.

Spiritual Work of Mercy

_____

_____

_____

_____

_____

Corporal Work of Mercy

_____

_____

_____

_____

_____

Our Church Makes a Difference

Volunteers (top and bottom photos) gleaning sweet potatoes, North Carolina Yam Jam

The Gleaning Network

Heroes and saints are not the only ones to take up the challenge to feed the poor and live the Works of Mercy. People in Catholic parish communities all over the world are working every day to help those in need.

The Gleaning Network is an organization that responds to the needs of many people who are without food. Its 32,000 volunteers provide more than 27 million servings of nourishing food to feed America's hungry each year.

The Gleaners in the Midwest saw that their fertile region produced an abundance of crops, such as tomatoes, oranges, onions, and carrots. Some of this food went to waste. The Gleaners contacted local farmers,

who helped them collect the unused crops. The Gleaners grew larger and larger, involved members of other churches, and purchased their own buildings. They now bring in fresh produce and canned goods from grocery stores and from food drives. They distribute food not just to people in their own community but to the needy throughout the county in which they live.

Remember Ruth in the Old Testament who stood by her mother-in-law, Naomi? The Gleaners chose their name to honor Ruth, who gleaned the fields for crops that were not harvested to support herself and Naomi.

 Who do you see living the Works of Mercy? Tell what they do.

What Difference Does Faith Make in My Life?

God created you to be holy. Living the Works of Mercy is one way you can strive to live a holy life.

Develop a list of three activities that you could do with others that would help you live a holy life. Choose one and draw up a plan to put it into action.

Signs of a Holy Life

1. _____

_____

2. _____

_____

3. _____

_____

Our Plan

_____

_____

_____

_____

_____

My Faith Choice

This week I will show that I believe I am called to live a life of holiness. I will

_____

_____.

We Pray

The Road Ahead

Leader: The road to living a holy life is not always an easy road to travel, but God always leads us along that road. Quiet yourself. Place your trust in God and quietly pray this prayer.

All:
Happy those whose way is blameless,
    who walk by the teaching of the LORD.
Happy those who observe God's decrees,
    who seek the LORD with all their heart.
May my ways be firm
    in the observance of your laws!
I will keep your laws;
    do not leave me alone.

With all my heart I seek you;
    do not let me stray from your commands.

Open my eyes to see clearly
    the wonders of your teachings.

Give me insight to observe your teaching,
    to keep it with all my heart.

Let your love come to me, LORD,
    salvation in accord with your promise.
I will keep your teachings always,
    for all time and forever.
I delight in your commands,
    which I dearly love.

Teach me wisdom and knowledge,
    for in your commands I trust.

Your word is a lamp for my feet,
    a light for my path.

PSALM 119:1–2, 5, 8, 10, 18, 34, 41, 44, 47, 66, 105

250

We Remember

What I Have Learned

Match each faith term with its description.

Faith Terms

____ **1.** holiness

____ **2.** love

____ **3.** theological virtues

____ **4.** sanctifying grace

____ **5.** Works of Mercy

Descriptions

a. acts of loving kindness

b. gift of God's life and love that makes us holy

c. virtue by which we love God above all else for his own sake and our neighbor as ourselves for the love of God

d. living in communion with God, being in the state of grace

e. gifts of God that enable us to live a holy life

Answer the following.

6. What are some ways God helps you live a holy life?

_____

_____

_____

7. Name and explain the theological virtues.

_____

_____

_____

8. Why is living the Works of Mercy part of living a holy life?

_____

_____

_____

_____

To Help You Remember

1. The theological virtues connect us with God and strengthen us to live a life of holiness in communion with God.

2. The grace of the Holy Spirit helps us to make choices to grow in holiness.

3. Living the Works of Mercy is a sign we are trying to live holy lives.

Growing in Faith

One important thing I learned this week is

_____

_____

_____.

This is important because

_____

_____

_____.

What will people see me doing as I live my faith choice this week?

_____

_____

_____

This Week . . .

In chapter 19, "Our Call to Holiness," your child learned more about the call of God to every person to live a holy life. Every person is created in the image and likeness of God. Made sharers in the life of Christ at Baptism, Christians are called to live the way of holiness Jesus lived and taught his disciples to live. Through Baptism we receive the gift of sanctifying grace. We are made sharers in the life and love of God the Father, the Son, and the Holy Spirit. We are joined to Christ and receive the gift of the Holy Spirit and the help to live as adopted sons and daughters of God the Father. God created us with free will and gives us the gift of faith to accept his invitation to live holy lives. Living the Corporal Works of Mercy and Spiritual Works of Mercy is one way that we cooperate with the Holy Spirit and strive to live holy lives.

For more on the teachings of the Catholic Church on grace and the universal call to holiness, see *Catechism of the Catholic Church* paragraph numbers 1699–1742, 1803–1832, and 1987–2016.

Sharing God's Word

Read together Leviticus 11:44–45. Emphasize that every person created by God is to live a holy life.

Praying

In this chapter your child quietly prayed a Psalm. Read and pray together this prayer on page 250.

Making a Difference

Choose one of the following activities to do as a family or design a similar activity of your own.

- Write a family pledge to live holy lives. Be sure that the pledge describes specific behaviors and attitudes that constitute holiness.

- Make a holiness banner. Use the word *Holiness.* Decorate the banner and hang it where it can remind all family members of their call to live holy lives.

- Pray the prayer of trust on page 250 as your family prayer this week. This prayer will remind the whole family that God is with you as you journey the road of holiness.

For more ideas on ways your family can live your faith, visit the "Faith First for Families" page at **www.FaithFirst.com**. Click on "Current Events" to find an article on an especially interesting topic.

Making Moral Choices

20

We Pray

I bless the LORD
    who counsels me. . . .
I keep the LORD always
    before me.   PSALM 16:7, 8

God our Father and
Creator, send us your
Holy Spirit to enlighten our
minds and to strengthen
our wills so that we may
walk in the way of Jesus
Christ, your Son.   Amen.

*What are some skills that you
would like to develop?*

When we need to learn and
develop athletic, dance, or
musical skills, we go to an
instructor and watch performers
who excel at those skills. The
same is true about growing in
the skills that enable us to
make better moral decisions.

*What steps do you follow to learn
how to make good decisions to
live a holy life?*

Morality

Faith Focus

Where can we find guidance for making moral decisions?

Faith Vocabulary

moral decisions. The decisions and choices we make to live as children of God and disciples of Jesus Christ.

morality. A way of judging, or evaluating, whether our choices lead us to God or away from him.

Where do we go when we want to get directions to someone's home? Visiting an on-line site that gives maps and driving directions is a good place to start. Our moral life is a journey of faith. Where do we go when we need direction in making wise moral decisions?

The Sources of Morality

Moral decisions are decisions and choices we make to live holy lives as children of God and disciples of Jesus Christ. Here are some practical starting points where we can look to make those decisions:

- the natural law, or the laws inscribed in creation and written in the human heart; for example, "Do good and not evil" and "Treat others as you want them to treat you";

- the Bible, especially the Great Commandment and the Ten Commandments;
- the life and teachings of Jesus Christ; and
- the teachings of the Catholic Church.

Knowing what determines things that make human acts good or evil will also help us make good moral decisions. There are three things that determine the **morality** of human acts, that is, whether they are good or evil. They are the:

- object of the act,
- intention of the act, and
- circumstances surrounding the act.

We call these three things the sources of the morality of a human act. Let us look at each one individually.

Object

The object of the act is what we do. It is the good or the bad we do or say. Some things are good in themselves, such as praying. Other things, such as abusing drugs, are evil in themselves.

Intention

The intention of a human act is what we want, or our purpose for doing or saying something. A good intention cannot change an evil act into something good. For example, if we steal something to give it to someone as a gift, the act of stealing is still wrong, even though we had a good intention.

Circumstances

The circumstances of a human act are those things that surround the decision. Circumstances do not change whether a human act is good or evil, but they might make a difference.

Circumstances can make something we do or say better or worse. For example, we might tell a lie because we do not want to hurt someone's feelings. The circumstance is kindness. The act of lying is still wrong. The circumstance may make the act of lying less evil. The better choice, of course, is not to lie.

 What three things determine the morality of our choices?

Making Moral Choices

Making a good choice is not always easy. What circumstances might make it difficult for people to choose to do something they know is right? Choose one of the circumstances you named and describe how that circumstance might affect your choice.

Circumstances	Affect on Choice
_____	_____
_____	_____
_____	_____
_____	_____
_____	_____
_____	_____
_____	_____

Faith Vocabulary

conscience. The gift of God that is part of every person that guides us to know and judge what is right and wrong.

Our life is filled with so many things that compete for our attention. Look here! Buy this! Wear this! Eat here! Shop here! We have so many choices that perhaps we really do not know how to go about making a moral decision. So the first thing we need to know is how to decide what is really the good thing to do.

Conscience

Every human being has another voice that calls for our attention. We have the God-given gift of **conscience**. Conscience is the gift of God that is part of every human person that guides a person to judge what is right and what is wrong, to know what is God's will and what is not his will. We have the responsibility to obey our conscience.

It is important that we form a good conscience so that our conscience guides us correctly in making moral decisions. The better we work at forming a good conscience, the better we will be at making wise and responsible decisions that help us live as followers of Jesus Christ.

Let us review four ways that we can develop a good conscience.
- Read, study, and pray over the Scriptures.

> LORD, teach me the way of your laws;
> I shall observe them with care.
> Give me insight to observe your teaching,
> to keep it with all my heart.
> PSALM 119:33–34

- Learn and study the teachings of the Catholic Church. The Church is our teacher.

- Seek the advice and wisdom of people of faith, people you can trust.

Not everyone forms a good conscience. People can have a conscience that does not know what is right or wrong. Conscience that is not well formed can lead a person to make wrong moral decisions. Such a conscience is called an erroneous conscience. It is a conscience that is filled with errors.

When a person deliberately does not work at forming a good conscience, they are forming an erroneous conscience. Because a person is responsible for their erroneous conscience, they are also responsible for the choices they make and the wrong caused by those choices.

When we exercise wisely, we build up the muscles of our body and develop our athletic skills. When we form our conscience wisely, we build up an inner resource that will guide us throughout our life.

QUESTION Why is it important to form a good conscience?

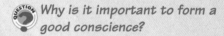

What to Do?

Your friend approaches you in the school yard and shows you a pack of firecrackers and a lighter.

1. What is your first reaction?

_____

_____

2. What will you do?

_____

_____

3. Why will you do it?

_____

_____

4. What might be the consequences of your decision?

_____

_____

Faith Vocabulary

capital sins. Seven sins named by the Church that are the sources of other sins—pride, covetousness, envy, anger, gluttony, lust, and sloth.

mortal sin. A serious or grave failure in our love and respect for God, our neighbor, creation, and ourselves.

The choices we make are not always easy. Sometimes we give in to our friends, or we take the easy, but wrong, way out of a tough situation. Sometimes we come close to doing what we know is against God's law and choose not to do it. At other times we give in to temptation and, at the last minute, we go along with the group as they get involved in doing something that our conscience tells us is just plain wrong. We sin.

Sin

We sin when we deliberately turn away from God and offend him. To help us understand more clearly what sin is all about, the Church speaks about capital sins, mortal sins, and venial sins.

Capital Sins

Capital sins are sins that lead to other sins. There are seven capital sins. They are pride, covetousness, envy, anger, gluttony, lust, and sloth.

Remember the Tenth Commandment, "You shall not covet your neighbor's goods." When we covet what someone else has and wrongfully desire it for ourself, it can lead to stealing, name calling, and even hatred. A false pride and wanting to appear better than others can lead us to telling lies about ourselves, gossiping, or spreading false rumors about others.

Mortal Sins

Mortal sins are serious offenses against God that break our relationship with him. Mortal sins are serious failures in our love for God, our neighbor, creation, and ourselves. Three things are necessary for a sin to be mortal. They are:

- The action involves a grave or serious matter.
- The choice is made with full knowledge of the gravity of our choice.
- The choice is made completely freely.

258

remain separated from him forever by our own choice. Being forever separated from God is what we call hell.

Venial Sins

Venial sins are less serious offenses against God. Sins may be venial when any or all of the conditions needed for a sin to be mortal are not present. Because all sin turns our heart away from God's love, we should seek forgiveness of all sins, including venial sins.

Whenever we think about sins, especially our own, we must remember that God wants to forgive us. If we are truly sorry for what we have done, we can always find forgiveness. Jesus died on the cross for our sins.

We can find forgiveness for all mortal sins through the Sacrament of Reconciliation. If we die in a state of separation from God, we

 Why do we need to seek forgiveness when we sin?

Forgiveness   **Yurushi**   **Danh tù**

Forgiveness Prayer

Write a prayer thanking God for his forgiveness.

_____

_____

_____

_____

_____

_____

_____

Perdón   **Wybaczenie**   **Perdono**

Saint John Bosco

The history of the Church is filled with people like John Bosco who helped others learn to make good choices. After he was ordained a priest, John Bosco became known as Don Bosco. "Don" is the title used by the diocesan clergy in Italy. Don Bosco studied the lives of people living in poverty in large cities. He tried to find out the answer to the question, How does living in poverty in a large city affect the moral decisions people make?

Don Bosco hearing confessions

Don Bosco came to realize that many people living in poverty in cities did not have the opportunities for a good education and a good job. Because education is an important part of training ourselves in making moral decisions, Don Bosco decided to create job training programs and professional schools. All the programs in the schools founded by Don Bosco were founded on three values: reason, religion, and kindness.

The followers of Saint John Bosco are called Salesians. Many religious priests, brothers, and sisters as well as lay volunteers carry on the work of Saint John Bosco today in more than two hundred schools around the world.

 Who helps you learn to make good moral choices?

Salesian Lay Missioners in Bolivia

What Difference Does Faith Make in My Life?

Many of the moral decisions you make are not always easy ones. The Holy Spirit is always with you to teach you and guide you to make good decisions. God has also created you and every person with a conscience. Your conscience helps you judge what is good and what is evil.

Look over this list of conscience builders. Mark a ✔ next to the actions you use to help build, or form, a good conscience.

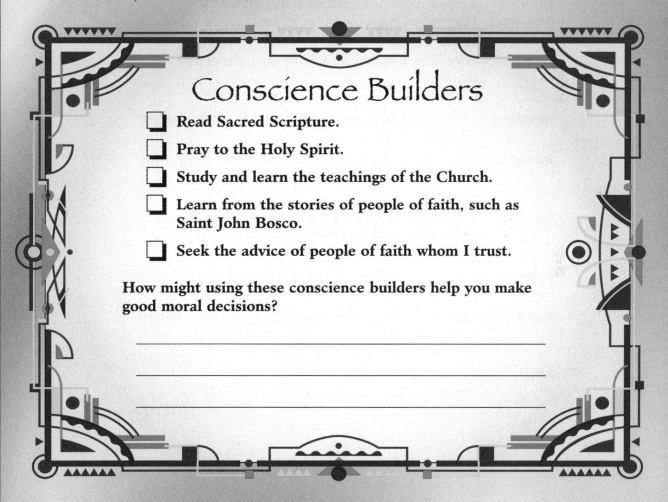

Conscience Builders

☐ **Read Sacred Scripture.**

☐ **Pray to the Holy Spirit.**

☐ **Study and learn the teachings of the Church.**

☐ **Learn from the stories of people of faith, such as Saint John Bosco.**

☐ **Seek the advice of people of faith whom I trust.**

How might using these conscience builders help you make good moral decisions?

_____

_____

_____

My Faith Choice

This week I will try to make moral decisions thoughtfully and responsibly. I will

_____

_____.

An Examination of Conscience

It is important to think about and evaluate our moral decisions. One way we do this is by examining our conscience.

Leader: Let us look into our hearts and think about the way we have loved or failed to love God and our neighbors as Jesus taught.

All: **Lord, I keep you always before me;**
You will show me the path to life.

BASED ON PSALM 116:8, 9

Leader: Reflect in silence after each question.

Reader: How have I kept God first in my life?
(Pause.)

Reader: How have I shown respect to my parents and teachers?
(Pause.)

Reader: How have I been kind and helpful to other people?
(Pause.)

Reader: How have my words and actions shown respect for my body and the bodies of others?
(Pause.)

Reader: How have I respected the truth and been honest in my dealings with others?
(Pause.)

Reader: How have I respected the property of others?
(Pause.)

Reader: How have I dealt with any feelings of anger, hatred, or envy?
(Pause.)

All: **Lord, I keep you always before me;**
You will show me the path to life.

BASED ON PSALM 116:8, 9

We Remember

What I Have Learned

Read this situation. Name the object, intention, and circumstances of the act. Then discuss the morality of the act.

Sarah and her teammates were playing in the championship game. In the final minutes of the game, Sarah swept by the defender. As she kicked the ball trying to break the 0–0 score, she slipped on the wet grass, and the ball struck the goalkeeper in the face. Stunned from the fall, she looked toward the goal and saw the goalkeeper running toward her.

1. **Object** _____

_____

2. **Intention** _____

_____

3. **Circumstances** _____

_____

Answer the following.

4. Compare capital sins, mortal sins, and venial sins.

_____

_____

_____

5 Explain the importance of forming a good conscience.

_____

_____

_____

6. Describe how you can form a good conscience.

_____

_____

_____

_____

To Help You Remember

1. The sources of the morality of our actions are the object of the act, the intention of the act, and the circumstances surrounding the act.

2. Our conscience guides us to judge whether an act is good or evil.

3. Sin is turning away from God's love, freely choosing to do or say what we know is against God's will or freely choosing not to do something we know God wants us to do.

Growing in Faith

One important thing I learned this week is

_____

_____

_____.

This is important because

_____

_____

_____.

What will people see me doing as I live my faith choice this week?

_____

_____

_____

20 With My Family

This Week . . .

In chapter 20, "Making Moral Choices," your child learned about the importance of making moral decisions. We journey through life as a member of the Church, which guides us in making wise decisions to live as faithful followers of Jesus Christ. The things that determine the morality of our acts are the good or evil deed we choose; the intention, or purpose, of doing the act; and the circumstances surrounding the act. A good conscience helps us judge correctly whether an act is good or evil. When we freely and knowingly choose an act that we know is evil, we sin. We turn away from God and offend him.

For more on the teachings of the Catholic Church on conscience, sin, and making moral decisions, see *Catechism of the Catholic Church* paragraph numbers 1749–1794 and 1846–1869.

Sharing God's Word

Read together Psalm 119:1–8. Emphasize that living the Ten Commandments guides us in loving God and our neighbors.

Praying

In this chapter your child used an examination of conscience. Read and use the examination of conscience on page 262 or another form of an examination of conscience.

Making a Difference

Choose one of the following activities to do as a family or design a similar activity of your own.

- Read the statement, "Right is right even if everyone is against it, and wrong is wrong even if everyone is for it." Discuss how the statement applies to making moral decisions.

- Create a banner for your home, using the above statement. Hang it inside your home near the entrance.

- Discuss the following questions: What circumstances might make it difficult for people to choose to do what they know is right? What can we do to help us choose to do what we know is right?

For more ideas on ways your family can live your faith, visit the "Faith First for Families" page at **www.FaithFirst.com**. Click on "Family Prayer." Plan to pray this prayer together this week.

Loving God

We Pray

The precepts of the LORD
    are right,
  rejoicing the heart.

PSALM 19:9

My God, I love you above
all else because you are
all good and worthy of
my love.   Amen.

*What signs let you know what is
important to people?*

Think about the people you
see every day. From what you
see people doing or hear them
saying, what seems to be most
important to them? Is it God,
or is it someone or something
other than God?

*How can you tell that a person
places God first?*

Faithfully Living as Children of God

Faith Focus

Why do we say that the basic rules for living as a good person are written in our hearts?

Faith Vocabulary

precepts. Rules or laws that detail responsibilities and impose standards of conduct.

When we say that we have faith in and trust our parents, what are we saying? One thing we are saying is that we know they love us and will always do what is best for us. While we might sometimes complain or object to the rules they laid down for us, we know deep down in our hearts that when they insist that we obey those rules, they are showing their love for us. Now shift your focus to God. God is Love. God is Truth. God is always faithful. God always does what is best for us!

The Natural Law

We have been created in the image and likeness of God. In God's fatherly love for us, he has etched into our hearts and minds a law, a pattern or design, that helps us live as images of God. This law guides us to discover the way to the true happiness that God has promised us. This law guides us to recognize the evil that leads us away from that happiness and away from God. There is something about the way God has created us that moves us naturally, or by nature, to choose what is good for us and others. The Church calls it the natural law.

What are some of the principles, or **precepts**, of this natural law? Here are three.
- Do good and avoid evil.
- Tell the truth to each other.
- Be respectful toward one another.

The Ten Commandments

To get a clearer picture of the precepts of the natural law, look at the Ten Commandments. When God made the Covenant with Moses and the Israelites, he gave them the Decalogue, or the Ten Commandments, which were ten laws, or precepts, that spelled out what they were to do to live the Covenant. Coming down from the mountain after God revealed the Ten Commandments to him, Moses said to the Israelites.

"Hear, O Israel, the statutes and decrees which I proclaim in your hearing this day, that you may learn them and take care to observe them. The LORD, our God, made a covenant with us at Horeb; not with our fathers did he make this covenant, but with us, all of us who are alive here this day. The LORD spoke with you face to face on the mountain from the midst of the fire. Since you were afraid of the fire and would not go up the mountain, I stood between the LORD and you at that time, to announce to you these words of the LORD.

DEUTERONOMY 5:1–5

Moses then named the Ten Commandments for the Israelites. He spelled out what the Lord God expected of them. Jesus told his disciples that they were to live the Commandments. He said that he came to fulfill the Commandments and not to do away with them. Jesus told us to live the Commandments as he did. We are to love God and one another as he did.

 What is the connection between the Ten Commandments and the natural law?

Naturally!

Choose one of the Ten Commandments. Describe how that Commandment makes good sense "naturally." Give specific examples.

_____

_____

_____

_____

_____

_____

_____

Faith Focus

What do the first two Commandments teach us about ourselves?

Faith Vocabulary

worship. Honor and respect we give God above all else; faith in, hope in, and love for God above all else.

The Pharisees and Sadducees Come to Tempt Jesus, James Tissot (1836–1902), French painter

Magazine, billboard, and television all promote material possessions, wealth, and power as items we should pursue with great vigor. We all know how easy it is to "worship" these things and make them the center of our life. When we do, we make these things idols, or "God-substitutes."

The First Commandment

I am the LORD your God; you shall not have strange gods before me.
BASED ON EXODUS 20:2–3

The First, Second, and Third Commandments teach us ways that we are to love God above all else. They teach us to love the Lord our God with our whole heart, soul, and mind as Jesus reminded a scholar of the law of God what the Torah taught.

[A scholar of the law] tested him by asking, "Teacher, which commandment in the law is the greatest?" He said to him, "You shall love the Lord, your God, with all your heart, with all your soul, and with all your mind. This is the greatest and the first commandment."
MATTHEW 22:35–38

The First Commandment teaches that we are to **worship** only God. We are to place our faith and hope in God and love him above all else.

Since most people today do not think they are into worshiping "strange gods," what is this Commandment teaching us?

The Second Commandment

You shall not take the name of the LORD, your God, in vain. BASED ON EXODUS 20:7

The Second Commandment teaches that we are to use the name of God and the names of Mary, Jesus, and the saints reverently and respectfully. Blasphemy is the use of the names of God, of Jesus Christ, of the Virgin Mary, and of the saints in an offensive way.

This Commandment also teaches that we are to take an oath only when it is necessary, as in a court of law. Whenever we call God as our witness, we must tell the truth. To use the name of

New citizens taking oath at naturalization ceremony

God or Jesus when we are angry, to show off, or to casually say "I swear to God" is against the Second Commandment.

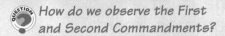 How do we observe the First and Second Commandments?

The Greatest Commandment

Read Matthew 22:34–40. Describe the importance of striving to live Jesus' teaching every day.

_____

_____

_____

_____

_____

_____

Faith Vocabulary

Precepts of the Church. Positive laws made by the Church guiding the faithful to meet their minimal responsibilities in prayer and moral living for their growth in living the Great Commandment of love of God and neighbor.

The photographs on this page show how some families make Sunday a special day. What are some of the ways your family celebrates Sunday?

The Third Commandment

> Remember to keep holy the LORD's Day.
> BASED ON EXODUS 20:8

In the Old Testament God rested from the work of creation on the seventh day, or the Sabbath. He commanded his people to do the same. The Israelites kept the Sabbath holy as the Lord's Day. They set it aside from all the other days of the week.

Sunday, the first day of the week, is the Lord's Day for Christians. It is the day on which the Lord Jesus was raised from the dead. It is the first day of the new creation of the world in Christ. It is the day on which we focus on keeping God first in our lives.

Sunday is to be kept as the most important holy day of obligation. Catholics have the obligation to take part in Mass on Sunday and on other holy days of obligation. We rest from all work that is not necessary and that turns our hearts and minds away from God.

Precepts of the Church

The Church has given us a list of laws to guide us in growing in our love for God and our neighbors. They are called the **Precepts of the Church**. They are:

- Participate in Mass on Sundays and holy days of obligation and rest from unnecessary work.
- Confess your sins at least once a year.
- Receive Holy Communion at least during the Easter season.
- Observe the prescribed days of fasting and abstinence.
- Provide for the material needs of the Church according to one's ability.

We can see that these precepts are both reasonable and minimal. They present us with the practical building blocks of prayer, penance, fasting, and generosity. On their foundation, we can build a life of living the Great Commandment as Jesus taught and as we promised to do at Baptism.

QUESTION *How do the Ten Commandments and Precepts of the Church help you show your love and respect for God?*

Make Sunday Special!

Think of some creative ways that you can keep the Lord's Day holy. Use them to design this placard.

World Mission Sunday

Each year the Church celebrates World Mission Sunday. On that Sunday a special collection is taken up in Catholic churches. This collection supports the Society for the Propagation of the Faith. The funds collected help mission bishops build churches and chapels, train and support catechists, build health clinics, house and feed missionaries, and support many other works. All these works help the Church fulfill Jesus' command, "Go into the whole world and proclaim the gospel to every creature" (Mark 16:15).

The Collection at Mass

When we take part in the celebration of Mass, we show our love both for God and for others. The collection at Mass is one sign of that love. This ancient tradition of the Church is one way we generously show our thanks to God and provide for the material needs of the Church.

In the early Church, wealthy people gave money to the Church. Others brought cheese, handwoven cloth, grain, animals, vegetables, bread, and other goods. After gathering at the entrance of the church, they walked in procession to an area near the altar where they left their gifts. After the celebration of the Mass concluded, these gifts were brought and shared with people in need.

QUESTION *What can you contribute to support your parish and the needs of the poor? What do you do now? What more can you do?*

What Difference Does Faith Make in My Life?

The Holy Spirit is always inviting you to place your faith, hope, and love in the Holy Trinity above all else. This may not always be easy to do. Many people and things try to take the place of God in your life. It is important that you recognize who these people and things might be.

On the pedestal, describe something that could make it difficult for you to place your trust in God. Then write how you can overcome that obstacle.

Name That Idol

Keeping God First

_____
_____
_____
_____
_____
_____
_____
_____
_____
_____

My Faith Choice

This week I will make God number one in my life. I will

_____
_____.

Shema

Leader: The Shema is prayed as a morning and evening prayer by Jewish people today. Praying the Shema is an ancient tradition found in the Old Testament. In the morning the Jewish people pray, in part: "Hear, O Israel, the Lord is our God, the Lord is One." In the evening they pray, in part: "Blessed be the Name of His glorious kingdom for ever and ever."

Let us pray in the spirit of the Shema,
using David's prayer from the First Book of Chronicles.

Group 1: "Blessed may you be, O LORD,
God of Israel our father,
from eternity to eternity.

Group 2: Yours, O LORD, are grandeur and power,
majesty, splendor, and glory.

All: **Blessed may you be, O LORD."**

Group 1: "For all in heaven and on earth is yours;
yours, O LORD, is the sovereignty;
you are exalted as head over all.

Group 2: Riches and honor are from you,
and you have dominion over all.

All: **Blessed may you be, O LORD."**

Group 1: "In your hand are power and might;
it is yours to give grandeur and strength to all.

Group 2: Therefore, our God, we give you thanks
and we praise the majesty of your name.

All: **Blessed may you be, O LORD."**

1 CHRONICLES 29:10–13

We Remember

What I Have Learned

Write First, Second, or Third beside the phrases that describe the Commandments.

1. _____ **a.** We call God to be our witness to the truth of what we are saying.

2. _____ **b.** We worship only God.

3. _____ **c.** Catholics take part in Mass on Sunday.

4. _____ **d.** We speak the name of God reverently and respectfully.

5. _____ **e.** We love God above all else.

Answer the following.

6. Compare the natural law and the Ten Commandments.

_____

_____

7. Describe the life of a person today who loves God above all else.

_____

_____

_____

8. Explain how the Precepts of the Church help us build a life of living the Great Commandment.

_____

_____

_____

_____

To Help You Remember

1. The First Commandment teaches us to worship only God and to believe in, hope in, and love God above all else.

2. The Second Commandment teaches us to use the name of God reverently and respectfully.

3. The Third Commandment teaches us to keep the Lord's Day as a holy day, a day set aside for God. Sunday is the Lord's Day for Christians.

Growing in Faith

One important thing I learned this week is

_____

_____

_____.

This is important because

_____

_____

_____.

What will people see me doing as I live my faith choice this week?

_____

_____

_____

This Week . . .

In chapter 21, "Loving God," your child learned more about the first three Commandments. The First Commandment teaches us that we are to worship only God. We are to believe in, hope in, and love God above all else. God alone is and should always be at the center of our lives. The Second Commandment teaches that we are to honor the name of God. We are to speak the name of God reverently and respectfully. The Third Commandment teaches that we are to set aside one day each week as the Lord's Day. For Christians Sunday is the Lord's Day. It is the most important holy day of obligation. On Sundays Catholics have the obligation to take part in the Mass. We are to avoid all work that prevents us from keeping God at the center of our lives.

For more on the teachings of the Catholic Church on the First, Second, and Third Commandments, see *Catechism of the Catholic Church* paragraph numbers 2084–2132, 2142–2159, and 2168–2188.

Sharing God's Word

Read together Exodus 20:1–17. Emphasize that we give glory to God when we live the Ten Commandments.

Praying

In this chapter your child learned to pray a prayer modeled on the Shema, an ancient prayer of the Jewish people. Read and pray together this prayer on page 274.

Making a Difference

Choose one of the following activities to do as a family or design a similar activity of your own.

- Talk about how your family can make God number one in the life of your family. Choose one thing you will do together as a family this week to show that God is number one in your lives.

- When you take part in Mass on Sunday, you keep the Lord's Day holy. After you take part in Mass, do something special to keep Sunday as the Lord's Day.

- Create table place mats proclaiming Sunday as the Lord's Day. Use these place mats at your Saturday evening and Sunday family meals.

For more ideas on ways your family can live your faith, visit the "Faith First for Families" page at **www.FaithFirst.com**. Check out "Bible Stories." Read and discuss the Bible story this week.

Loving One Another

We Pray

Trust in the LORD and
do good.   PSALM 37:3

Make known to me
your ways, Lord,
teach me your paths.
                    Amen.

*What does it mean to be a
disciple of Christ?*

We sometimes ask "Why?"
when we are told or asked to
do something. But even if we
know "why," we often need
to know "how." At the Last
Supper, Jesus gave the answer
to the "how" behind his
teachings on the way he wanted
his disciples to live. He said,
"[L]ove one another as I love
you" (John 15:12).

*What does it mean to love as
Jesus did?*

Loving Others and Ourselves

Faith Focus

What do the Fourth and Fifth Commandments teach us about showing love for ourselves and for others?

Faith Vocabulary

respect. The virtue, or good habit, of giving esteem to others due to them because they are images of God.

obey. To follow the advice and commands of others who use their lawful authority properly to guide us in living according to the Law of God.

Our family is where life is really at. Our day begins there and ends there. Our family makes all things possible, in one way or another. The Fourth Commandment focuses on our family, especially our relationship with our parents.

The Fourth Commandment

"Honor your father and your mother." EXODUS 20:12

The Fourth Commandment commands that all family members contribute to the family's well-being. Children, even when they are adults, are to honor their parents. They are to **respect** and **obey** their parents. The Old Testament Book of Sirach, also known as the Book of

Ecclesiasticus, describes the wisdom of living this Commandment:

> Children, pay heed to a
>   father's right;
>   do so that you may live.
> For the LORD sets a father in
>   honor over his children;
>   a mother's authority he
>   confirms over her [children].
> SIRACH 3:1–2

Parents are to teach that the first calling of a Christian is to follow Jesus Christ. They are to care for the physical and spiritual needs of their children.

The Fourth Commandment also teaches, in a general way, about our responsibilities as citizens. As long as lawful authority follows God's law, we must obey those who have lawful authority over us for the common good of everyone.

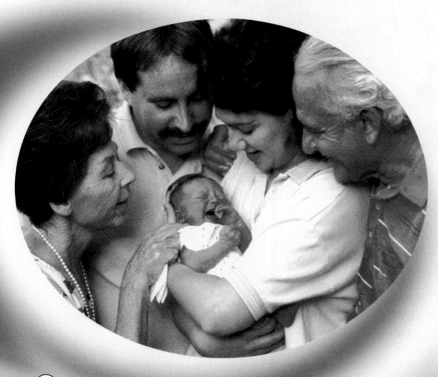

The Fifth Commandment

"You shall not kill." EXODUS 20:13

The principle underlying the Fifth Commandment is: All life is sacred. This Commandment teaches that we must protect and nurture all human life, from the first moment of its conception. We are to respect and care for our own lives, health, and bodies, and those of others. We are to act safely and not put ourselves or others in unnecessary danger. We are to live as peacemakers.

The Fifth Commandment forbids (1) the abuse and misuse of food, alcohol, tobacco, or drugs; (2) the direct and intentional killing, or murder, of another human person, born or unborn; (3) the ending of our own life by suicide; (4) the ending of the lives of handicapped, sick, or dying persons; (5) bullying; and (6) acts of terrorism or hostage-taking.

The command not to kill, however, does not prohibit the defending of human life with appropriate force. All people have the right to live safely and securely. A nation may legitimately and justly defend the lives of its citizens. A person may use the force necessary to stop a person or people from unjustly harming him or her.

 How do the Fourth and Fifth Commandments teach us to live the Great Commandment?

Living the Fifth Commandment

Read Matthew 5:38–41 and Luke 6:27–36. Describe how this teaching of Jesus guides us to live the Fifth Commandment.

_____

_____

_____

_____

_____

_____

_____

_____

_____

Faith Vocabulary

sexuality. The gift of being male or female—a boy or a man, or a girl or a woman.

covet. To unjustly desire what rightfully belongs to someone else.

Music, television sitcoms, magazine ads—there are so many voices, so many words and pictures trying to advise us on how to live our relationships with others. There is so much out there telling us how to live the gift of our **sexuality**.

Sexuality is the gift given to us by God of being male or female—of being a boy or a man, or of being a girl or a woman. The Sixth Commandment guides us in living the gift of our sexuality.

The Sixth Commandment

"You shall not commit adultery."
EXODUS 20:14

The Sixth Commandment commands everyone to live a chaste life. It guides Christians to follow Christ as our model in the way we express our love and friendship with one another. We are always to use our sexuality in appropriate ways.

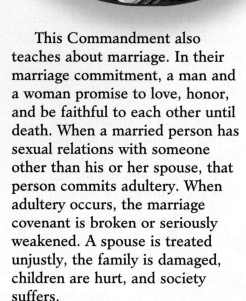

This Commandment also teaches about marriage. In their marriage commitment, a man and a woman promise to love, honor, and be faithful to each other until death. When a married person has sexual relations with someone other than his or her spouse, that person commits adultery. When adultery occurs, the marriage covenant is broken or seriously weakened. A spouse is treated unjustly, the family is damaged, children are hurt, and society suffers.

Among other sins which that are gravely contrary to the Sixth Commandment are masturbation, fornication, pornography, sterilization, the use of unnatural means to prevent the conception of a child, and homosexual activity.

Everyone experiences temptations to misuse their sexuality. To dwell on these thoughts and desires can easily lead us to a misuse of our sexuality. God's grace is always there to help us deal with these temptations.

The Ninth Commandment

"You shall not covet your neighbor's wife." EXODUS 20:17

Many television sitcoms and blockbuster movies would have us believe that it is natural for a man or a woman to tempt a married person to "cheat" on their spouse. Jesus taught differently. He taught that the marriage commitment is so sacred that it is sinful even to think about being unfaithful and desiring to do so. He taught:

"You have heard that it was said, 'You shall not commit adultery.' But I say to you, everyone who looks at a woman [or a man] with lust has already committed adultery . . . in his [her] heart." MATTHEW 5:27–28

The Ninth Commandment commands that everyone respect and honor the promises a man and a woman make to one another in marriage. We are not to do anything, not even desire to do anything, that would break up a marriage.

This Commandment also guides us to train ourselves to be pure in mind and heart, and in our actions. Covetousness is one of the capital sins. To **covet** something is to have an unjust and inordinate desire for something that belongs to someone else.

We need to be careful about what we watch, what we read, and what we listen to. We need to be responsible in the way we talk to one another. We need to train our eyes, ears, and mouth. We need to do and say only those things that show respect for people.

 QUESTION *Why is it important to honor and respect our own sexuality and the sexuality of others?*

What's the Message?

Name a popular TV show or a popular song that depicts people in a relationship. How are the people in that relationship living or not living according to the Commandments? How might the show or song affect people viewing or listening to it?

Faith Focus

How can the Seventh, Eighth, and Tenth Commandments help us imitate Jesus?

Faith Vocabulary

justice. One of the moral, or cardinal, virtues; the good habit of giving to God and to all people what is rightfully due to them.

Good laws and their enforcement are necessary to guide people to live together justly and peacefully. The Seventh, Eighth, and Ninth Commandments are the final three of the Ten Commandments that teach us how to live as just, honest, and peaceful people as God created us to do.

The Seventh Commandment

"You shall not steal."
EXODUS 20:15

The Seventh Commandment commands that we live the virtues of **justice** and charity in our relationships with other people. We are to use the goods of the earth responsibly. How we treat the environment and use water and other natural resources has an impact not only on our own generation but on future generations.

This Commandment also teaches us about the importance of work. Human work is a

participation in the work of God the Creator. Because we are joined to Christ in Baptism, our work is joined to his, and we give honor and glory to God.

This Commandment forbids stealing, cheating, misusing or damaging the property of other people, paying unjust wages, and treating people as if they were objects to be bought and sold—in other words, making them our slaves. If we break this Commandment, we have the obligation to repair whatever damage we have caused or to restore what we have unjustly taken.

The Eighth Commandment

"You shall not bear false witness against your neighbor."
EXODUS 20:16

The Eighth Commandment is about truth. It commands that we live honest and truthful lives. We are to respect the good name of others. We are truthful and loyal followers of Jesus who is "full of grace and truth" (John 1:14) and who is "the way and the truth and the life" (John 14:6).

Breaking this Commandment weakens our trust and respect for others. If we break it, we have the obligation to repair the damage that our misuse of the truth has caused. A person's good name is one of their most valued possessions. If we have told lies about a person by spreading false rumors or damaging gossip, we need to get the truth out.

The Tenth Commandment

You shall not covet your neighbor's goods.
BASED ON EXODUS 20:17

The Tenth Commandment commands us to treat others fairly and justly. We are to share the blessings God has given us with others. We are to be thankful and generous with what we have.

Jesus taught about what this Commandment teaches when he said:

"Blessed are the poor in spirit, for theirs is the kingdom of heaven." MATTHEW 5:3

The "poor in spirit" praise God as the source of all blessings—their own blessings and the blessings of others. The poor in spirit are not envious, greedy, or jealous. They are those who "renounce all things" (Luke 14:33) to be a disciple of Jesus.

 How do you observe the Seventh, Eighth, and Tenth Commandments?

Honesty Is the Best Policy

What do we mean by the expression "Honesty is the best policy"?

_____

_____

_____

_____

_____

Blessed Are the Peacemakers

Living the Ten Commandments prepares the way for the Kingdom of God, the kingdom of peace. The Church has the responsibility to help us understand and guide us in living the Ten Commandments as Jesus taught. One way the popes fulfill this responsibility is by writing encyclicals. An encyclical is a teaching letter written to the whole Church.

In 1963 Blessed Pope John XXIII wrote *Pacem in Terris*, or "Peace on Earth." Pope John was very troubled about the many ways human life was being abused. So he wrote this encyclical to remind the world that all human life, the life of every person, without exception, is sacred.

Pope John pointed out clearly that warfare, unjust wages, the misuse of authority, and poverty violate the sacred dignity of people. We must work to correct these injustices and build the kingdom of peace that Jesus announced. We must love one another as Jesus did.

The road to peace is the way of justice. Everyone, people and governments, needs to respect the life and dignity of all people as sacred. We sometimes treat people unjustly because we fear the diversity and differences among people. We need to see that fear as an evil and to embrace diversity and differences as expressions of the infinite beauty of God, who created everyone as a sacred image of himself.

The Holy Spirit teaches us the way of justice. The more we listen, accept his help, and act justly, the more we are building a world of peace as Blessed John XXIII reminded us we are obligated to do.

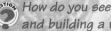
How do you see people living justly and building a world of peace?

Blessed Pope John XXIII (1881–1963), beatified, or named a Blessed of the Church, by Pope John Paul II on September 3, 2000

What Difference Does Faith Make in My Life?

Each day you cooperate with the Holy Spirit and show respect for yourself and others in many ways. Making such choices builds friendships, families, and safe communities.

Describe several ways you would like others to treat you. Then use them as a guide to the way you treat others.

Living the Golden Rule

My Faith Choice

This week I will look for opportunities to live the Golden Rule. I will

_____

_____ .

Prayer for Peace

Lord, make me an instrument of your

Peace.

Leader: Peace is one of the Fruits of the Holy Spirit.
We live as peacemakers when we live the
Ten Commandments as Jesus taught.

Let us pray for the grace to live as peacemakers.

All: **Lord, make me an instrument of your** *(sign peace).*

Group 1: Where there is hatred, let me sow love.
All: **Lord, make me an instrument of your** *(sign peace).*

Group 2: Where there is injury, pardon.
All: **Lord, make me an instrument of your** *(sign peace).*

Group 1: Where there is doubt, faith.
All: **Lord, make me an instrument of your** *(sign peace).*

Group 2: Where there is despair, hope.
All: **Lord, make me an instrument of your** *(sign peace).*

Group 1: Where there is darkness, light.
All: **Lord, make me an instrument of your** *(sign peace).*

Group 2: Where there is sadness, joy.
All: **Lord, make me an instrument of your** *(sign peace).*

Leader: Let us share with each other a sign of peace.

We Remember

What I Have Learned

Mark the true statements T and the false statements F. Change the false statements into true statements.

1. Adult children who live away from home have less responsibility to honor their parents than do younger children who live at home.   **F   T**

2. All human life is sacred from the first moment a person is conceived in their mother's womb.   **F   T**

3. Everyone is called to live a chaste life.   **F   T**

4. The virtues of justice and generosity help us live the Seventh and Tenth Commandments.   **F   T**

5. The Eighth Commandment is all about living honest and truthful lives.   **F   T**

Answer the following.

6. How do we show that all life is sacred?

_____

_____

7. How do we honor and respect our sexuality?

_____

_____

_____

8. How does the virtue of justice help us show our love and respect for others?

_____

_____

_____

To Help You Remember

1. The Fourth Commandment teaches us that family members are to respect and honor one another.

2. The Fifth Commandment teaches us to treat all life as sacred.

3. The Sixth through Tenth Commandments teach us to live as just, honest, and peaceful people.

Growing in Faith

One important thing I learned this week is

_____

_____

_____.

This is important because

_____

_____

_____.

What will people see me doing as I live my faith choice this week?

_____

_____

_____

This Week . . .

In chapter 22, "Loving One Another," your child learned more about the teachings of the Ten Commandments. The Fourth Commandment teaches that all family members are to contribute to the well-being of the family. Children, young and adult, are to honor and respect their parents. The Fifth Commandment teaches us to respect all human life as sacred and to live as peacemakers. The taking of a human life, even when justified, is a grave evil. The Sixth and Ninth Commandments command all Christians to live a chaste life as Jesus did. The Seventh and Tenth Commandments command that we are to be just and generous. We are to use and care for creation wisely. The Eighth Commandment commands us to live honest and truthful lives.

For more on the teachings of the Catholic Church on the Fourth through Tenth Commandments, see *Catechism of the Catholic Church* paragraph numbers 2196–2550.

Sharing God's Word

Read together John 14:15–21. Emphasize that faithfully living the Ten Commandments is a sign of a faithful disciple of Christ.

Praying

In this chapter your child learned to sign a prayer. Read and sign this prayer on page 286 together.

Making a Difference

Choose one of the following activities to do as a family or design a similar activity of your own.

- Talk about how your family lives as good stewards of creation. Do one thing this week as a family to live as good stewards of creation.

- When we live as peacemakers, we live the Ten Commandments. Talk about how you all live as peacemakers at home, at school or work, and in your community.

- When we show love and respect for others, we live the Ten Commandments. Share stories with each other about times when you were not treated with love or respect. How did being treated this way make you feel?

For more ideas on ways your family can live your faith, visit the "Faith First for Families" page at **www.FaithFirst.com**. Click on "Games" and make learning fun for your child.

The Wisdom Books
A Scripture Story

We Pray

The fear of the LORD is the
   beginning of wisdom;
   prudent are all who live by it.
                           PSALM 111:10

Mary, Mother of God,
Seat of Wisdom, pray
for us.   Amen.

*Who do you consider to be a
person of wisdom?*

The good advice of wise people
is often passed on from one
generation to the next. The
wisdom of the Israelites has
been gathered and handed on
in the wisdom books in the
Old Testament.

*What words of wisdom from the
Old Testament do you know?*

Bible Background

Faith Focus

What is the wisdom literature found in the Bible?

Faith Vocabulary

oral tradition. The passing on of stories and teachings by word of mouth.

People living in the Middle East before the time of Christ had an interesting way of gathering, preserving, and expressing common sense. They put their **wisdom** into forms they could learn by heart and pass on by word of mouth.

The Oral Tradition

The Israelites collected and passed on their wisdom in stories, poems, chants, sayings, proverbs, and prayers. These insights were first passed on by word of mouth. This word-of-mouth way of doing things is called **oral tradition**. It is one generation passing on verbally what the previous one had passed on to them. Eventually, many of the pieces of the oral tradition of the Israelites were collected and written down.

God obviously was the focal point of these writings, which describe wisdom as a gift of God, and a wise person was the person who lived a holy and virtuous life. In the Old Testament, wisdom is practical. It is a skill in action. The chief topics of wisdom are the problem of suffering, the origin and destiny of humans, the meaning of happiness, good and evil actions, and death.

The Wisdom Books

There are seven wisdom books in the Old Testament. They are Job, Psalms, Proverbs, Ecclesiastes, the Song of Songs, Wisdom, and Sirach.

The Book of Job is really a long poem that is like a play. In it, both Job and his friends try to understand the problem of human suffering. The wisdom of Job leads us to a sense of God's mystery and wonder. It helps us understand the problem of suffering in our life.

The Book of Psalms is a collection of prayers in the form of poetry. The Psalms spring from life experiences, such as suffering, a desire for God, a deep feeling of gratitude for what God has done, and a sense of awe before the beauty of his creation. The wisdom of the Psalms is to refer everything back to God—all our joy, all our sorrow, all our hope.

The Book of Ecclesiastes is a long reflection on the emptiness of life. Its wisdom is to identify that our feeling of emptiness can only be filled, in the end, by God.

The Song of Songs is a poetic hymn portraying the love of God for his people.

The Book of Wisdom and the Book of Sirach (Ecclesiasticus) help people understand the wisdom of staying faithful to God's law and walking in his path.

 How does the gift of wisdom guide you in living as a follower of Jesus?

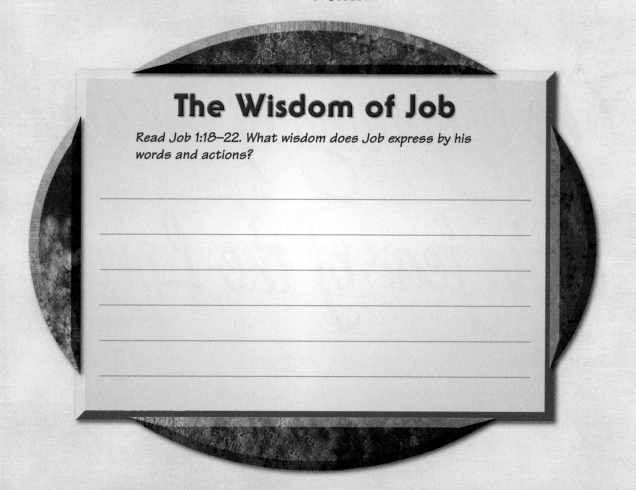

The Wisdom of Job

Read Job 1:18–22. What wisdom does Job express by his words and actions?

_____

_____

_____

_____

_____

_____

Reading the Word of God

Faith Focus

What do the sayings in the Book of Proverbs teach us?

Faith Vocabulary

proverb. A short, concise saying stating a well-accepted fact or criterion for making a wise decision.

Coaches need to give good, practical advice in short, clear, and concise statements. Such advice helps aspiring athletes, musicians, dancers, and other artists become skilled at what they are learning. We need similar advice to help us live as children of God. The Book of Proverbs provides us with such advice.

The Book of Proverbs

The Book of Proverbs is a collection of relatively brief sayings, called proverbs. Proverbs are meant to guide people through life. A **proverb** is a short, concise saying stating a well-accepted fact or criterion for making a wise decision. These sayings are "skills in action." Training oneself to live by these proverbs turns wisdom into a practical skill.

This is how the Book of Proverbs describes wisdom:

> Wisdom has built her house,
>   she has set up her seven
>   columns;
> She has dressed her meat,
>   mixed her wine,
>   yes, she has spread her
>   table.
> She has sent out her
>   maidens; she calls
>   from the heights out over
>   the city:

The beginning of wisdom is the fear of the Lord.

PROVERBS 9:10

292

"Let whoever is simple turn
   in here;
   to him who lacks
   understanding, I say,
Come, eat of my food,
   and drink of the wine
   I have mixed!
Forsake foolishness that you
   may live;
   advance in the way of
   understanding." . . .
The beginning of wisdom is
   the fear of the LORD,
   and knowledge of the Holy
   One is understanding.

If you are wise, it is to your
   own advantage;
   and if you are arrogant,
   you alone shall bear it.
               PROVERBS 9:1–6, 10–12

   Throughout the Book of
Proverbs we are given a series of
maxims, or rules of conduct, to
make wise decisions. For example:
   A mild answer calms wrath,
      but a harsh word stirs up
      anger.   PROVERBS15:1

You have probably already
experienced the wisdom of that
proverb.

Wise Person on Board!

Design a license plate, using your favorite proverb.

Understanding the Word of God

Wisdom enables us to decide well. It guides us in making decisions that will have lasting good effects. To grow in wisdom is to be open to the Holy Spirit and to see all things in relationship to God's plan.

Jesus, the Wisdom of God

Jesus, the Word of God, is the key to discovering and understanding God's wisdom. He is, according to Saint Paul the Apostle:

The power of God and the wisdom of God.
1 CORINTHIANS 1:24

Jesus told this proverb to help us understand true wisdom. He said:

"[W]here your treasure is, there also will your heart be."
LUKE 12:34

He also taught about true wisdom in the parable of the Ten Virgins. He said:

"[T]he kingdom of heaven will be like ten virgins who took their lamps and went out to meet the bridegroom. Five of them were foolish and five were wise. The foolish ones, when taking their lamps, brought no oil with them, but the wise brought flasks of oil with their lamps. . . . At midnight, there was a cry, 'Behold, the bridegroom! Come out to meet him!'" MATTHEW 25:1–4, 6

You can easily supply the ending. The message is clear. Be prepared! Be ready when the bridegroom comes. Always live as a true disciple of Jesus. Keep God first in your life as Jesus kept his Father first in his life and you will receive the promise of the Kingdom of Heaven.

QUESTION What is an example of a proverb of your own that you follow to make good choices?

Jesus at Prayer

Dove, symbol of the Holy Spirit

Saint Paul tells us that the Holy Spirit teaches us the gift of God's wisdom. He writes:

We have not received the spirit of the world but the Spirit that is from God, so that we may understand the things freely given us by God. And we speak about them not with words taught by human wisdom, but with words taught by the Spirit.

1 CORINTHIANS 2:12–13

When we keep our eyes fixed on Jesus, we will live wisely. To grow in wisdom we need to be open to the Holy Spirit, who helps us understand everything Jesus taught. This will make a difference in our lives each and every day.

 What does Jesus' parable of the Ten Virgins teach us about wisdom?

Doctors of the Church

The wisdom of the great teachers of the Church is recognized in a unique way. These saints are named Doctors of the Church. Saint Bonaventure and Saint Thérèse of Lisieux are two of the thirty-three saints honored with the title of Doctor of the Church.

TRUE WISDOM

In the right column describe a value that is important to you as a follower of Jesus.
In the left column describe how that value guides you in making wise decisions.

VALUE	INFLUENCES
_____	_____
_____	_____
_____	_____
_____	_____
_____	_____
_____	_____

Mary, Mother of the Savior

Mary, Queen of Heaven and Earth

Madonna and Child

Seat of Wisdom

Christians honor and respect Mary for her wisdom. She always kept God at the center of her life. Mary's love for God was the driving force behind all her decisions.

One of the titles Christians honor Mary with is Seat of Wisdom. Mary is called the Seat, or Bearer, of Wisdom because she is the Mother of Jesus, who is "the power and wisdom of God." We honor Mary as the Seat of Wisdom because she lived out her life according to the plan of God. Mary was eager to hear God's word and to act upon it. Even when she did not understand everything that God asked of her, Mary trusted and believed in God. She believed and trusted in the larger plan of God's wisdom.

We also honor Mary with the title Mother of Good Counsel. We turn to her for advice, or counsel. We ask her to help us make wise decisions.

QUESTION How does reflecting on the life of Mary help guide you in living as a follower of Christ?

What Difference Does Faith Make in My Life?

There is a difference between acting wisely and acting foolishly. Before you act, ask the Holy Spirit to help you make a wise decision.

Think of someone in a movie or a television program who acts wisely or acts foolishly. Describe how this character's wise or foolish actions affect others.

Actions Have Consequences

My Faith Choice

This week I will begin each day by praying to the Holy Spirit for the gift of wisdom. I will use this gift to help me make decisions about

_____

_____ .

Mary, Pray for Us

Leader: Let us pray to Mary whom Jesus asked to care for us, his disciples.

Reader:

	All:
Holy Mary	**pray for us**
Holy Mother of God	**pray for us**
Most honored of virgins	**pray for us**
Mother of Christ	**pray for us**
Mother of the Church	**pray for us**
Mother most pure	**pray for us**
Mother of good counsel	**pray for us**
Mother of our Creator	**pray for us**
Mother of our Savior	**pray for us**
Virgin most wise	**pray for us**
Mirror of justice	**pray for us**
[Seat] of wisdom	**pray for us**
Cause of our joy	**pray for us**
Shrine of the Spirit	**pray for us**
Tower of David	**pray for us**
Ark of the covenant	**pray for us**
Morning Star	**pray for us**
Help of Christians	**pray for us**
Queen of angels	**pray for us**
Queen of patriarchs and prophets	**pray for us**
Queen of apostles and martyrs	**pray for us**
Queen of all saints	**pray for us**
Queen of peace	**pray for us**

Leader: Pray for us, holy Mother of God

All: **That we may become worthy of the promises of Christ.**

Leader: Eternal God,
let your people enjoy constant health in mind and body.
Through the intercession of the Virgin Mary
free us from the sorrows of life
and lead us to happiness in the life to come.
Grant this through Christ our Lord.

All: **Amen.**

FROM THE LITANY OF THE BLESSED VIRGIN MARY

We Remember

What I Have Learned

Write a foolish decision and a wise decision for the following situation. Compare the consequences of the decisions.

> The temperature outdoors has just hit 104° F. Two teammates e-mail you to join them to practice your basketball skills on the court outside your school.

1. **Foolish Decision** _____

   _____

   _____

   _____

2. **Wise Decision** _____

   _____

   _____

   _____

Answer the following.

3. Describe how wisdom guides us in living our life.

   _____

   _____

4. Explain how the Book of Proverbs describes wisdom.

   _____

   _____

   _____

5. Describe how you might grow in using the gift of wisdom.

   _____

   _____

To Help You Remember

1. Wisdom is the Gift of the Holy Spirit that helps us know God's plan of creation and salvation, and make decisions according to that plan.

2. The wisdom writings of the Old Testament contain seven books.

3. Jesus Christ, the Word of God, is the fullest Revelation of the wisdom of God.

Growing in Faith

One important thing I learned this week is

_____

_____

_____.

This is important because

_____

_____

_____.

What will people see me doing as I live my faith choice this week?

_____

_____

_____

23 With My Family

This Week . . .

In chapter 23, "The Wisdom Books: A Scripture Story," your child learned more about Sacred Scripture, in particular the wisdom writings of the Old Testament. This short collection of seven books includes the books of Job, Psalms, Proverbs, Ecclesiastes, Song of Songs, Wisdom, and Sirach. Originally passed on from one generation to the next by word of mouth, this collection of writings contains stories, poems, chants, sayings, proverbs, and prayers. The chief topics of these writings are the problem of suffering, our origin and destiny, the meaning of happiness, the conflict between good and evil, and death.

For more on the teachings of the Catholic Church on Sacred Scripture, see *Catechism of the Catholic Church* paragraph numbers 101–133.

Sharing God's Word

Read together Proverbs 9:10–12. Emphasize that in the Book of Proverbs the sayings are the inspired Word of God and guide us through life by helping us make wise choices.

Praying

In this chapter your child prayed a prayer from the Litany of the Blessed Virgin Mary. Read and pray together this prayer on page 298.

Making a Difference

Choose one of the following activities to do as a family or design a similar activity of your own.

- Create a proverb for living as a family. Post it in your home where everyone can see it.

- Brainstorm as many sayings as you can that help you live as children of God. Write one each month on your family calendar to help you make wise family decisions.

- Watch a movie or television show together. List the names of the characters on a sheet of paper. Keep track of the wise and foolish decisions the characters make. Talk about what the characters who made foolish decisions could have done to make wise decisions.

For more ideas on ways your family can live your faith, visit the "Faith First for Families" page at **www.FaithFirst.com**. Check out this week's "Just for Parents" article.

Catholic Social Teaching

Sister Rose's Passion

One day, in the early 1930s when she was eleven years old, Rose Thering and her father were driving through the farming town where they lived. "There's a new pharmacist in town," her father told her. Then he whispered, "He's Jewish." Rose was confused. When they arrived home, Rose asked her mother, "Why did Daddy whisper that?" Rose's mother would not answer.

Sister Rose Thering

As Rose grew older, she heard more and more comments about Jews. She discovered that there was a deep "anti-Jewishness," as she called it, in her country. Some people, and even some religion books, called Jews "children of the devil" and "Christ-killers."

"Jesus was a Jew," Rose thought to herself. "Mary was a Jew. I can't imagine God not loving people who are Jewish."

Rose became a Dominican sister. She wanted to teach and help others love God. Sister Rose has worked hard her whole life to change people's attitudes about the Jewish people. Her work even helped change the Catholic Church's views toward Jewish people. Everywhere she goes, Sister Rose reminds people of what intolerance, prejudice, and bigotry can do. She tells about how these things led to the extermination of millions of people in the Holocaust.

In a documentary about her life, *Sister Rose's Passion*, which was nominated for an Academy Award, Sister Rose is meeting with a group of schoolchildren. She tells the children that they can make a difference by standing up for what is right. "When you see a bully on the playground you say, 'Enough. No more.'"

Sister Rose is an example of a person who has spent her life defending basic human dignity and human rights of people. How will you stand up for human rights for everyone, everywhere?

We Respect the Dignity of Every Person

Each person possesses a basic dignity that comes from God. We do not have to earn this dignity through any special human qualities or accomplishments. No one, no matter how they treat us, can take this dignity away from us.

Making Connections . . .

There are many situations today in which people's human dignity is not shown the respect it deserves and where the basic human rights of people need to be defended. All people deserve dignity and respect.

with Social Studies

Do a research project on the history of the Jewish people during the first and second centuries. Pay particular attention to how they were treated by the Roman Empire and by the early Church.

with Math and Science

During the Holocaust close to six million Jewish people out of a Jewish population of more than nine-and-a-half million people in thirteen countries were put to death. Use your math skills to complete the "Statistics of the Holocaust" chart on the handout. Report your findings to the class.

with Language Arts

Read *Number the Stars* by Lois Lowry. This book emphasizes the qualities of courage and caring and standing up for what is right. The story, based on fact, is set in Denmark during World War II and tells of that country's efforts to save their Jewish citizens. Share what you learned with your class.

⊃ **Faith Action** *Write a journal entry this week based on this question: How can I make a difference for good in my world?*

Name _____

A. Best Response

Read each statement and circle the best answer.

1. Which of these virtues is one of the theological virtues?

   a. wisdom   b. prudence

   c. faith   d. courage

2. Which one is not an effect of the grace of the Holy Spirit?

   a. We grow in our ability to make right choices.   b. We turn toward God and away from sin.

   c. We gain the confidence to grow in holiness.   d. We reject God's gift of forgiveness.

3. The sources of morality are _____.

   a. object, intention, purpose   b. intention, reason, effect

   c. object, intention, circumstances   d. object, circumstances, effect

4. Which one of the following is not the result of an informed conscience?

   a. judging what is right and wrong   b. making good moral decisions

   c. choosing to do what is against God's Law   d. living as a follower of Jesus Christ

5. _____ are serious offenses against God.

   a. Venial sins   b. Moral virtues

   c. Temptations   d. Mortal sins

6. Which of the Ten Commandments focus on our relationship with God?

   a. First   b. First and Second

   c. First, Second, and Third   d. First, Second, Third, and Fourth

7. Which of the Ten Commandments teaches us not to cheat on a test?

   a. Fifth   b. Eighth

   c. Seventh   d. Tenth

8. Which of the Ten Commandments teaches us to live chaste lives?

   a. First   b. Fifth

   c. Seventh   d. Ninth

9. Which of the Ten Commandments teaches us to respect all human life as sacred?

   a. First   b. Fourth

   c. Fifth   d. Tenth

10. The Book of Proverbs is one of the Old Testament _____.

    a. historical books   b. books of the prophets

    c. books of wisdom   d. epistles

B. Completing the Paragraph

Fill in the blanks in the paragraph by using the terms in the word bank.

> **cardinal** **conscience**
> **mortal** **venial**
> **holiness** **moral**

God gives each person the grace to make wise choices and to live a life of

_____. Making choices to live according to God's will is

called living a _____ life. By developing and practicing the four

_____ virtues, we develop good habits and grow in holiness.

Our _____ guides us in judging whether an act is right or

wrong and whether it agrees or does not agree with God's Law. When we

deliberately choose to do or say something that we know is against God's Law, we

sin. _____ sins are grave or serious sins that break our

relationship with God. _____ sins weaken but do not break

our relationship with God.

C. What I Have Learned

*Write three things you learned in this unit.
Share them with the group.*

_____

_____

_____

*Look at the list of faith terms in "Words to Know" on page 164.
Circle the terms you know now.*

D. From a Scripture Story

*Explain how the following proverb makes a difference
in our daily lives.*

> A mild answer calms wrath,
> but a harsh word stirs up anger.
> PROVERBS 15:1

How do we grow as people of prayer?

Getting Ready

What I Have Learned

What is something you already know about these faith terms?

praying the Psalms

_____

_____

prayer of adoration

_____

_____

prayer of contemplation

_____

_____

Words to Know

Put an X next to the faith terms you know. Put a ? next to the faith terms you need to know more about.

Faith Vocabulary

_____ prayer

_____ Book of Psalms

_____ prayer life

_____ vocal prayer

_____ Sermon on the Mount

_____ Lord

Questions I Have

What questions would you like to ask about the Catholic tradition of prayer?

_____

_____

_____

_____

A Scripture Story

Jesus praying in the Garden of Gethsemane

How is Jesus the model of prayer for Christians?

People of Prayer

We Pray

Blessed be God, who did not
   refuse me
   the kindness I sought
   in prayer.   PSALM 66:20

**As morning breaks
I look to you, O God,
to be my strength
this day.   Amen.**

*What do you like to do with
friends?*

Friends like to spend time
with each other. God is the
closest Friend we have. He is
always with us. He wants us to
spend time with him.

*What are some of the ways you
spend time with God in prayer?*

The Prayer of God's People

Faith Focus

What is prayer and how do we pray?

Faith Vocabulary

invocations.
Brief prayers we can learn by heart and pray throughout the day.

We talk a lot and sometimes listen a lot to our closest friends. On the phone, by e-mail, as we walk down the corridors of our school, we talk and talk, and listen and listen. People of prayer do the same with God. God is always with us for a good chat wherever we are available.

Prayer

Prayer can be described in many ways. Simply put, prayer is talking and listening to God. It is the expression of our hearts to God. It is lifting our minds and hearts to God. It is "talking with God." Prayer is an invitation from God to spend time with him. He eagerly awaits and listens for our response as he waited for young Samuel to recognize his presence and respond:

> When Samuel went to sleep in his place, the LORD came and revealed his presence, calling out as before, "Samuel, Samuel!" Samuel answered, "Speak, for your servant is listening." 1 SAMUEL 3:9–10

We do not need to use fancy words when we pray. We just need to talk from our heart. We do not need to impress God. He is always interested in what we have to share with him.

308

Prayer and the Trinity

Christians' prayer is most often directed to the Father. Of course, we can and do also pray at times directly to Jesus, God the Son, and to God the Holy Spirit. We pray as Jesus did:

> At that very moment he rejoiced [in] the holy Spirit and said, "I give you praise, Father, Lord of heaven and earth, for although you have hidden these things from the wise and the learned you have revealed them to the childlike. Yes, Father, such has been your gracious will." LUKE 10:21

Jesus leads us in prayer. In our prayer, Jesus joins us, the Holy Spirit moves us, and the Father listens with loving attention.

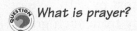 **What is prayer?**

A Message About Prayer

Christians have always prayed short prayers, called invocations, throughout the day. Use this code to decipher this invocation. Find the letter in the puzzle in the bottom row of letters and match it to the letter in the top row. Pray the prayer often during the day.

| A B C D E F G H I J K L M N O P Q R S T U V W X Y Z , . |
| E T M Z F I O 2 B H L U Y P K Q S C G J R D V W A 3 X N |

U K C Z X B T F U B F D F B P A K R N

L _ _ _ _ _ _ _ _ _ _ _ _ _ _ _ _ _ _

U K C Z X B 2 K Q F B P A K R N

_ _ _ _ _ _ _ _ _ _ _ _ _ _ _ _

U K C Z X B U K D F A K R N

_ _ _ _ _ _ _ _ _ _ _ _ _ _

Faith Vocabulary

Book of Psalms. The Old Testament book of the Bible containing 150 prayers in the form of poems and songs.

forms of prayer. The five types of prayer revealed in Sacred Scripture that are the norm for Christian prayer, namely, blessing and adoration, petition, intercession, thanksgiving, and praise.

Talking and learning the language we use to talk is first learned at home. This seems to just happen naturally, without much effort on our part. As we grow older, however, we learn the skill of talking well from both our family and from other people.

Christians can learn about prayer by returning to the Old Testament. There we can learn from our ancestors in faith. We can learn to pray from such great people of prayer as Abraham and Sarah, Jacob and Rebecca, Moses and Miriam, Ruth and Naomi, Judith, David, and Job.

Abraham, Our Father in Faith

Among all the people of prayer in the Old Testament, Christians recognize and honor Abraham as our father in faith. When God first revealed himself to Abram, his name before it was changed to Abraham, Abraham prayed by the simple action of being present with God and walking with him in the path that God had shown him. This is what God promised:

The LORD said to Abram: . . .
"I will make of you a great
   nation,
  and I will bless you;
I will make your name great,
  so that you will be a blessing.
. . . All the communities of
   the earth
  shall find blessing in you."
GENESIS 12:1–3

With deep faith, Abraham brought his questions and concerns honestly and directly to God. He placed everything in God's hands and placed himself in his care. The Book of Genesis says of Abraham:

"[He] put his faith in the LORD, who credited it to him as an act of righteousness." GENESIS 15:6

King David is also a model of prayer for Christians. David is considered the author of many of the prayers in the **Book of Psalms**. Filled with emotion, these prayers flow from the heart.

The Psalms

In the Book of Psalms we can find five basic **forms of prayer.** They are:

- **Blessing and adoration.** We declare that God is our almighty Creator. Read Psalm 95:1, 6.
- **Petition.** We ask for God's forgiveness and help in all our needs. Read Psalm 38:22–23.
- **Intercession.** We pray that God will help others in their need. Read Psalm 67:2.
- **Thanksgiving.** We express our gratitude to God for all his many blessings. Read Psalm 100:4–5.
- **Praise.** We give glory to God simply because he is God and is deserving of our honor and respect. Read Psalm 29:1–2.

Jesus and Mary and the early Church would have prayed the Psalms. Today, the Church prays the Psalms every day.

 What do Abraham and David teach us about prayer?

Creating a Psalm Prayer

In a few verses create your own psalm, using one or more of the five basic prayer forms.

_____

_____

_____

_____

_____

_____

_____

_____

Faith Vocabulary

distractions.
Thoughts and ideas that pull us away from prayer.

Christians are people of prayer as were Abraham, King David, and the other faith-filled people of prayer in the Old Testament and New Testament. It is within our families that we first learn to pray. In and with our families, the Holy Spirit first calls us and teaches us to pray.

Growing as People of Prayer

The Church is a people of prayer. How can we continue to grow as people of prayer? There are a number of things we can do.

- **Be humble.** Sometimes we hesitate to pray because we feel unworthy. We need not worry. Our prayers, like those of the tax collector, are most welcomed by God. (Read Luke 18:9–14.)

- **Prepare for prayer.** Set aside a special time for prayer. Go to a special place. For example, make a visit to the church or sit before a holy image of Jesus or Mary.

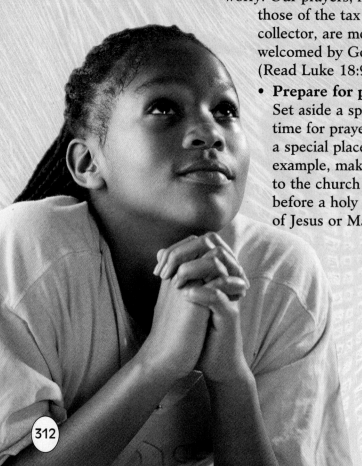

- **Focus on praying.** Sometimes we are faced with a variety of **distractions** to our prayer. Turn your distracting thoughts and ideas over to the Holy Spirit.

- **Have courage and trust.** Sometimes we are not sure if God is listening. We begin to feel discouraged. Even when you are not clear how things will work out, trust God. Jesus reminded us of this important truth about prayer. He taught:

"Ask and it will be given to you; seek and you will find; knock and the door will be opened to you. For everyone who asks, receives; and the one who seeks, finds; and to the one who knocks, the door will be opened. Which one of you would hand his son a stone when he asks for a loaf of bread, or a snake when he asks for a fish? . . . how much more will your heavenly Father give good things to those who ask him." MATTHEW 7:7–11

The prayer of Christians begins with our loving faith and trust in God the Father. Our prayer is like that of the man in the Gospel who said:

"I do believe, help my unbelief!"

MARK 9:24

Prayer strengthens our faith, hope, and love for God. It deepens our communion with the Holy Trinity. There is no deep secret to praying. We just need to respond to the invitation of the Holy Spirit. We need to want to pray and then continue praying—even when praying is difficult.

? What are some of the things that can get in the way of our growing as people of prayer?

Our Catholic Identity

Prayer Groups

Jesus promised that when his followers come together to pray he will be there with them. Christians often form prayer groups, which the Church calls "schools of prayer." Prayer groups often center their prayer on the Bible. These groups are aware that Jesus, the Word of God, is with them and that it is with and through Jesus that they pray.

Overcoming Obstacles to Prayer

Describe one of the things that makes praying difficult for you. Then name two ways that you can deal with that obstacle to prayer.

Obstacle to Prayer	Dealing with Obstacle

The Jesus Prayer

Since the days of the early Church, Christians have prayed in many ways. To help keep in touch with God, Christians have prayed **invocations**. The word *invocation* means "calling on someone." Invocations are brief prayers we can say throughout the day.

One invocation that has been popular for more than six hundred years is called the Jesus Prayer. The words of the prayer are simple and often are uttered with a special breathing technique.

The Jesus Prayer is a simple prayer to use whenever you want and wherever you are. Memorize the prayer. Pray it often. Teach it to your family and friends. Become a model of prayer for them.

QUESTION *How often do you pray throughout the day? How can you pray more often?*

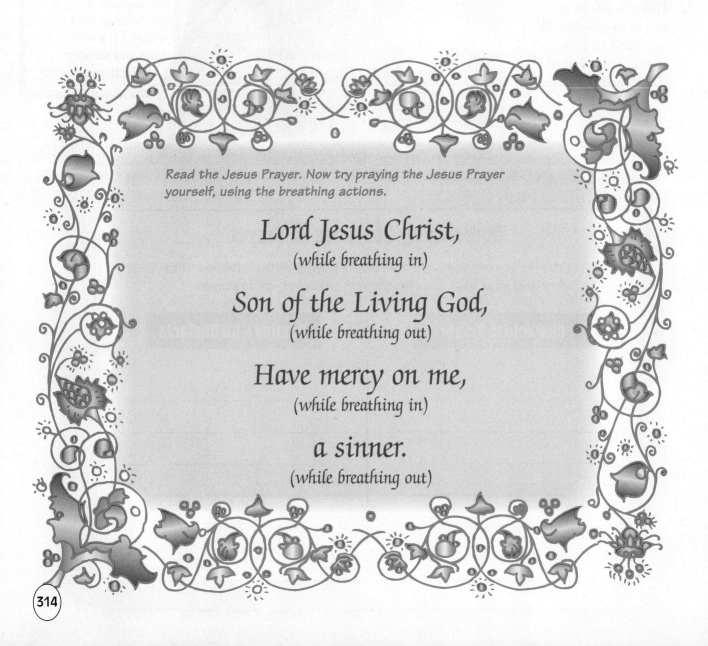

Read the Jesus Prayer. Now try praying the Jesus Prayer yourself, using the breathing actions.

Lord Jesus Christ,
(while breathing in)

Son of the Living God,
(while breathing out)

Have mercy on me,
(while breathing in)

a sinner.
(while breathing out)

What Difference Does Faith Make in My Life?

The Holy Spirit invites you to pray often throughout the day. He invites you to pray with your family and friends and to pray when you are alone.

Take the time to fill out this daily planner. Set aside several different times during the day for praying.

Times for Praying

7:00
7:30
8:00
8:30
9:00
9:30
10:00
10:30
11:00
11:30
12:00
12:30
1:00
1:30
2:00
2:30
3:00
3:30
4:00
4:30
5:00

My Faith Choice

This week I will try to spend more time with God in prayer. I will

_____

_____ .

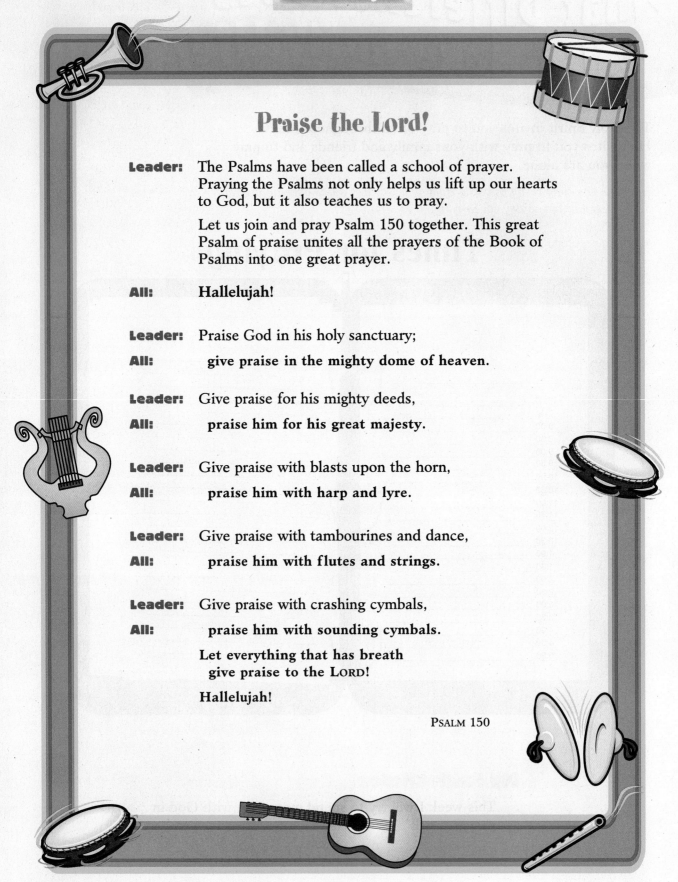

Praise the Lord!

Leader: The Psalms have been called a school of prayer.
Praying the Psalms not only helps us lift up our hearts
to God, but it also teaches us to pray.

Let us join and pray Psalm 150 together. This great
Psalm of praise unites all the prayers of the Book of
Psalms into one great prayer.

All: **Hallelujah!**

Leader: Praise God in his holy sanctuary;

All: **give praise in the mighty dome of heaven.**

Leader: Give praise for his mighty deeds,

All: **praise him for his great majesty.**

Leader: Give praise with blasts upon the horn,

All: **praise him with harp and lyre.**

Leader: Give praise with tambourines and dance,

All: **praise him with flutes and strings.**

Leader: Give praise with crashing cymbals,

All: **praise him with sounding cymbals.**

**Let everything that has breath
give praise to the Lord!**

Hallelujah!

PSALM 150

We Remember

What I Have Learned

1. Unscramble the words in the word bank. Use the words to write a brief paragraph about the prayer life of Christians.

usJes   onraadoti   ylHo   pStiri

tracdistions   saPlms   ocatinvions

The Prayer Life of Christians

_____

_____

_____

_____

_____

_____

Answer the following.

2. Describe prayer as a conversation with God.

_____

_____

_____

3. Name and describe the five forms of prayer found in the Bible.

_____

_____

_____

4. Compare the prayer of Abraham and the Psalms with the prayer of Christians.

_____

_____

_____

_____

To Help You Remember

1. The prayer of Christians is most often addressed to God the Father in the name of the Son through the power of the Holy Spirit.

2. Christian prayer finds its roots in the prayer of the Jewish people, our ancestors in faith.

3. Christians grow as people of prayer their whole life long.

Growing in Faith

One important thing I learned this week is

_____

_____

_____ .

This is important because

_____

_____

_____ .

What will people see me doing as I live my faith choice this week?

_____

_____

_____

This Week . . .

In chapter 24, "People of Prayer," your child learned more about the Church as a people of prayer. They discovered that the tradition of Christian prayer is rooted in the Old Testament. Christians can learn how to pray from Old Testament models of faith such as Abraham and Sarah. Today, Christians express themselves in prayer following the model of praying found in the Old Testament Psalms. We pray prayers of blessing and adoration, petition, intercession, thanksgiving, and praise. Like our ancestors in faith, we need to work at growing as people of prayer.

For more on the teachings of the Catholic Church on prayer, see *Catechism of the Catholic Church* paragraph numbers 2566–2589, 2598–2619, 2623–2643, and 2725–2745.

Sharing God's Word

Read together Luke 10:21. Emphasize that Christians learn to pray from the way Jesus prayed.

Praying

In this chapter your child prayed a prayer of praise. Read and pray together this prayer on page 316.

Making a Difference

Choose one of the following activities to do as a family or design a similar activity of your own.

- Read 1 Samuel 3:1–10. This Bible story is about Samuel listening to God. As you read this story, remember that we all need to spend time in prayer listening to God.

- Saint Ignatius of Loyola is one of the great spiritual guides in the Catholic tradition of prayer. Look on the Internet or at the library to find out more about this great saint.

- When you take part in Mass this week, listen carefully for the doxology, "Through him, and with him, and in him, O God, almighty Father, in the unity of the Holy Spirit." As you hear and pray these words, recall that the Church prays with and in the name of Jesus to the Father and that it is the Holy Spirit who teaches us how and what to pray.

For more ideas on ways your family can live your faith, visit the "Faith First for Families" page at **www.FaithFirst.com**. Take a look at "Just for Parents" this week.

The Gift of Prayer

25

We Pray

The LORD is my shepherd;
  there is nothing I lack.

PSALM 23:1

God our Father,
send the Holy Spirit
to teach and guide us,
to preach the Gospel,
the way of Salvation
and love. We ask this
in Jesus' name.   Amen.

What have you practiced and become good at doing?

Champions become champions by taking the time and making the effort to develop their gifts and abilities. God gives everyone the gift of prayer. We need to take the time to develop that gift.

How can you develop the gift of prayer?

Pray Without Ceasing

Faith Vocabulary

prayer life. The habit of making prayer part of the rhythm of our day.

There is truth to the statement "Champions are made, not born." Becoming a person of prayer also results from developing the gift of prayer. We need to take the time and use that gift daily, many times each day.

The Christian Prayer Life

Jesus is our model of prayer. He is the one who best shows us how to develop our **prayer life.** Jesus often spent time in conversation with his Father. He especially did this at important moments in his life. With trust he presented his needs and concerns to the Father. With gratitude he blessed and thanked his Father.

Prayer is so important in our lives as followers of Christ. Saint Paul reminds us:

Pray without ceasing.
1 THESSALONIANS 5:17

The Church lives by Saint Paul's advice. She makes prayer a regular part of her life each day. We pray as the psalmist prayed, at "dusk, dawn, and noon" (Psalm 55:18).

Morning Prayer

Throughout the world the Church welcomes each new day with prayer. We join Zechariah, the father of Saint John the Baptist, in thanking God for the dawn of Salvation in Jesus Christ. We pray:

"Blessed be the Lord,
the God of Israel,
for he has visited and
brought redemption
to his people.
He has raised up a horn
for our salvation
within the house of David
his servant,
even as he promised through
the mouth of his holy
prophets from of old."
LUKE 1:68–70

Evening Prayer

As the sun sets, the Church throughout the world also gathers in prayer. We join Mary in praising God for the wonders of his grace-filled ways.

> "My soul proclaims the
> greatness of the Lord;
> my spirit rejoices in God
> my savior. . . .
> His mercy is from age to age
> to those who fear him. . . .
> He has helped Israel his servant,
> remembering his mercy,
> according to his promise to our
> fathers,
> to Abraham and to his
> descendants forever."
>
> LUKE 1:46–47, 50, 54–55

Every time we try to make prayer a regular part of each day, we show that God is at the center of our lives. He is the One in whom we place our faith, hope, and love. We show that we value our friendship with God more than anything else in our lives.

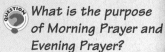 **What is the purpose of Morning Prayer and Evening Prayer?**

Praying Always

Make some practical suggestions on how you could "pray without ceasing."

_____

_____

_____

_____

_____

_____

_____

_____

Faith Focus

What role does the prayer of adoration have in our prayer life?

When have you heard the expression "I adore him"? Parents often use the term to express the depth of their love for their children.

The Prayer of Adoration

Christians use the term adoration to express the depth of their love for God. When we say to God, "We adore you," we are saying that we love him above all else.

In our **prayer of adoration** we stand before God as his creatures. We praise God's greatness and acknowledge that he is our Creator. We worship him and admit that we depend on him for everything.

Psalm 95 is an example of a prayer of adoration. Leading the people into the Temple in Jerusalem, the psalmist sings out:

> Come, let us sing joyfully
>   to the LORD;
>   cry out to the rock of our
>   salvation.
> Let us greet him with a song
>   of praise,
>   joyfully sing out our psalms.
> For the LORD is the great God,
>   the great king over all gods,
> Whose hand holds the depths
>   of the earth;
>   who owns the tops of the
>   mountains.
> The sea and dry land belong
>   to God,
>   who made them, formed
>   them by hand.
> Enter, let us bow down in
>   worship;
>   let us kneel before the LORD
>   who made us.
>   PSALM 95:1–7

A prayer of adoration proclaims the depth of our love and homage for the God who made us.

322

Holy, Holy, Holy

The Church's greatest prayer of adoration is the Eucharist. At Mass we worship God as the community of followers of Jesus. At every Mass, at the end of the Preface, we sing or pray aloud the acclamation "Holy, Holy, Holy Lord":

Holy, Holy, Holy Lord
    God of hosts.
Heaven and earth are full
    of your glory.
    Hosanna in the highest.
Blessed is he who comes in
    the name of the Lord.
Hosanna in the highest.

PREFACE ACCLAMATION,
ROMAN MISSAL

The words of this prayer of adoration are from the Old Testament Book of the Prophet Isaiah. We join in this great act of adoration with the Church on earth and with all the angels and the saints.

"Holy, holy, holy is the LORD of hosts!" they cried one to the other. "All the earth is filled with his glory!"

ISAIAH 6:3

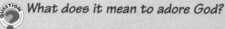 **What does it mean to adore God?**

Giving Glory to God

Gestures are a form of prayer. Think about these prayer gestures we use during the celebration of the Eucharist. Describe how each is a prayer of adoration.

Standing _____

_____

_____

Kneeling _____

_____

_____

Bowing _____

_____

_____

Faith Vocabulary

meditation. An expression of prayer using our imagination, mind, and desire to live our new life in Christ.

contemplation. An expression of prayer in which the mind and heart focus on the love and infinite goodness of God in loving adoration.

Think of the many ways you can communicate with others. Many of these use words—but not all. Sometimes our silence communicates our message more clearly than words ever could. You have heard the expression "A picture is worth a thousand words." It's true. Sometimes the right picture communicates what we could never put into words. Prayer is like that too.

Expressions of Prayer

The Holy Spirit teaches us to pray. Christians respond to the Holy Spirit by saying, or expressing, our prayers in three basic ways. They are vocal prayer, meditation, and contemplation. They all share one thing in common—all prayer is a communication that flows from our mind and heart.

Vocal Prayer

We use words all day long. How natural for us to use words when we pray. Vocal prayer is prayer that uses words. Vocal prayers are prayed aloud or silently. They are prayed alone or with others.

The words we speak in our prayers express our thoughts and feelings. They flow from our mind and our heart. They enable us to share with God our joys and sorrows, our achievements and our dreams. They give us the power to share with him everything about ourselves.

But remember, words are not necessary. God knows our innermost thoughts. He knows what we want to say before we put it into words.

Meditation

God is a loving Father who every moment is an active part of our life. In a prayer of **meditation** we connect our lives more closely with God. We use our imagination, mind, and desire to live the new life in Christ that we have received in Baptism. We seek not only to know about Christ, but also to grow in our love and friendship with him. We spend time with God the Father and give him all

our attention. We listen as the Holy Spirit shows us how to live as children of God and disciples of Jesus.

Contemplation

Saint Teresa of Avila (1515–1582), Doctor of the Church and Spanish mystic, describes the prayer of **contemplation** as "nothing less than a close sharing between friends." In a prayer of contemplation we take time to be alone with him who we know loves us. The prayer of contemplation uses few if any words. It is the closest of friends being in the presence of each other. Time seems to disappear. Contemplation is communion with God the Father, in Christ, through the power of the Holy Spirit.

 What do vocal prayer, meditation, and contemplation tell us about prayer?

Our Catholic Identity

Spiritual Direction

Everyone needs help to lead a life of prayer. Living a life of prayer is not something we can do on our own. Christians who desire to live a life of prayer seek spiritual direction. They seek the advice of a spiritual director, a person of prayer, who has received the gifts of wisdom, faith, and discernment from the Holy Spirit. The Holy Spirit gives spiritual directors the charism to guide members of the Church in living a life of prayer.

Giving Jesus All Your Attention

Choose one of these Gospel passages. Place yourself in the presence of Jesus. Describe your thoughts and feelings.

Luke 14:7–11 • Luke 15:1–10 • John 2:1–11

_____

_____

_____

_____

_____

Hildegard of Bingen

The history of the Church is filled with examples of people of prayer. Many have turned and continue to turn to these people. They pray for advice and direction on how to make their lives more prayerful.

Hildegard of Bingen (1098–1179) was blessed with a sense of God's closeness to her and all people. She had a great love of creation as God's great gift to us. At the age of thirty-eight, Hildegard was elected as abbess, or leader, of a group of women who lived together in a religious community. They had joined together to live their lives according to the Rule of Saint Benedict.

Hildegard kept prayer at the heart and center of her life. Through the example of her life she continues to teach people today that through prayer we deepen

Abbey Saint Hildegard, Ruedesheim, Germany, sisters praying (top left), sister working in art studio (bottom)

Saint Hildegard of Bingen

our friendship with God. Through prayer we speak to God as friend to Friend. The Church honors Hildegard of Bingen as a saint. We celebrate her feast day on September 17.

QUESTION What can you do to make prayer a regular part of your day?

What Difference Does Faith Make in My Life?

The Holy Spirit teaches you to pray. He is always by your side in everything you do. He is always inviting you to share your life with God.

Prayer can become part of everything you do. Here is a list of things that are part of our lives. Describe how you can make prayer a part of each of them.

Pray Always

STUDYING _____

EATING _____

PLAYING _____

READING _____

LISTENING TO MUSIC _____

WATCHING TELEVISION_____

My Faith Choice

This week I will try to be more aware that God is always inviting me to spend time with him, friend with Friend. I will

_____

_____.

A Prayer of Meditation

Pray a prayer of meditation following these steps.

1. Remind yourself that you are in the presence of God. Ask the Holy Spirit to teach you to pray.

2. Select and prayerfully read a passage from the Gospel, for example, Luke 10:38–42.

3. Imagine yourself in a scene from the Gospel.

4. Reread the passage. Pay careful attention to the conversation between the characters in the Gospel scene. What is Jesus saying to you?

5. Make a decision to put into practice what Jesus is asking of you.

6. Pray a short prayer to the Holy Spirit. Ask the Holy Spirit to help you live as a disciple of Jesus.

We Remember

What I Have Learned

Match the prayer terms in the word box with their descriptions.

> 1. vocal prayer   2. meditation   3. contemplation
> 4. prayer life   5. adoration

_____ The habit of making prayer a regular part of our day.

_____ A prayer that uses words that we say aloud or quietly in our hearts.

_____ A prayer that is a close sharing between friends, and being alone with God who we know loves us.

_____ A prayer that uses our imagination, mind, and desire to live as a faithful disciple of Christ.

_____ A prayer acknowledging that God is God alone, the Creator and source of all that is.

Answer the following.

6. Explain why "Pray without ceasing" is a description of the Christian life of prayer.

_____

_____

_____

7. Describe the Mass as a prayer of adoration.

_____

_____

_____

8. Compare vocal prayer and contemplation.

_____

_____

_____

To Help You Remember

1. We learn best to pray from Jesus, our model of prayer.

2. In a prayer of adoration we worship God and make him the center of our lives.

3. We often use words to pray. Sometimes we do not use words but just spend time with God.

Growing in Faith

One important thing I learned this week is

_____

_____

_____.

This is important because

_____

_____

_____.

What will people see me doing as I live my faith choice this week?

_____

_____

_____

25 With My Family

This Week . . .

In chapter 25, "The Gift of Prayer," your child learned more about the Church as a people of prayer. Jesus is our model of prayer. He is the One who best shows us how to develop our prayer life. Saint Paul the Apostle reminds us that we are to pray without ceasing (see 1 Thessalonians 5:17). The Church follows the advice of Saint Paul and prays throughout the day. Each time we make prayer a regular part of our day, we keep God at the center of our lives. We grow to worship God and value our friendship with him more than all else. We often speak our prayers, either aloud or silently in our heart. As we grow in prayer, we come to realize that prayer is simply spending time with God, and words are not always necessary.

For more on the teachings of the Catholic Church on prayer, see *Catechism of the Catholic Church* paragraph numbers 2598–2619 and 2700–2719.

Sharing God's Word

Read together Luke 1:46–55, 68–75. Emphasize that prayer is important to our lives as followers of Christ.

Praying

In this chapter your child prayed a prayer of meditation. Read and pray together this prayer on page 328.

Making a Difference

Choose one of the following activities to do as a family or design a similar activity of your own.

- Blessed Mother Teresa of Calcutta used this image to describe prayer. She said, "Prayer enlarges the heart until it is capable of containing God's gift of himself." Ask family members to share how they invite God into their hearts.

- Saint Hildegard of Bingen always felt close to God. Look on the Internet or at the library for more information about this wonderful saint.

- This week when you pray, pray that all your actions will be a reflection of God's love for the world.

For more ideas on ways your family can live your faith, visit the "Faith First for Families" page at **www.FaithFirst.com**. Click on "Family Prayer" and pray the prayer together this week.

The Lord's Prayer
A Scripture Story

We Pray

Answer when I call,
    my saving God. . . .
    [S]how me favor;
    hear my prayer.   PSALM 4:2

Our Father,
hallowed be your name.
Your kingdom come.
                    Amen.

*What event have you attended
or seen that began with people
praying?*

Beginning special events and
celebrations with prayer is a
widespread custom. Many
Christians pray the Lord's
Prayer, or the Our Father,
every day. Christians pray the
Our Father all over the world,
in all languages.

*What do we pray for when we
pray the Lord's Prayer?*

When you were younger, did you have your own special prayer book? Perhaps you were given one as a gift when you made your First Holy Communion. If you had such a prayer book, one of the first prayers in the book was the Our Father. You will find the Our Father in almost every Christian prayer book. Why is that? The Our Father is the prayer of all Christians.

The Prayer of All Christians

In the Gospels the Our Father comes to us in two forms. A shorter form is found in the Gospel of Luke (Luke 11:2–4).

A longer form is found in the Gospel of Matthew (Matthew 6:9–13). It is Matthew's version on which the Church bases the form of the Our Father we pray today. Both versions address God by name, honor him, and ask him to respond to our needs.

The Our Father in Matthew's Gospel follows this pattern:

1. God is addressed, or called upon: *Our Father*.

2. Three prayer verses give glory to the Father. We pray that:
   - God's name be made holy;
   - God's kingdom come;
   - God's will be done.

3. Four petitions present our needs to God. We pray that:
- God will provide for our deepest needs;
- God will forgive our sins;
- God will help us overcome temptation;
- God will help us win the struggle over evil.

The Lord's Prayer is a vast treasure chest of wisdom condensed into a small jewelry box. An ancient Roman Christian writer from Roman Africa, Tertullian (A.D. 160–225), called it a summary of the whole Gospel. Saint Augustine (A.D. 354–430), the bishop of Hippo in North Africa, described it this way:

Run through the words of the holy prayers [in Scripture], and I do not think that you will find anything in them that is not contained and included in the Lord's Prayer.

QUESTION *What are the parts of the Lord's Prayer?*

A Portrait of the Lord's Prayer

For centuries, artists have tried to depict the feelings they have when they hear and pray the Lord's Prayer. Your artist easel awaits. Create your own depiction of what the Lord's Prayer means to you.

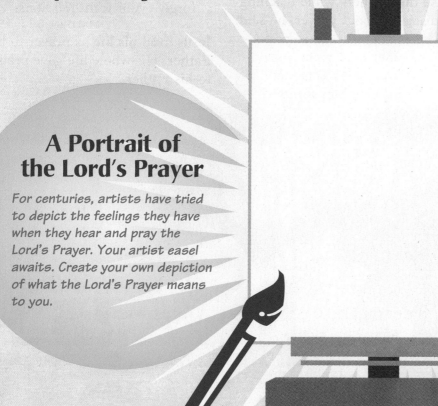

Faith Vocabulary

Sermon on the Mount. The summary of the teachings of Jesus on discipleship that are grouped in chapters 5, 6, and 7 of Matthew's Gospel.

Like most Catholics, the Our Father was one of the first prayers you prayed with your family and learned by heart. Catholics pray the Our Father at every celebration of the Mass. When do you pray the Our Father alone? When do you pray it with others?

The Lord's Prayer

In Matthew's account of the Gospel, the Lord's Prayer is part of the **Sermon on the Mount.** Jesus had just finished warning his disciples about doing good deeds so that everyone could praise them. Then, while teaching his disciples about prayer, he said:

"This is how you are to pray:
Our Father in heaven,
hallowed be your name,
your kingdom come,
your will be done,
on earth as in heaven.
Give us today our daily bread;
and forgive us our debts,
as we forgive our debtors;
and do not subject us
to the final test,
but deliver us from
the evil one."

MATTHEW 6:9–13

Jesus then concluded:
"If you forgive others their transgressions, your heavenly Father will forgive you. But if you do not forgive others, neither will your Father forgive your transgressions."

MATTHEW 6:14–15

Jesus lived his life as prayer to the Father. His whole life gave praise to his Father.

Jesus placed total trust in the Father. Everything he did was to fulfill his Father's will and the work his Father sent him to do. This trust is especially clear as he approached his death on the cross. Facing death, he prayed:

"I am troubled now. Yet what should I say? 'Father, save me from this hour'? But it was for this purpose that I came to this hour. Father, glorify your name." JOHN 12:27–28

All Jesus did gave glory and honor to the Father. The Lord's Prayer teaches us not only how to pray but also how to live so that we too give glory and honor to the Father as Jesus did. We are to live as people who place all our trust in God our Father, Abba.

 How does praying the petition "your will be done" help you live as a disciple of Jesus?

AND NOW...FOR TODAY'S
NEWS HEADLINES

Create headlines for a newspaper that tell about:
a. a parish that supports an orphanage in Central America
b. teens who raise money for hurricane victims
c. families who collect clothes and toys for homeless children.

Understanding the Word of God

Faith Focus

How does the Lord's Prayer teach us to pray?

The Meaning of the Lord's Prayer

The Lord's Prayer teaches us not only how to pray but also how to live a life of total trust in God the Father as Jesus did.

1. *OUR FATHER*
   Through our Baptism we are joined to Jesus and become one with him and one another. The Holy Spirit is poured into our hearts, enabling us to call God Abba, or Father, as Jesus did.

2. *WHO ART IN HEAVEN*
   The word *heaven* points to God's majesty and glory. The Church on earth joins with the angels and saints in heaven in praising God.

3. *HALLOWED BE THY NAME*
   Glory and praise truly belong to God, the All-Holy One, who creates, redeems, and sanctifies us.

4. *THY KINGDOM COME*
   We pray that the Kingdom announced by Jesus may come to completion when he comes again in glory at the end of time. We promise to prepare a way for the coming of that kingdom.

5. *THY WILL BE DONE ON EARTH AS IT IS IN HEAVEN*
   God's will is for all people to live in communion with him forever. When we pray "thy will be done," we promise to live according to God's will and plan.

6. *GIVE US THIS DAY OUR DAILY BREAD*
Our daily bread is Christ himself, who said, "I am the living bread that came down from heaven" (John 6:51). We ask God to watch over our physical and spiritual needs.

7. *AND FORGIVE US OUR TRESPASSES AS WE FORGIVE THOSE WHO TRESPASS AGAINST US*
Forgiveness is a two-way street. Those who receive God's forgiveness and mercy must be willing to be forgiving and merciful. They must forgive others as God so generously forgives them. They must be as merciful toward others as God is toward them.

8. *AND LEAD US NOT INTO TEMPTATION*
Temptation tries to convince us that there is something better than God's will. We ask God for the courage to face temptation with strong faith, confident hope, and generous love.

9. *BUT DELIVER US FROM EVIL*
Satan and the forces of evil in the world try to lead us away from God's love. There is no one, no power, stronger than Jesus. We pray with confidence that God's victory in Jesus Christ will be our victory as well.

 What do the petitions of the Our Father tell us about prayer?

Our Catholic Identity

Ecumenism

Jesus prayed that his followers would be one as he and the Father are one. But divisions have arisen in the Church. The followers of Jesus are divided into many churches. Ecumenism is the work of the Church striving to restore unity among all Christians.

On The Road Again

Create a billboard for the Lord's Prayer. Remember, you have to compete with a lot of other messages out there. Grab people's attention with the good news of the Lord's Prayer!

Our Church Makes a Difference

Share the Good News

Jesus gave the Church the command to share the good news of God's saving love with the whole world. We are to make disciples of all nations. We are to evangelize the whole world. We are to invite all people to be baptized and join with Jesus in calling God Abba, Father.

This work is called evangelization. It is the most important work of the Church. We carry out this work by preaching the Word of God and by living as faithful witnesses for Christ. We celebrate the sacraments and live the Great Commandment. We do all these things and more so that the Good News will enter every heart of every person on earth.

When this happens, the human family will be renewed. Our prayer "Thy kingdom come" will be fully answered. All people will live as children of God, whom we all honor and love as the one Father of all.

 How does each image in the illustration connect to the themes in the Our Father?

What Difference Does Faith Make in My Life?

Jesus gave the Church the Lord's Prayer, or Our Father. That means he gave it to you. The Holy Spirit gives you the power to call God Abba, Father. What a wonderful privilege! Stay in touch with God your Father today.

You have been given the job of webmaster of a new Web site that tells the world all about the Lord's Prayer. Design the home page.

My Faith Choice

Each morning this week I will pray one petition of the Our Father. I will think about what it means and I will

_____

_____.

The Lord's Prayer

The Our Father, or Lord's Prayer, is the prayer of all Christians. Take time every day to pray it alone.

Reader: Our Father, who art in heaven,
hallowed be thy name;

Group 1: thy kingdom come;
thy will be done on earth
as it is in heaven.

Group 2: Give us this day our daily bread;
and forgive us our trespasses

Group 1: as we forgive those
who trespass against us;

Group 2: and lead us not into temptation,
but deliver us from evil.

All: Amen.

We Remember

What I Have Learned

1. Use the code to discover why the Church says that the Our Father teaches us both how to pray and how to live as children of God.

A .–	F ..–.	K –.–	P .––.	U ..–	Z ––..
B –...	G ––.	L .–..	Q ––.–	V ...–	
C –.–.	H	M ––	R .–.	W .––	
D –..	I ..	N –.	S ...	X –..–	
E .	J .–––	O –––	T –	Y –.––	

___ ___ ___ ___ ___ ___ ___ ___ ___
... .–. ––. – .– .–. –.–.

___ ___ ___ ___
––. .–.. – ....

___ ___ ___ ___ ___ ___
––. ––– .– ..–. . .–.

Answer the following.

2. In the Lord's Prayer, what does the phrase "who art in heaven" mean?

_____

_____

_____

3. What do we promise when we pray "thy will be done"?

_____

_____

_____

4. How do we give glory to the Father when we pray the Lord's Prayer?

_____

_____

_____

To Help You Remember

1. The Lord's Prayer is the prayer of all Christians.

2. The Lord's Prayer teaches us to make our whole life a prayer.

3. The Lord's Prayer shows us how to live as people who place our trust in God above all else. (see page 387)

Growing in Faith

One important thing I learned this week is

_____

_____

_____.

This is important because

_____

_____

_____.

What will people see me doing as I live my faith choice this week?

_____

_____

_____

This Week . . .

In chapter 26, "The Lord's Prayer: A Scripture Story," your child learned more about the Our Father. In Matthew's Gospel, Jesus' teaching of the Our Father, or Lord's Prayer, is part of the Sermon on the Mount. Many biblical scholars think that the version of the Our Father in Matthew is close to the version the early Christians prayed. Saint Thomas Aquinas called the Lord's Prayer the "most perfect of prayers." He said, "This prayer not only teaches us to ask for things, but also in what order we should desire them." When we pray the Our Father, the Holy Spirit teaches us how to pray and how to live the Gospel.

For more on the teaching of the Catholic Church on the Our Father, see *Catechism of the Catholic Church* paragraph numbers 2759–2856.

Sharing God's Word

Read together Matthew 6:9–13. Emphasize that Jesus lived his life as a prayer.

Praying

In this chapter your child prayed the Lord's Prayer. Read and pray together the Lord's Prayer on page 340.

Making a Difference

Choose one of the following activities to do as a family or design a similar activity of your own.

- Many of the communities in the early Church prayed the Our Father three times a day. This week use the Our Father for family prayer at least once a day.

- Visit the supermarket as a family. Purchase some basic food items and deliver them to a local food bank. Your parish can give you a location.

- Saint Thomas Aquinas wrote that the Our Father "not only teaches us to ask for things, but also in what order we should desire them." Look at the Our Father and discuss what you think Saint Thomas Aquinas meant.

For more ideas on ways your family can live your faith, visit the "Faith First for Families" page at **www.FaithFirst.com**. "Gospel Reflections" will continue to change each week over the summer. Don't forget to check it out.

Catholic Social Teaching

Family Values

Mr. Harper and his sixth grade class were in an intense discussion about values. "What is a value?" he asked them.

"Something important," John answered. "A quality that is important," added Rosario.

"An ideal. A value is a belief we have about what is important," summarized Katie.

"Very good," said Mr. Harper. "So what values are important to you?" he challenged the class.

"Listening." "Respect." "Honesty." The class shouted out a lot of words.

"Now," Mr. Harper continued as he handed out a 3 x 5 inch card to each student, "write down what you think are the top five values in family life. Think about what is most important for families and what families want to hold up as their standard for how members treat each other."

When the class was finished, Mr. Harper collected the cards. He and the students tallied the responses. How do you think they responded?

We Live in Community

In our families we learn about and act on our values. We build up family life and promote Jesus' way of living by acting on Christian values.

Making Connections . . .

Mr. Harper posed some challenging questions to his class about what is most important to them.

with Math and Science

Find out what the top five family values are of the students in your class. Create a graph or data chart that indicates what those values are.

with Social Studies

Choose a situation from your history studies that tells about people who were involved in a situation in their country, as well as the values they held. Describe how the situation would have been different if the values of the people involved were different.

with Creative Arts

Using the list of family values your class chooses as important, act out scenarios depicting those values in action in a home situation.

⊃ **Faith Action** *There is a saying, "You have to walk the walk and talk the talk." This means that if we say we value something, our actions should reflect that value. This week, reflect on how your actions at home reflect the things you value.*

Name _____

A. The Best Response

Read each statement and circle the best answer.

1. Which of the following is not a definition of prayer?

   a. lifting our minds and hearts to God

   b. an invitation from God to spend time with him

   c. talking and listening to God

   d. impressing God with our words

2. The prayer in which we use our imagination to connect our lives more closely with God is _____.

   a. contemplation

   b. intercession

   c. Psalms

   d. meditation

3. Paul taught us to pray _____.

   a. only in the morning

   b. with fear of God

   c. without ceasing

   d. mainly during the evening hours

4. Which is not a form of prayer found in the Psalms?

   a. blessing and adoration

   b. petition

   c. thanksgiving

   d. letters

5. Which prayer did Tertullian call a summary of the whole Gospel?

   a. Nicene Creed

   b. Our Father

   c. Glory Be

   d. Apostles' Creed

6. When we pray "Give us this day our daily bread," we _____.

   a. ask God for the courage to face temptation

   b. promise to live according to God's will

   c. ask God to watch over our physical and spiritual needs

   d. give glory and praise to God

7. Which of the following people is not a good model of prayer?

   a. Mary

   b. Judas

   c. Abraham

   d. David

8. In the prayer of invocation, we _____.

   a. express our sorrow

   b. call on someone to assist us with our needs

   c. complain when things go wrong

   d. praise God for his blessings

9. Which of these is not a true statement about prayer?

   a. When we pray we show that God is the center of our lives.

   b. The Eucharist is the greatest prayer of adoration.

   c. Jesus is the best model of prayer.

   d. All prayer uses words.

10. In Matthew's Gospel, Jesus taught the Our Father _____.

    a. in the Temple in Jerusalem

    b. at the beginning of his ministry

    c. in the Sermon on the Mount

    d. at his Crucifixion

B. Completing the Paragraph

Fill in the blanks in the paragraph using the words in the word bank.

> vocal   contemplation   communion
> meditation   prophets   petition
> adoration

  The Christian tradition of prayer has its roots in the Old Testament. Abraham, whom we recognize as our father in faith, King David, and the _____ are some of the Old Testament's models of prayer for Christians. The Old Testament also reveals five basic forms of prayer that Christians use. They are prayers of _____, _____, intercession, praise, and thanksgiving. Christians express our prayers in three ways. We pray _____ prayers, prayers of _____, and prayers of _____. By praying regularly each day we grow in friendship and _____ with God.

C. What I Have Learned

Write three things you learned in this unit. Share them with the group.

_____

_____

_____

Look at the faith terms in "Words to Know" on page 208. Circle the terms you know now.

D. From a Scripture Story

The Lord's Prayer teaches us not only how to pray but also how to live as Jesus did. Describe three ways you live the Our Father.

_____

_____

_____

What do the celebrations of the liturgical year help us remember and share in?

The Liturgical Year

The Church gathers throughout the year to remember and share in the saving work of Christ. Each day of the year is made holy by the Church gathering together with Christ, the Head of the Church, to give praise, honor, and glory to the Father through the power of the Holy Spirit. Each week the Church, the new People of God, gathers on Sunday, or the Lord's Day, to celebrate and share in the Paschal Mystery. In addition to Sunday celebrations, the liturgical year of the Church is made up of a cycle of seasons, solemnities, feasts, and memorials. The lessons in this unit focus on the seasons of the liturgical year of the Church. This page lists many of the solemnities, feasts, and memorials that are celebrated throughout the year.

JANUARY
Mary, the Mother of God (January 1)
Elizabeth Ann Seton, Religious (January 4)
John Neumann, Bishop (January 5)
Agnes, Virgin and Martyr (January 21)
Conversion of Saint Paul, Apostle (January 25)
Thomas Aquinas, Priest and Doctor (January 28)

FEBRUARY
Presentation of the Lord (February 2)
Blase, Bishop and Martyr (February 3)
Agatha, Virgin and Martyr (February 5)
Our Lady of Lourdes (February 11)
Chair of Saint Peter, Apostle (February 22)

MARCH
Perpetua and Felicity, Martyrs (March 7)
Patrick, Bishop (March 17)
Joseph, Husband of Mary (March 19)
Annunciation (March 25)

APRIL
Mark, Evangelist (April 25)
Catherine of Siena, Virgin and Doctor (April 29)

MAY
Joseph the Worker (May 1)
Athanasius, Bishop and Doctor (May 2)
Philip and James, Apostles (May 3)
Matthias, Apostle (May 14)
Isidore (May 15)
Visitation (May 31)
Holy Trinity (First Sunday after Pentecost)

Body and Blood of Christ (Sunday after Holy Trinity)
Sacred Heart (Friday following Second Sunday after Pentecost)

JUNE
Charles Lwanga and Companions, Martyrs (June 3)
Barnabas, Apostle (June 11)
Anthony of Padua, Priest and Doctor (June 13)
Birth of John the Baptist (June 24)
Peter and Paul, Apostles (June 29)

JULY
Thomas, Apostle (July 3)
Blessed Kateri Tekakwitha, Virgin (July 14)
Our Lady of Mount Carmel (July 16)
Mary Magdalene (July 22)
James, Apostle (July 25)
Joachim and Ann, Parents of Mary (July 26)
Martha (July 29)
Ignatius of Loyola, Priest (July 31)

AUGUST
Transfiguration (August 6)
Lawrence, Deacon and Martyr (August 10)
Clare, Virgin (August 11)
Assumption (August 15)
Queenship of Mary (August 22)
Rose of Lima, Virgin (August 23)
Bartholomew, Apostle (August 24)
Monica (August 27)
Augustine of Hippo, Bishop and Doctor (August 28)

SEPTEMBER
Birth of Mary (September 8)
Peter Claver, Priest (September 9)
Triumph of the Cross (September 14)
Our Lady of Sorrows (September 15)
Matthew, Apostle and Evangelist (September 21)
Michael, Gabriel, and Raphael, Archangels (September 29)

OCTOBER
Theresa of the Child Jesus, Virgin (October 1)
Francis of Assisi (October 4)
Our Lady of the Rosary (October 7)
Teresa of Jesus, Virgin and Doctor (October 15)
Luke, Evangelist (October 18)
Isaac Jogues and John de Brébeuf, Priests and Martyrs, and Companions (October 19)
Simon and Jude, Apostles (October 28)

NOVEMBER
All Saints (November 1)
All Souls (November 2)
Martin de Porres, Religious (November 3)
Frances Xavier Cabrini, Virgin (November 13)
Elizabeth of Hungary (November 17)
Presentation of Mary (November 21)
Cecilia, Virgin and Martyr (November 22)
Andrew, Apostle (November 30)
Christ the King (Last Sunday in Ordinary Time)

DECEMBER
Immaculate Conception (December 8)
Our Lady of Guadalupe (December 12)
Christmas (December 25)
Stephen, First Martyr (December 26)
John, Apostle and Evangelist (December 27)
Holy Innocents (December 28)

Faith Focus

How does the Jesse tree help us celebrate Advent?

The Word of the Lord

These are the Gospel readings for the First Sunday of Advent. Choose this year's reading. Read and discuss it with your family.

Year A
Matthew 24:37–44

Year B
Mark 13:33–37

Year C
Luke 21:25–28, 34–36

The Family Tree of Jesus

All families have a history and a story to tell. All the people who are part of your family history make up your family tree—your parents, brothers and sisters, grandparents, aunts, uncles, and family members who lived generations ago.

Jesus has a family tree too. We Christians use it to help us celebrate Advent. We call it the Jesse tree. The tree is named for Jesse, a shepherd from Bethlehem. He lived about one thousand years before Jesus. Jesse was the father of David, who grew up to be the greatest king of the people of Israel. David is an ancestor of Jesus.

During Advent we remember the people—like Jesse and David—who are part of Jesus' family tree. We decorate the Jesse tree with symbols of these Old and New Testament figures. The Jesse tree is like our family tree. Each person on the Jesse tree is part of the long story of God's loving plan of Salvation that is fulfilled in Jesus.

Remembering the faith stories of the people on the Jesse tree helps us remember God's great love for us—and for all people.

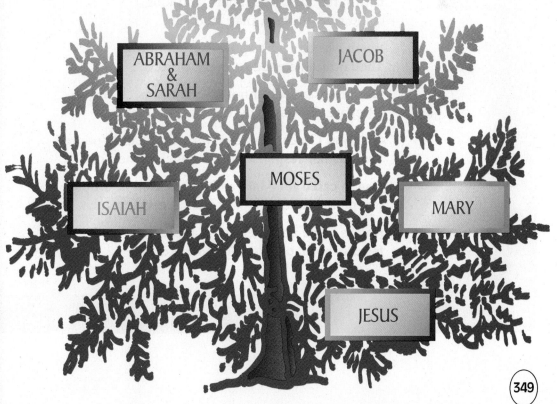

ADAM & EVE

ABRAHAM & SARAH

JACOB

MOSES

ISAIAH

MARY

JESUS

Remembering
the Story of Salvation

Make your own Jesse tree. You can use a small evergreen tree or just some branches. Make a symbol for each of these figures. Add others of your own. Put the symbols on your Jesse tree.

When **Adam** and **Eve** refused to obey,
God promised a savior would come someday.

Noah is a man to note;
while others laughed he built a boat.

Abraham and **Sarah** obeyed God's call.
Their faith is an example for one and for all.

When **Isaac** was born, Sarah was old.
Her laughter rang out, so we are told.

Isaac's son **Jacob** was rich and able;
soon twelve healthy sons sat at his table.

Joseph saved his family from starvation.
In Egypt they grew into a very strong nation.

Moses, leader and man of God,
led Israel through the Red Sea dryshod.

David, the Lord's shepherd and king,
could rule, protect, play, and sing.

Isaiah was one who spoke for his Lord.
The faithful listened to every word.

John the Baptist's announcement was clear.
"Prepare the way! The Lord draws near!"

On **Mary** God's blessings were abundantly poured.
Yes was her response to the angel of the Lord.

Joseph cared for Mary as he promised he would,
Joseph the mild, the patient, the good.

Angels came and shepherds adored,
Jesus is born, our Savior and Lord!

The Second Week of Advent

Faith Focus

What do we prepare for during Advent?

The Word of the Lord

These are the Gospel readings for the Second Sunday of Advent. Choose this year's reading. Read and discuss it with your family.

Year A
   Matthew 3:1–12

Year B
   Mark 1:1–8

Year C
   Luke 3:1–6

Day of the Lord

Advent reminds us of three things:

- The Lord comes in history at Christmas.
- The Lord comes in mystery each day.
- The Lord comes in majesty at the end of time.

The prophets of the Old Testament often used the phrase *day of the Lord* to describe the Lord's coming. Through the prophets, God encouraged the people of Israel to seek out and welcome his Promised One.

Through the prophet Isaiah, God described a day when the Messiah, the Promised One, would come. (See Isaiah 11:6–9.) Then even enemies would come and live together in peace.

During Advent we make room for the Lord in our lives and hearts. We pray with Mary and Joseph as they prepare to welcome Jesus into their family.

On Christmas Eve, the last day of Advent, we listen to the Scripture, and God speaks to us about that great day, the birthday of Jesus the King and Savior promised to David. We pray:
   Come quickly, we pray, Lord Jesus, and do not delay, . . .
FROM COLLECT
THE MORNING MASS
DECEMBER 24

When we faithfully keep the Advent season, we are ready to welcome Jesus on Christmas Day. Peace rules our hearts and our homes. Peace rules the earth. God's Promised One has come.

On the Day of the Lord . . .

Look up and read Isaiah 11:6–9. Then fill in the spaces with symbols or pictures for the missing words. Prayerfully reflect on the words of Isaiah.

The   shall be the guest of the   ,

and the   shall lie down with the   ;

The calf and the young   shall browse together,

with a little   to guide them.

The   and the   shall be neighbors;

together their young shall rest;

the   shall eat hay like the   .

The   shall play by the   's den. . . .

There shall be no harm or ruin on all my holy   ;

for the   shall be filled with knowledge of the Lord.

BASED ON ISAIAH 11:6–9

The Third Week of Advent

Faith Focus

How does celebrating Advent strengthen our faith in Jesus' presence with us?

The Word of the Lord

These are the Gospel readings for the Third Sunday of Advent. Choose this year's reading. Read and discuss it with your family.

Year A
Matthew 11:2–11

Year B
John 1:6–8, 19–28

Year C
Luke 3:10–18

What You See

The Third Sunday of Advent is the midpoint of the Advent season. In some dioceses the priest may wear rose-colored vestments and the rose-colored candle on the Advent wreath is lit. The color rose signifies our joy at the hope of the coming of our Savior, Jesus Christ.

The Lord's Coming

With joy we welcome new people into our lives. We may prepare for them by cooking special foods and sharing a meal with them. Advent is the time the Church helps us get ready to welcome Jesus. We pray:

O God, who see how your people faithfully await the feast of the Lord's Nativity, enable us, we pray, to attain the joys of so great a salvation and to celebrate them always with solemn worship and glad rejoicing.

FROM THE COLLECT
THIRD SUNDAY OF ADVENT

As we prepare for something wonderful in our lives, we experience many different feelings. We feel excitement and anticipation. We feel happiness and joy. We can hardly wait for the wonderful time that is to come!

During Advent we prepare for our celebration of the birth of Jesus. We remember that the Son of God took on flesh and lived among us. Our faith tells us that this coming of the Son of God among us is a sign that he is with us each moment of every day.

All throughout Advent the Church recalls Israel's waiting for the coming of the Lord. Our hearts are filled with the hope of the prophet Zephaniah:

Shout for joy, O daughter Zion!
sing joyfully, O Israel!
The LORD, your God, is in
your midst,
a mighty savior;
He will rejoice over you with
gladness,
and renew you in his love.

ZEPHANIAH 3:14, 17

We believe that Jesus is our Lord and the promised Messiah. We remember his birth at Christmas. We also look forward to the time when he will come again in glory. During Advent we seek to grow more loving day by day. We pray that we will be ready when the Lord comes to welcome us into the Kingdom of heaven.

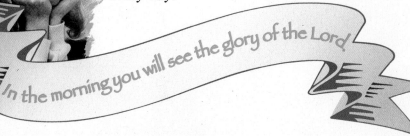

In the morning you will see the glory of the Lord

The Lord Is Near

"Rejoice in the Lord always. I shall say it again: rejoice! Your kindness should be known to all. The Lord is near" (Philippians 4:4–5).

Joy is a gift of a loving person. Joy is yours to keep and yours to spread. Plan three ways your presence and actions will spread joy during Advent this year.

Action	When I Will Do It
_____	_____
_____	_____
_____	_____
_____	_____
_____	_____
_____	_____
_____	_____
_____	_____

Faith Focus

What are the Gospel stories of the Annunciation and the Visitation?

The Word of the Lord

These are the Gospel readings for the Fourth Sunday of Advent. Choose this year's reading. Read and discuss it with your family.

Year A
Matthew 1:18–24

Year B
Luke 1:26–38

Year C
Luke 1:39–45

The Annunciation

The Visitation

Stories About Jesus' Birth

We like to hear stories about our birth: who visited us just after we were born, why our parents gave us our name. We also like to hear stories about when we were infants and toddlers. Our parents know all these stories, and they share them with us.

The Gospel accounts of Luke and Matthew tell us the stories about Jesus' birth and infancy. Both Luke and Matthew tell us the story of the angel Gabriel's announcement of the birth of Jesus. In Luke we read the story of the angel's announcement to Mary. She said yes to God and agreed to become the Mother of Jesus. We call this announcement to Mary the Annunciation.

In Matthew we read the story of the announcement to Joseph. An angel helped him understand that Mary's child would be the Savior promised by God. Many years before, through the prophet Isaiah, God had announced that "the virgin shall be with child, and bear a son" (Isaiah 7:14). The angel helped Joseph understand that this virgin was Mary. When the angel asked Joseph to take care of Mary, he agreed, and immediately he took her into his home.

During Advent Christians listen to these stories and remember the events. These events help us celebrate Advent.

Luke's account of the Gospel also tells us the story of Zechariah and Elizabeth. For a long time they had prayed for a child. God heard their prayer, and Elizabeth gave birth to a son, whom they named John.

Zechariah praised God for their son and announced John's future work: "'And you, child, will be called prophet of the Most High, / for you will go before the Lord to prepare his ways'" (Luke 1:76).

After Mary learned about Zechariah and Elizabeth's good news, she went to visit them. We call this story the Visitation. When Mary visited her cousin, Elizabeth said, "'Most blessed are you among women'" (Luke 1:42).

Praying the Story of Mary

The story of the Annunciation also became a prayer called the Angelus. This prayer is customarily said three times a day: morning, noon, and night. Take the time to pray it now.

Leader: The Angel of the Lord declared unto Mary,
All: **And she conceived of the Holy Spirit.**
Hail Mary . . .

Leader: Behold the handmaid of the Lord,
All: **Be it done unto me according to your Word.**
Hail Mary . . .

Leader: And the Word was made flesh,
All: **And dwelt among us.**
Hail Mary . . .

Leader: Pray for us, O holy Mother of God,
All: **That we may be made worthy of the promises of Christ.**

Leader: Let us pray.
Pour forth, we beseech you, O Lord, your grace into our hearts: that we, to whom the Incarnation of Christ your Son was made known by the message of an Angel, may by his Passion and Cross be brought to the glory of his Resurrection. Through the same Christ our Lord.
All: **Amen.**

Christmas

Faith Focus

What do we learn from the Gospel story of the angel's announcement to the shepherds of the birth of Jesus?

The Word of the Lord

These are the Gospel readings for Mass on Christmas Day. Choose one reading. Read and discuss it with your family.

John 1:1–18 or
John 1:1–5, 9–14

Shepherds First

Sometimes the people in our lives surprise us. They do something we do not expect. When that happens, we learn a new thing about them. What happened on the night Jesus was born tells us something new about him.

Luke's account of the Gospel includes the announcement of the birth of Jesus to the shepherds. They were the first to receive the good news of Jesus' birth. As the shepherds watched their sheep, an angel appeared to them and said:

"[T]oday in the city of David a savior has been born for you who is Messiah and Lord."

LUKE 2:11

The shepherds hurried to Bethlehem. There they found Jesus and Mary and Joseph as the angel said they would.

Throughout the history of Israel, the writers of the Sacred Scripture used the image of shepherds to speak about God. For the Israelites God was a shepherd who watched over them, his sheep. They often prayed:

The LORD is my shepherd.

PSALM 23:1

However, at the time of Jesus' birth, many people thought that shepherds were of little worth. Their hard, dangerous work kept them in the fields day and night. This meant that they were unable to observe religious practices. Because of this, religious leaders thought shepherds were unfaithful, unimportant people.

But it was to shepherds, Luke tells us, that God announced the birth of the Savior. Jesus is the Messiah and Lord of all.

The Lord Is Our Shepherd

For each letter of the word shepherd, write a word or phrase that tells us about who Jesus is. Then use your words and phrases and write a paragraph telling others about Jesus.

S
H
E
P
H
E
R
D

_____
_____
_____
_____
_____
_____
_____

_____
_____
_____
_____
_____
_____
_____

The First Week of Lent

Faith Focus

What are we called to do during Lent?

The Word of the Lord

Choose this year's Gospel reading for the First Sunday of Lent. Read and discuss it with your family.

Year A
Matthew 4:1–11

Year B
Mark 1:12–15

Year C
Luke 4:1–13

What You See

In our churches we see signs that Lent is a season of discipline. The color of Lent is purple, the color of penitence. No flowers or brightly colored decorations greet us. We sing no joyous Alleluia or Gloria.

Lent

For many of us, the winter landscape seems bare. Leaves fall from trees, flowers die, and grass turns brown. But we trust that after winter, spring will come and bring new life. Each year during Lent we renew the new life of Christ we received in Baptism.

Lent begins on Ash Wednesday. On Ash Wednesday the Church gathers to begin our Lenten journey. As ashes are placed on our head, we hear the words:
Repent, and believe in the Gospel.

During Lent the Church calls us to enter more fully into Jesus' death and Resurrection. We make sacrifices to do this. We may decide to share more of our time and talents with others. We may give up something that we enjoy. We want habits of goodness to live in us. We support one another in our decisions during Lent. Together we look forward to celebrating the joy of Easter.

Choose two small twigs or pieces of wood and tie them with twine to form a simple cross. Place your cross on the prayer table as you gather for prayer. Then pray the prayer together.

Take Up Your Cross

Introduction

LEADER: During Lent we walk with Jesus. We hope to share in his Resurrection at Easter.

The Word of God

READER: *Proclaim Mark 10:35–45.*

LEADER: Jesus looked ahead at the cross he would bear. Are you willing to take up your small cross this Lent?

ALL: **We are.**

Lenten Commitment

LEADER: Let us pause and decide on one thing we know we need to do to be more like Jesus. *(Pause.)*

As I call your name, please come forward.

(Name), will you strive to take up your Lenten cross and follow Jesus?

STUDENT: I will.

Closing Prayer

(Choose a wooden cross from the prayer table.)

LEADER: May the cross of Christ remind us to open our minds and hearts to God.

ALL: **Amen!**

LEADER: May we all walk with Jesus and enter into the joy of Easter.

ALL: **Amen!**

LEADER: May we pray for one another. May we support one another as we take up our cross as a sign of our love of Jesus, who carried his cross because of his love for us.

ALL: **Amen!**

Faith Focus

How did God show his compassion through Jesus?

The Word of the Lord

Choose this year's Gospel reading for the Second Sunday of Lent. Read and discuss it with your family.

Year A
Matthew 17:1–9

Year B
Mark 9:2–10

Year C
Luke 9:28–36

What You Hear

During Lent only a Psalm verse is used before the Gospel reading. The Alleluia that is sung in every season outside of Lent is not said or sung.

The Compassion of God

When something sad or bad happens to someone we love, we feel compassion for that person. The word *compassion* means "to suffer with" another person. Can you remember a time you felt the suffering of another person?

The story of Jesus is the story of a man of compassion. When we see the compassion of Jesus, we see God's compassion for us. At the beginning of his public ministry, Jesus urged his followers to be filled with compassion, just as their heavenly Father was filled with compassion (see Luke 6:36). All through his life, Jesus suffered with people who came to him for healing and forgiveness.

Toward the end of his life, Jesus looked over the city of Jerusalem. Deeply saddened that so many people turned away from God, he wept and prayed:

"Jerusalem, . . . how many times I yearned to gather your children together, as a hen gathers her young under her wings, but you were unwilling!"

MATTHEW 23:37

During Lent the Church invites us to imitate the compassion of God. He asks us to reach out to those who need our help. Find out what your parish is doing during Lent to help others. As a class, choose a way you will participate in this Lenten outreach. Then pray the prayer together.

The Lord Is Compassionate

LEADER: Bless the Lord, O my soul.

ALL: **Bless the Lord, O my soul.**

BOYS: Bless the Lord, O my soul; bless the Lord, all my being.

GIRLS: Bless the Lord, O my soul; never forget the Lord's greatness.

BOYS: The Lord pardons our offenses and heals our ills.

GIRLS: The Lord redeems us from death and crowns us with goodness and compassion.

BOYS: The Lord fills us with good and renews our strength like the eagle's.

GIRLS: The Lord upholds the poor; the Lord guards the oppressed.

BOYS: Merciful and gracious is the Lord, slow to anger, quick to bless.

GIRLS: The Lord does not treat us with anger; the Lord treats us with mercy and compassion.

BOYS: As high as the heavens are above the earth, so is God abundant in mercy.

GIRLS: Just as parents are compassionate toward their children, so the Lord is compassionate toward those who show reverence to him.

LEADER: The compassion of the Lord lasts forever. May the Lord have compassion on us.

ALL: **Bless the Lord, O my soul. Amen.**

Faith Focus

What does praying make us more aware of?

The Word of the Lord

Choose this year's Gospel reading for the Third Sunday of Lent. Read and discuss it with your family.

Year A
John 4:5–42, or
John 4:5–15,
19–26, 39,
40–44

Year B
John 2:13–25

Year C
Luke 13:1–9

God Is Near

We like to spend time with our friends, talking and playing and laughing together. But most of us like to spend time alone too. We enjoy a quiet moment to think our own thoughts.

One friend who is with us all the time is God. Faith tells us that God is always near. Prayer helps us become more aware of how close God is to us. Sometimes we pray with others; sometimes we pray alone in the quiet of our heart.

When we pray together, we are sometimes silent together. In fact, our prayer together includes and depends on moments of silence. In silence we are better able to pay close attention to God. The psalmist tells us:

Be still before the LORD;
wait for God.
PSALM 37:7

During Lent we sharpen our awareness of how Jesus taught us to pray. Jesus told us to pray quietly without drawing attention to ourselves. He taught us that prayer should be a normal part of our life. He taught us to pray and to trust that God is near and listens to our prayer.

Lent is a good time to resolve to pray frequently. In prayer you draw near to God, who is always near to you.

Be Still and Wait for God

Pray this prayer together. Then choose one of the petitions and make a bookmark as a reminder to pray always.

LEADER: Let us come together and worship the Lord, our God, who is always near.

ALL: **Be still before the Lord; wait for God.**

LEADER: Let us pray for peace in the world.

ALL: **Be still before the Lord; wait for God.**

LEADER: Let us pray for those who are doing good works during Lent.

ALL: **Be still before the Lord; wait for God.**

LEADER: Let us pray to continue our own prayers and good works during Lent.

ALL: **Be still before the Lord; wait for God.**

LEADER: Lord, hear our prayer that we may be ready to celebrate Easter. We ask this in Jesus' name. Amen.

The Fourth Week of Lent

Faith Focus

Why do we give up things during Lent?

The Word of the Lord

Choose this year's Gospel reading for the Fourth Sunday of Lent. Read and discuss it with your family.

Year A
John 9:1–41 or
John 9:1, 6–9,
13–17,
34–38

Year B
John 3:14–21

Year C
Luke 15:1–3, 11–32

The Eye of a Needle

In Jesus' time, Jerusalem was a city surrounded by a wall. The people there called one of its narrow gates the "Eye of a Needle." So when a rich man asked Jesus what he had to do to get to heaven, Jesus told a parable about a camel passing through the eye of a needle. The camel carried so much baggage on its back that it could not get through the narrow gateway.

In this story Jesus reminds us that things we have can sometimes get in our way on our journey to God. Jesus told the man to give away what he had and follow Jesus. But the man couldn't do it. He went away sad. Remembering this story during Lent helps us remember to share our possessions with others. This is one way we can live as Jesus wants us to live.

Giving and Giving Up

Sometimes we enjoy giving our time to help others. But giving time to others is not always easy. Sometimes we enjoy giving up something that matters to us when someone else needs it. But that is not always easy either.

During Lent the Church invites us to give to others, especially to people who are poor. To give a little more is called almsgiving. Long ago an alms was an amount of money. Almsgiving today includes sharing our time, talents, and goods, as well as our money.

Fasting is another way of doing penance or giving up something for a greater good. When we fast, we voluntarily give up food for a certain amount of time. Following the example of Christ, who fasted often, this practice has long been a part of Catholic tradition. Lent and each Friday of the year, in honor of Jesus' death, are special times of fasting in the Church. On Ash Wednesday and Good Friday, Catholics between the ages of 18 and 59 fast by eating only one full meal a day. Fasting can help us make up for our sins and deepen our relationship with God and others. Some people fast in order to identify more closely with the poor and hungry of the world.

But we can think of fasting in a bigger way. Fasting can include giving up bad habits, such as eating and drinking unhealthy foods, or giving up our greedy desires.

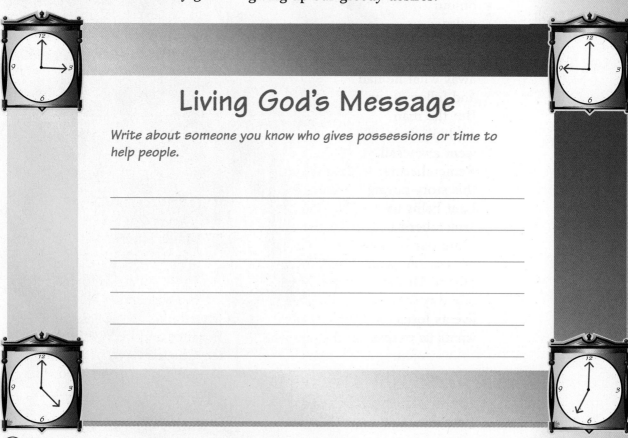

Living God's Message

Write about someone you know who gives possessions or time to help people.

_____

_____

_____

_____

_____

_____

Faith Focus

What does Jesus teach us about repentance?

The Word of the Lord

Choose this year's Gospel reading for the Fifth Sunday of Lent. Read and discuss it with your family.

Year A
John 11:1–45 or
John 11:3–7, 17,
20–27,
33–45

Year B
John 12:20–33

Year C
John 8:1–11

Turn and Live

Think of a time you hurt someone you really care about. How did you feel? What did you want to do? We just want to be forgiven. We wish we had never hurt that person. We just want things to be fixed. We want to change.

Jesus told us over and over again that God always forgives us. He always wants things to be just right between himself and us.

What we need to do is trust God and repent. We need to turn *from* unloving and hurtful words, actions, and attitudes. We need to turn *to* loving words, actions, and attitudes that bring harmony and life.

In the parable of the Good Shepherd, Jesus told of a shepherd who searched for a single lost sheep. The shepherds of Israel often faced great danger from howling hyenas, baying wolves, sly jackals, and sharp-toothed bears. When a sheep wandered away, the shepherd went out to battle these wild animals and rescue the one who had strayed.

In his parable Jesus said that as the good shepherd in the parable, he would risk his life

The Finding of the Lost Sheep, painting on wood. Emanuel Vigeland (1875–1948), Norwegian artist.

for his sheep. He is our Good Shepherd, and we are his sheep.

We stray when we sin. Jesus will come after us. He will come in search of us to forgive us and bring us home.

During Lent we celebrate the Sacrament of Penance and Reconciliation. We recognize and admit our hurtful actions. We confess our sins.

These special celebrations are the welcoming arms of Jesus today. The Sacrament of Penance and Reconciliation is the Church's way of helping us choose life with God and with one another in harmony and community.

A Litany of Repentance

Lent is a season of repentance. We think about how we are living as followers of Jesus and try to do better. Pray this prayer together with your classmates and with your family.

LEADER: Lord, you announced the good news of God's love for us.

ALL: Lord, have mercy.

LEADER: You announced the coming of the Kingdom of God.

ALL: Lord, have mercy.

LEADER: You preached a message of repentance.

ALL: Lord, have mercy.

LEADER: You forgave and healed the sinful man who could not walk.

ALL: Lord, have mercy.

LEADER: You invited the tax collectors Levi and Zacchaeus and the good thief into the kingdom.

ALL: Lord, have mercy.

LEADER: You forgave the woman who sinned.

ALL: Lord, have mercy.

LEADER: You will surely forgive us our sins, especially . . . *(Pause.)* Help us forgive others as abundantly as you forgive us.

ALL: Lord, have mercy.

Palm Sunday of the Lord's Passion

Faith Focus

Why do we celebrate Palm Sunday of the Lord's Passion?

The Word of the Lord

Choose this year's Gospel reading for Palm Sunday of the Lord's Passion. Read and discuss it with your family.

Year A
  Matthew 26:14–
        27:66 or
        27:11–54
Year B
  Mark 14:1–15:47
      or 15:1–39
Year C
  Luke 22:14–23:56
      or 23:1–49

Holy Week

When a well-known person comes to your school or town, you welcome them with a marching band and banners and balloons. When Jesus entered the city of Jerusalem, the people gave him a special welcome.

On that day, the people of Jerusalem welcomed Jesus as a messiah. He did not ride on a mighty horse or in a gilded chariot as a great soldier or a conquering hero. Jesus entered Jerusalem riding a donkey. But as he entered, the people cheered him as they would a great king:

> "Hosanna to the Son of David;
> blessed is he who comes in
> the name of the Lord;
> hosanna in the highest."
> MATTHEW 21:9

The people proclaimed *Hosanna*, a greeting of joy and praise, which means "Lord, grant salvation."

The people spread cloaks on the road to make the path smooth and less dusty for Jesus. They waved branches taken from palm trees. This welcome of Jesus, as the Messiah riding on a donkey, reminds us that Jesus is the king of everyone, even the lowly. Jesus is a king filled with compassion and care.

The celebration of Palm Sunday begins Holy Week. We begin our celebration with a procession. Everyone walks into church carrying palm branches. This recalls the day Jesus rode into Jerusalem.

Jesus' Final Entry into Jerusalem, stained-glass triptych, or three-paneled window

Blessing of palm fronds
before the entrance
procession into the church,
Liturgy of Palm Sunday
of the Lord's Passion

Hosanna! A Meditation

Sit quietly.

Close your eyes and breathe slowly.

Remember the story of Jesus' entry into Jerusalem.

Compare the meaning of this story to your own life and share your thoughts with Jesus. Take the time to praise him for the gifts he has brought to your life.

After a few quiet moments, write down any key words or phrases that will help you remember this prayer experience.

_____

_____

_____

_____

Faith Focus

Why is Easter the most important season of the Church's year?

The Word of the Lord

These are the Gospel readings for Easter Sunday. Choose this year's reading. Read and discuss it with your family.

Year A
John 20:1–9
    or
Matthew 28:1–10
    or
Luke 24:13–35

Year B
John 20:1–9
    or
Mark 16:1–8
    or
Luke 24:13–35

Year C
John 20:1–9
    or
Luke 24:1–12
    or
Luke 24:13–35

This Is the Day

There is something special about the farm when crops begin to grow and fill the field. The air is filled with new scents as the smell of winter dirt is transformed into the fresh aroma of new, green life. What signs of spring and new life fill the places where you live and play?

Signs of the new life we have in Christ fill our churches during Easter. At the Easter Vigil the newly lighted Easter candle stands tall and shines in the darkness. Standing and holding lighted candles that flood the church with light, the worshiping assembly listens as the Church proclaims:

Exult, let them exult,
    the hosts of heaven,
exult, let Angel ministers
    of God exult, . . .

Everyone rejoices. Easter is the Church's season of new life. On Easter Sunday the Church around the world breaks into joyful song and sings, "This is the day the Lord has made; let us be glad and rejoice in it" (Responsorial Psalm, The Mass of Easter Day).

We fill our homes and lives with signs of joy and new life. Flowers and candles decorate our homes. Special foods, such as Easter breads and colored eggs, remind us that this is a life-giving feast. Throughout this day and for fifty days afterward, our celebration of Easter continues. We sing aloud and in the quiet of our hearts, "Alleluia! Alleluia! Alleluia!"

Alleluia! Christ Is Risen

Create a design for an Easter banner in this space. Then, using your design, work with your family to create a banner and hang it in your home.

The Second Week of Easter

Faith Focus

How does the story of Thomas remind us of our gift of faith?

The Word of the Lord

This is the Gospel reading for the Second Sunday of Easter each year. Read and discuss it with your family.

John 20:19–31

Thomas's Profession of Faith

When someone tells us about an event they have witnessed, we believe them. We believe them because they were there.

When Jesus first appeared to the disciples, Thomas the Apostle was not with them. The disciples told Thomas that Jesus appeared to them, but Thomas refused to believe them. He said he would believe only when he saw the Risen Jesus himself—when he could see Jesus' wounds. This refusal of Thomas to believe the other disciples has become so famous that someone who demands evidence before they believe others is now called a "doubting Thomas."

John's account of the Gospel tells us that a week later the Risen Jesus again appeared to his disciples. This time Thomas was with them. Jesus showed Thomas his wounds and said to him:

"[D]o not be unbelieving, but believe." Thomas answered and said to him, "My Lord and my God!"
JOHN 20:27–28

He then became a strong believer in Jesus, the Risen Lord.

We believe that Jesus was raised from the dead and lives in a new way. This is a gift of faith.

Doubting Thomas, detail from stained-glass window

373

We Believe in Christ

Look up and read 1 John 5:1–6 in the New Testament. Create a
symbol of your faith in the Risen Christ. Profess your faith in Jesus.
Share and explain your symbol to a partner and to your family.

Called and Sent

At home most of us have chores to do. Our tasks help all our family members and create happiness and harmony within our family. The Gospel tells us that Jesus asks the members of the Church family to serve one another:

> "[A]s I have done for you, you should also do."
>
> JOHN 13:15

The Gospel clearly tells us that Jesus told the Apostles that they were to serve others and not want to be served by others. This was a new type of leadership. It was the way Jesus taught them to live through his own life. They were to lead as he led as a good shepherd.

Today bishops are ordained to serve the Church as Christ served others. They are called to serve as Peter and the other Apostles did. All the baptized are also called to live a life in service of others. This service is lived out daily in our homes, in our schools, and in our communities. Each day is filled with opportunities to serve others as Jesus asked us to do.

Faith Focus

How do members of the Church serve one another?

The Word of the Lord

Choose this year's Gospel reading for the Third Sunday of Easter. Read and discuss it with your family.

Year A
Luke 24:13–35

Year B
Luke 24:35–48

Year C
John 21:1–19 or 21:1–14

Live to Serve

Look at the photos on page 375. Think about how you might live Jesus' command to serve others. Write down some of your ideas. Then choose one and do it.

Ideas

_____
_____
_____
_____

My Choice   When I Will Do It

_____   _____
_____   _____
_____   _____
_____   _____
_____   _____
_____   _____

The Fourth Week of Easter

Faith Focus

How has water brought life to God's people?

The Word of the Lord

Choose this year's Gospel reading for the Fourth Sunday of Easter. Read and discuss it with your family.

Year A
John 10:1–10

Year B
John 10:11–18

Year C
John 10:27–30

Water Brings Us Life

At the Easter Vigil the presider blesses water. The prayers of this blessing remind us of waters that brought life to God's people throughout their history. We celebrate that life when we bless ourselves with holy water.

In the beginning God created the vast seas and the rains that nourish the earth and all its creatures. God led the Hebrews to freedom through the waters of the Red Sea. God brought refreshing waters as his people wandered in the dry, stony desert.

The prophet Ezekiel spoke of water when he wrote of a new Covenant between the people and God:

I will sprinkle clean water upon you . . . . I will cleanse you. I will give you a new heart and place a new spirit within you. . . . [Y]ou shall be my people, and I will be your God. EZEKIEL 36:25–26, 28

The blessing of water at the Easter Vigil also recalls Jesus' baptism in the Jordan River. Water reminds us of our Baptism in the death and Resurrection of Jesus. It reminds us of how we are made new again through the death and Resurrection of Jesus.

Water and New Life

Write a chapter title for a book about ways that water has brought life to God's people. Explain why you chose your title. Share your explanation with a classmate and with your family.

_____

_____

_____

_____

_____

_____

_____

_____

_____

_____

_____

_____

_____

_____

_____

_____

_____

_____

Faith Focus

How can we learn from the early Church to be true followers of Jesus?

The Word of the Lord

Choose this year's Gospel reading for the Fifth Sunday of Easter. Read and discuss it with your family.

Year A
   John 14:1–12

Year B
   John 15:1–8

Year C
   John 13:31–35

Love One Another

When we see someone in need, we can talk about what we have seen. Or we can do something for the person in need. The Church calls us to put our words into action.

During the Sundays of Easter, the first reading of the Liturgy of the Word is always from the Acts of the Apostles. These readings tell us how the early Christians put their faith and words into action.

The early Church remembered that on the night before he died, Jesus gave his disciples a new commandment. He said:

"[L]ove one another. As I have loved you, so you also should love one another. This is how all will know that you are my disciples, if you have love for one another."   JOHN 13:34–35

The First Letter of John in the New Testament reminded the early Christians that their love for God must show in their love for one another. If we refuse to love a person we can see, how can we say that we love God, whom we cannot see?

The first followers of Jesus showed this love in many ways. They took care of those who were most in need. They forgave one another.

They welcomed travelers. They gave them food, clothing, and a warm place to live. They prayed for one another. They brought the healing presence of Christ to those who were sick and troubled.

These welcoming and loving followers of Jesus attracted others who wanted to live in this new way. This is still true today. True followers do not simply talk about the good news of Jesus' Resurrection. They show their love for one another.

Bless this House

This blessing is found on the door of Saint Stephen's Church in London.

O God, make the door of this house wide enough
to receive all who need human love and fellowship,
narrow enough to shut out all envy, pride, and strife.

Make its threshold smooth enough to be no stumbling
block to children, nor to straying feet, but rugged and
strong enough to turn back the tempter's power.

God, make the door of this house
the gateway to your eternal kingdom.

Write a blessing to put on the door of your home.

_____

_____

_____

_____

_____

_____

_____

_____

_____

_____

The Sixth Week of Easter

Faith Focus

How were the Apostles to be witnesses to Jesus?

The Word of the Lord

Choose this year's Gospel reading for the Sixth Sunday of Easter. Read and discuss it with your family.

Year A
John 14:15–21

Year B
John 15:9–17

Year C
John 14:23–29

Ascension of Christ, unknown German painter

Promise of the Holy Spirit

Waiting can be hard. But when someone we love promises to give us something, we trust that the waiting will lead to good things. The Apostles waited for the gift Jesus promised to send them.

After his Resurrection, Jesus appeared to many of his followers. He told them that he would send them the Holy Spirit.

One day Jesus led the Apostles to Bethany outside Jerusalem. He reminded them that he had fulfilled all that was written in the Scriptures: He suffered, died, and was raised to new life.

Jesus reminded the Apostles that they had witnessed all that he had done. He told them that they would be his witnesses throughout Judea and Samaria and to the very ends of the earth. They were to tell others about him.

Then Jesus asked them to wait for the coming of the promised Holy Spirit. He then blessed the Apostles and returned to his Father in heaven.

Witnessing Today

Read each modern-day saying. Look up the matching Scripture passage that tells you how Jesus wants you to be a witness to his life today. Then choose one saying and make up an ad featuring some of Jesus' words.

Modern Sayings	Jesus' Advice
Shop 'til you drop.	Matthew 6:19–21
You can have it all!	Luke 9:57–62
Don't get mad. Get even.	Matthew 5:38–41
Might makes right.	Luke 9:46–48

Faith Focus

What is proclaimed in the Gospel readings during the Easter season?

The Word of the Lord

Choose this year's Gospel reading for the Seventh Sunday of Easter. Read and discuss it with your family.

Year A
 John 17:1–11

Year B
 John 17:11–19

Year C
 John 17:20–26

Good News!

Christ is risen to new life! Alleluia! During the seven weeks in the Easter season, we praise God with greater joy than ever before. We celebrate new life with the Risen Jesus.

The Gospel readings for the seven Sundays of Easter tell us of the appearances Jesus made after his Resurrection.

In John's Gospel, we read that Mary Magdalene saw Jesus and proclaimed to the disciples:

"I have seen the Lord."
JOHN 20:18

In Luke's account of the Gospel, we read that two disciples recognized their Risen Lord in the breaking of bread.

Jesus' Resurrection is good news for us too. We share in the new life of Jesus' Resurrection.

Jesus is our Lord and Savior. Each time we gather to celebrate the Eucharist, we celebrate our faith. We profess our faith in Jesus, our Risen Lord and God.

Easter

Alleluia! He Is Risen!

Share your Easter joy. Sing your Alleluia!

All: **Alleluia. Alleluia. Alleluia.**

First Reader: Give thanks to the Lord, for he is good,
                          for his mercy endures forever.
                   Let the house of Israel say,
                          "His mercy endures forever."

All: **Alleluia. Alleluia. Alleluia.**

Second Reader: The right hand of the Lord has struck
                          with power;
                          the right hand of the Lord is exalted.
                   I shall not die, but live,
                          and declare the works of the Lord.

All: **Alleluia. Alleluia. Alleluia.**

Third Reader: The stone which the builders rejected
                          has become the cornerstone.
                   By the Lord has this been done;
                          it is wonderful in our eyes.

All: **Alleluia. Alleluia. Alleluia.**

BASED ON RESPONSORIAL PSALM
SECOND SUNDAY OF EASTER

Faith Focus

How did the gift of the Holy Spirit on Pentecost strengthen the disciples?

The Word of the Lord

Choose this year's Gospel reading for Pentecost. Read and discuss it with your family.

Year A
John 20:19–23

Year B
John 20:19–23 or John 15:26–27, 16:12–15

Year C
John 20:19–23 or John 14:15–16, 23–26

The Holy Spirit

Can you think of a day when you felt as if you could do anything you set your mind to? What had happened to make you feel that way? Did someone say something to you or give you a gift?

The disciples knew a day like that. They received a great gift that made them strong in their belief in the Risen Lord. That day was Pentecost.

Pentecost is a Jewish harvest festival. On this holy day the Jewish people offer the first fruits of the new harvest to God. At the time of Jesus, Jews traveled to Jerusalem for this great feast.

Detail from stained-glass window depicting Pentecost

The disciples gathered in Jerusalem too. As they prayed together in an upper room, they heard the noise of a great wind. Flames gently settled over their heads.

They were filled with the Holy Spirit. They felt new and strong. They went out and boldly proclaimed the Risen Lord. As they spoke, all the people in the crowd heard the message in their own language. People who could not understand one another before suddenly did! People who were separated drew together. The Holy Spirit came upon the disciples as Jesus promised. The work of the Church, filled with the Holy Spirit, had begun.

My Proclamation

What do you wish all people could know about Jesus?
Write here the Good News you would like to proclaim.
Then pray to the Holy Spirit to help you tell others.

_____

_____

_____

_____

_____

Come, Holy Spirit,
fill the hearts of your faithful
and enkindle in them
the fire of your love.
Send forth your Spirit and
they shall be created, and you
shall renew the face of the earth.

Catholic Prayers and Practices

Sign of the Cross

In the name of the Father,
and of the Son,
and of the Holy Spirit. Amen.

Glory Be

Glory be to the Father
and to the Son
and to the Holy Spirit,
as it was in the beginning
is now, and ever shall be
world without end. Amen.

Lord's Prayer

Our Father, who art in heaven,
hallowed be thy name;
thy kingdom come,
thy will be done
    on earth as it is in heaven.
Give us this day our daily bread,
and forgive us our trespasses,
as we forgive those who trespass
    against us;
and lead us not into temptation,
but deliver us from evil. Amen.

Hail Mary

Hail, Mary, full of grace,
the Lord is with thee.
Blessed art thou among women
and blessed is the fruit of thy
    womb, Jesus.
Holy Mary, Mother of God,
pray for us sinners,
now and at the hour of our death.
Amen.

Signum Crucis

In nómine Patris,
et Fílii,
et Spíritus Sancti. Amen.

Gloria Patri

Glória Patri
et Fílio
et Spirítui Sancto.
Sicut erat in princípio,
et nunc et semper
et in sæcula sæculórum. Amen.

Pater Noster

Pater noster, qui es in cælis:
sanctificétur nomen tuum;
advéniat regnum tuum;
fiat volúntas tua, sicut in cælo,
    et in terra.
Panem nostrum cotidiánum da
    nobis hódie;
et dimítte nobis débita nostra,
sicut et nos dimíttimus
    debitóribus nostris;
et ne nos indúcas in tentatiónem;
sed líbera nos a malo. Amen.

Ave, Maria

Ave, María, grátia plena,
Dóminus tecum.
Benedícta tu in muliéribus,
et benedíctus fructus ventris
    tui, Jesus.
Sancta María, Mater Dei,
ora pro nobis peccatóribus,
nunc et in hora mortis nostræ.
Amen.

The four prayers on this page are in English
and in Latin. Latin is the universal language
of the Roman Catholic Church.

Apostles' Creed

I believe in God,
the Father almighty,
Creator of heaven and earth,
and in Jesus Christ,
 his only Son, our Lord,

*(At the words that follow, up to and
including the Virgin Mary, all bow.)*

who was conceived by the Holy Spirit,
born of the Virgin Mary,
suffered under Pontius Pilate,
was crucified, died and was buried;
he descended into hell;
on the third day he rose again
 from the dead;
he ascended into heaven,
and is seated at the right hand
 of God the Father almighty;
from there he will come to judge
 the living and the dead.

I believe in the Holy Spirit,
the holy catholic Church,
the communion of saints,
the forgiveness of sins,
the resurrection of the body,
and life everlasting. Amen.

Nicene Creed

I believe in one God,
the Father almighty,
maker of heaven and earth,
of all things visible and invisible.

I believe in one Lord Jesus Christ,
the Only Begotten Son of God,
born of the Father before all ages.
God from God, Light from Light,
true God from true God,
begotten, not made, consubstantial
 with the Father;
through him all things were made.
For us men and for our salvation
he came down from heaven,

*(At the words that follow, up to and
including* **and became man,** *all bow.)*

and by the Holy Spirit
 was incarnate of the Virgin Mary,
and became man.

For our sake he was crucified under
 Pontius Pilate,
he suffered death and was buried,
and rose again on the third day
in accordance with the Scriptures.
He ascended into heaven
and is seated at the right hand
 of the Father.
He will come again in glory
to judge the living and the dead
and his kingdom will have no end.

I believe in the Holy Spirit, the Lord,
 the giver of life,
who proceeds from the Father and the Son,
who with the Father and the Son
 is adored and glorified,
who has spoken through the prophets.

I believe in one, holy, catholic and
 apostolic Church.
I confess one Baptism
 for the forgiveness of sins
and I look forward to the resurrection
 of the dead
and the life of the world to come.
Amen.

Morning Prayer

Dear God,
as I begin this day,
keep me in your love and care.
Help me to live as your child today.
Bless me, my family, and my friends
   in all we do.
Keep us all close to you. Amen.

Evening Prayer

Dear God,
I thank you for today.
Keep me safe throughout the night.
Thank you for all the good I did today.
I am sorry for what I have chosen
   to do wrong.
Bless my family and friends. Amen.

Grace Before Meals

Bless us, O Lord,
   and these thy gifts,
which we are about to receive
   from thy bounty,
through Christ our Lord.
Amen.

Grace After Meals

We give thee thanks, for all thy benefits,
   almighty God,
who lives and reigns forever.
Amen.

A Vocation Prayer

God, I know you will call me
for special work in my life.
Help me follow Jesus each day
and be ready to answer your call.

Act of Faith

O my God, I firmly believe that you are
one God in three divine Persons, Father,
Son, and Holy Spirit; I believe that your
divine Son became man and died for our
sins, and that he will come to judge the
living and the dead. Amen.

Act of Hope

O my God, relying on your infinite
goodness and promises, I hope to obtain
pardon of my sins, the help of your grace,
and life everlasting, through the merits of
Jesus Christ, my Lord and Redeemer.
Amen.

Act of Love

O my God, I love you above all things,
with my whole heart and soul, because
you are all good and worthy of all my love.
I love my neighbor as myself for the love
of you. I forgive all who have injured me
and I ask pardon of all whom I have
injured. Amen.

The Divine Praises

Blessed be God.
Blessed be his holy name.
Blessed be Jesus Christ, true God
   and true man.
Blessed be the name of Jesus.
Blessed be his most Sacred Heart.
Blessed be his most precious Blood.
Blessed be Jesus in the most holy Sacrament
   of the altar.
Blessed be the Holy Spirit, the Paraclete.
Blessed be the great Mother of God,
   Mary most holy.
Blessed be her holy and Immaculate
   Conception.
Blessed be her glorious Assumption.
Blessed be the name of Mary, Virgin
   and Mother.
Blessed be Saint Joseph, her most
   chaste spouse.
Blessed be God in his angels and in his saints.

Prayer of Saint Francis

Lord, make me an instrument
   of your peace:
where there is hatred,
   let me sow love;
where there is injury, pardon;
where there is doubt, faith;
where there is despair, hope;
where there is darkness, light;
where there is sadness, joy.

O divine Master, grant that
   I may not so much seek
to be consoled as to console,
to be understood as to understand,
to be loved as to love.
For it is in giving that we receive,
it is in pardoning that
   we are pardoned,
it is in dying that we are born
   to eternal life.
Amen.

The Angelus

Leader: The Angel of the Lord declared
   unto Mary,
Response: And she conceived of the
   Holy Spirit.
All: Hail Mary . . .

Leader: Behold the handmaid of the Lord,
Response: Be it done unto me according to
   your Word.
All: Hail Mary . . .

Leader: And the Word was made flesh
Response: And dwelt among us.
All: Hail Mary . . .

Leader: Pray for us, O holy Mother
   of God,
Response: That we may be made worthy of the
   promises of Christ.

Leader: Let us pray.
Pour forth, we beseech you,
O Lord, your grace into our
hearts: that we, to whom the
Incarnation of Christ your
Son was made known by the
message of an Angel, may
by his Passion and Cross be
brought to the glory of his
Resurrection. Through the
same Christ our Lord.
All: Amen.

The Great Commandment

"You shall love the Lord, your God, with all your heart, with all your soul, and with all your mind. . . . You shall love your neighbor as yourself."

MATTHEW 22:37, 39

The New Commandment

[Jesus said:] "I give you a new commandment: love one another. As I have loved you, so you also should love one another. This is how all will know that you are my disciples, if you have love for one another."

JOHN 13:34–35

The Ten Commandments

1. I am the LORD your God: you shall not have strange gods before me.
2. You shall not take the name of the LORD your God in vain.
3. Remember to keep holy the LORD's Day.
4. Honor your father and your mother.
5. You shall not kill.
6. You shall not commit adultery.
7. You shall not steal.
8. You shall not bear false witness against your neighbor.
9. You shall not covet your neighbor's wife.
10. You shall not covet your neighbor's goods.

The Beatitudes

"Blessed are the poor in spirit,
for theirs is the kingdom of heaven.
Blessed are they who mourn,
for they will be comforted.
Blessed are the meek,
for they will inherit the land.
Blessed are they who hunger
and thirst for righteousness,
for they will be satisfied.
Blessed are the merciful,
for they will be shown mercy.
Blessed are the clean of heart,
for they will see God.
Blessed are the peacemakers,
for they will be called children of God.
Blessed are they who are persecuted
for the sake of righteousness,
for theirs is the kingdom of heaven.

Blessed are you when they insult you
and persecute you and utter every kind
of evil against you [falsely] because of me.
Rejoice and be glad, for your reward will
be great in heaven."

MATTHEW 5:3–12

Corporal Works of Mercy

Feed people who are hungry.
Give drink to people who are thirsty.
Clothe people who need clothes.
Visit prisoners.
Shelter people who are homeless.
Visit people who are sick.
Bury people who have died.

Spiritual Works of Mercy

Help people who sin.
Teach people who are ignorant.
Give advice to people
    who have doubts.
Comfort people who suffer.
Be patient with other people.
Forgive people who hurt you.
Pray for people who are alive and for
    those who have died.

Gifts of the Holy Spirit

Wisdom
Understanding
Right judgment (Counsel)
Courage (Fortitude)
Knowledge
Reverence (Piety)
Wonder and awe (Fear of the Lord)

Cardinal Virtues

Prudence
Justice
Fortitude
Temperance

Precepts of the Church

1. Participate in Mass on Sundays and holy days of obligation and rest from unnecessary work.

2. Confess sins at least once a year.

3. Receive Holy Communion at least during the Easter season.

4. Observe the prescribed days of fasting and abstinence.

5. Provide for the material needs of the Church, each according to one's abilities.

Basic Principles of the Church's Teaching on Social Justice

The Church's teaching on social justice guides us in living lives of holiness and building a just society. These principles are:

1. All human life is sacred. The basic equality of all people flows from their dignity as human persons and the rights that flow from that dignity.
2. The human person is the principle, the object, and the subject of every social group.
3. The human person has been created by God to belong to and to participate in a family and other social communities.
4. Respect for the rights of people flows from their dignity as persons. Society and all social organizations must promote virtue and protect human life and human rights and guarantee the conditions that promote the exercise of freedom.
5. Political communities and public authority are based on human nature. They belong to an order established by God.
6. All human authority must be used for the common good of society.
7. The common good of society consists of respect for and promotion of the fundamental rights of the human person; the just development of material and spiritual goods of society; and the peace and safety of all people.
8. We need to work to eliminate the sinful inequalities that exist between peoples and for the improvement of the living conditions of people. The needs of the poor and vulnerable have a priority.
9. We are one human and global family. We are to share our spiritual blessings, even more than our material blessings.

Based on the *Catechism of the Catholic Church*

Rosary

Catholics pray the Rosary to honor Mary and remember the important events in the lives of Jesus and Mary. There are twenty mysteries of the rosary. Follow the steps from 1 to 5.

3. Think of the first mystery. Pray an Our Father, 10 Hail Marys, and the Glory Be.

5. Pray the Hail, Holy Queen prayer. Make the Sign of the Cross.

2. Pray an Our Father, 3 Hail Marys, and the Glory Be.

4. Repeat step 3 for each of the next 4 mysteries.

1. Make the Sign of the Cross and pray the Apostles' Creed.

Joyful Mysteries

1. The Annunciation
2. The Visitation
3. The Nativity
4. The Presentation in the Temple
5. The Finding of the Child Jesus After Three Days in the Temple

Luminous Mysteries

1. The Baptism at the Jordan
2. The Miracle at Cana
3. The Proclamation of the Kingdom and the Call to Conversion
4. The Transfiguration
5. The Institution of the Eucharist

Sorrowful Mysteries

1. The Agony in the Garden
2. The Scourging at the Pillar
3. The Crowning with Thorns
4. The Carrying of the Cross
5. The Crucifixion and Death

Glorious Mysteries

1. The Resurrection
2. The Ascension
3. The Descent of the Holy Spirit at Pentecost
4. The Assumption of Mary
5. The Crowning of the Blessed Virgin as Queen of Heaven and Earth

Hail, Holy Queen

Hail, holy Queen, Mother of mercy:
Hail, our life, our sweetness and our hope.
To you do we cry, poor banished
    children of Eve.
To you do we send up our sighs,
mourning and weeping
    in this valley of tears.
Turn then, most gracious advocate,
your eyes of mercy toward us;
and after this our exile
show unto us the blessed fruit
    of your womb, Jesus.
O clement, O loving, O sweet Virgin Mary.

Stations of the Cross

1. Jesus is condemned to death.

2. Jesus accepts his cross.

3. Jesus falls the first time.

4. Jesus meets his mother.

5. Simon helps Jesus carry the cross.

6. Veronica wipes the face of Jesus.

7. Jesus falls the second time.

8. Jesus meets the women.

9. Jesus falls the third time.

10. Jesus is stripped of his clothes.

11. Jesus is nailed to the cross.

12. Jesus dies on the cross.

13. Jesus is taken down from the cross.

14. Jesus is buried in the tomb.

Some parishes conclude the Stations by reflecting on the Resurrection of Jesus.

The Seven Sacraments

Jesus gave the Church the seven sacraments. The sacraments are the main liturgical signs of the Church. They make the Paschal Mystery of Jesus, who is always the main celebrant of each sacrament, present to us. They make us sharers in the saving work of Christ and in the life of the Holy Trinity.

Sacraments of Christian Initiation

Baptism

Through Baptism we are joined to Christ and become members of the Body of Christ, the Church. We are reborn as adopted children of God the Father and receive the gift of the Holy Spirit. Original sin and all personal sins are forgiven.

Confirmation

Confirmation completes Baptism. In this sacrament the gift of the Holy Spirit strengthens us to live our Baptism.

Eucharist

Sharing in the Eucharist joins us most fully to Christ and to the Church. We share in the one sacrifice of Christ. The bread and wine become the Body and Blood of Christ through the power of the Holy Spirit and the words of the priest. We receive the Body and Blood of Christ.

Sacraments of Healing

Penance and Reconciliation

Through the ministry of the priest we receive forgiveness of sins committed after our Baptism. We need to confess all mortal sins.

Anointing of the Sick

Anointing of the Sick strengthens our faith and trust in God when we are seriously ill, dying, or weak because of old age.

Sacraments at the Service of Communion

Holy Orders

Through Holy Orders a baptized man is consecrated to serve the whole Church as a bishop, priest, or deacon in the name of Christ. Bishops, who are the successors of the Apostles, receive this sacrament most fully. They are consecrated to teach the Gospel, to lead the Church in the worship of God, and to guide the Church to live holy lives. Bishops are helped by priests, their coworkers, and by deacons in their work.

Matrimony

Matrimony unites a baptized man and a baptized woman in a lifelong bond of faithful love to always honor each other and to accept the gift of children from God. In this sacrament the married couple is consecrated to be a sign of Christ's love for the Church.

We Celebrate the Mass

The Introductory Rites

**We remember that we are the members
of the Church. We prepare to listen to the Word of God
and to celebrate the Eucharist.**

The Entrance

We stand as the priest, deacon, and other ministers enter the assembly. We sing a gathering song. The priest and deacon kiss the altar. The priest then goes to the chair where he presides over the celebration.

Sign of the Cross and Greeting

The priest leads us in praying the Sign of the Cross. The priest greets us, and we say,
"And with your spirit."

The Penitential Act

We admit our wrongdoings.
We bless God for his mercy.

The Gloria

We praise God for all the good he has done for us.

The Collect

The priest leads us in praying the Collect. We respond, **"Amen."**

The Liturgy of the Word

**God speaks to us today.
We listen and respond to God's word.**

The First Reading from the Bible

We sit and listen as the reader reads from the Old Testament or from the Acts of the Apostles. The reader concludes, "The word of the Lord." We respond,
"Thanks be to God."

The Responsorial Psalm

The song leader leads us in singing a psalm.

The Second Reading from the Bible

The reader reads from the New Testament, but not from the four Gospels. The reader concludes, "The word of the Lord." We respond,
"Thanks be to God."

Acclamation

We stand to honor Christ present with us in the Gospel. The song leader leads us in singing **"Alleluia, Alleluia, Alleluia"** or another chant during Lent.

The Gospel

The deacon or priest proclaims, "A reading from the holy Gospel according to (name of Gospel writer)." We respond,
"Glory to you, O Lord."

He proclaims the Gospel. At the end, he says, "The Gospel of the Lord." We respond,
"Praise to you, Lord Jesus Christ."

The Homily

We sit. The priest or deacon preaches the homily. He helps the whole community understand the Word of God spoken to us in the readings.

The Profession of Faith

We stand and profess our faith.
We pray the Nicene Creed together.

The Prayer of the Faithful

The priest leads us in praying for our Church and its leaders, for our country and its leaders, for ourselves and others, for the sick and those who have died. We can respond to each prayer in several ways. One way we respond is,
"Lord, hear our prayer."

The Liturgy of the Eucharist
We join with Jesus and the Holy Spirit to give thanks and praise to God the Father.

The Preparation of the Gifts

We sit as the altar table is prepared and the collection is taken up. We share our blessings with the members of the Church and especially with those in need. The song leader may lead us in singing a song. The gifts of bread and wine are brought to the altar.

The priest lifts up the bread and blesses God for all our gifts. He prays, "Blessed are you, Lord God of all creation, . . ."
We respond,
"Blessed be God for ever."

The priest lifts up the cup of wine and prays, "Blessed are you, Lord God of all creation, . . ." We respond,
"Blessed be God for ever."

The priest invites us,
"Pray, brethren (brothers and sisters),
   that my sacrifice and yours
may be acceptable to God,
   the almighty Father."

We stand and respond,
**"May the Lord accept the sacrifice at your hands
for the praise and glory of his name,
for our good and the good of all his holy Church."**

The Prayer over the Offerings

The priest leads us in praying the Prayer over the Offerings. We respond, **"Amen."**

Preface

The priest invites us to join in praying the Church's great prayer of praise and thanksgiving to God the Father.
Priest: "The Lord be with you."
Assembly: **"And with your spirit."**
Priest: "Lift up your hearts."
Assembly: **"We lift them up to the Lord."**

Priest: "Let us give thanks to the Lord our God."
Assembly: **"It is right and just."**

After the priest sings or prays aloud the Preface, we join in acclaiming,
**Holy, Holy, Holy Lord God of hosts.
Heaven and earth are full of
   your glory.
Hosanna in the highest.
Blessed is he who comes in
   the name of the Lord.
Hosanna in the highest.**

The Eucharistic Prayer

The priest leads the assembly in praying the Eucharistic Prayer. We call upon the Holy Spirit to make our gifts of bread and wine holy and that they become the Body and Blood of Jesus. We recall what happened at the Last Supper. The bread and wine become the Body and Blood of the Lord. Jesus is truly and really present under the appearances of bread and wine.

The priest sings or says aloud,
"The mystery of faith." We respond using this or another acclamation used by the Church,
**"We proclaim your Death, O Lord,
and profess your Resurrection
until you come again."**

The priest then prays for the Church. He prays for the living and the dead.

Doxology

The priest concludes the praying of the Eucharistic Prayer. He sings or prays aloud,
Through him, and with him, and in him,
O God, almighty Father,
in the unity of the Holy Spirit,
all glory and honor is yours,
for ever and ever.
We stand and respond, **"Amen."**

The Communion Rite

The Lord's Prayer

We pray the Lord's Prayer together.

The Rite of Peace

The priest invites us to share a sign of peace, saying, "The peace of the Lord be with you always." We respond, **"And with your spirit."** We share a sign of peace.

The Fraction, or the Breaking of the Bread

The priest breaks the host, the consecrated bread. We sing or pray aloud,

**"Lamb of God, you take away
the sins of the world,
have mercy on us.
Lamb of God, you take away
the sins of the world,
have mercy on us.
Lamb of God, you take away
the sins of the world,
grant us peace."**

Communion

The priest raises the host and says aloud, "Behold the Lamb of God, behold him who takes away the sins of the world. Blessed are those called to the supper of the Lamb." We join with him and say,

"Lord, I am not worthy that you should enter under my roof, but only say the word and my soul shall be healed."

The priest receives Communion. Next, the deacon and the extraordinary ministers of Holy Communion and the members of the assembly receive Communion.

The priest, deacon, or extraordinary minister of Holy Communion holds up the host. We bow and the priest, deacon, or extraordinary minister of Holy Communion says, "The Body of Christ." We respond, **"Amen."** We then receive the consecrated host in our hand or on our tongue.

If we are to receive the Blood of Christ, the priest, deacon, or extraordinary minister of Holy Communion holds up the cup containing the consecrated wine. We bow and the priest, deacon, or extraordinary minister of Holy Communion says, "The Blood of Christ." We respond, **"Amen."** We take the cup in our hands and drink from it.

The Prayer after Communion

We stand as the priest invites us to pray, saying, "Let us pray." He prays the Prayer after Communion. We respond, **"Amen."**

The Concluding Rites

**We are sent forth to do good works,
praising and blessing the Lord.**

Greeting

We stand. The priest greets us as
we prepare to leave. He says, "The
Lord be with you." We respond,
"And with your spirit."

Blessing

The priest or deacon may invite us,
  "Bow down for the blessing."
The priest blesses us, saying,
  "May almighty God bless you,
  the Father, and the Son, and the Holy
    Spirit."
We respond, **"Amen."**

Dismissal of the People

The priest or deacon sends us forth,
using these or similar words,
  "Go and announce
    the Gospel of the Lord."
We respond,
  "Thanks be to God."

We sing a hymn. The priest and the
deacon kiss the altar. The priest, deacon,
and other ministers bow to the altar and
leave in procession.

We Celebrate Penance and Reconciliation

Individual Rite

Greeting

Scripture Reading

Confession of Sins and Acceptance
  of Penance

Act of Contrition

Absolution

Closing Prayer

Communal Rite

Greeting

Scripture Reading

Homily

Examination of Conscience with a litany
  of contrition and the Lord's Prayer

Individual Confession and Absolution

Closing Prayer

Act of Contrition

My God,
I am sorry for my sins
  with all my heart.
In choosing to do wrong
and failing to do good,
I have sinned against you
whom I should love above all things.
I firmly intend, with your help,
to do penance,
to sin no more,
and to avoid whatever leads me to sin.
Our Savior Jesus Christ
suffered and died for us.
In his name, my God, have mercy.

FROM RITE OF PENANCE

The Books of the Bible

The Old Testament

Law (Torah) or Pentateuch

Genesis	(Gn)
Exodus	(Ex)
Leviticus	(Lv)
Numbers	(Nm)
Deuteronomy	(Dt)

Historical Books

Joshua	(Jos)
Judges	(Jgs)
Ruth	(Ru)
First Book of Samuel	(1 Sm)
Second Book of Samuel	(2 Sm)
First Book of Kings	(1 Kgs)
Second Book of Kings	(2 Kgs)
First Book of Chronicles	(1 Chr)
Second Book of Chronicles	(2 Chr)
Ezra	(Ezr)
Nehemiah	(Neh)
Tobit	(Tb)
Judith	(Jdt)
Esther	(Est)
First Book of Maccabees	(1 Mc)
Second Book of Maccabees	(2 Mc)

The Poetry and Wisdom Books

Job	(Jb)
Psalms	(Ps)
Proverbs	(Prv)
Ecclesiastes	(Eccl)
Song of Songs	(Sg)
Wisdom	(Wis)
Sirach/Ecclesiasticus	(Sir)

Prophets

Isaiah	(Is)
Jeremiah	(Jer)
Lamentations	(Lam)
Baruch	(Bar)
Ezekiel	(Ez)
Daniel	(Dn)
Hosea	(Hos)
Joel	(Jl)
Amos	(Am)
Obadiah	(Ob)
Jonah	(Jon)
Micah	(Mi)
Nahum	(Na)
Habakkuk	(Hb)
Zephaniah	(Zep)
Haggai	(Hg)
Zechariah	(Zec)
Malachi	(Mal)

The New Testament

The Gospels

Matthew	(Mt)
Mark	(Mk)
Luke	(Lk)
John	(Jn)

Early Church

Acts of the Apostles	(Acts)

Letters of Paul and Other Letters

Romans	(Rom)
First Letter to the Corinthians	(1 Cor)
Second Letter to the Corinthians	(2 Cor)
Galatians	(Gal)
Ephesians	(Eph)
Philippians	(Phil)
Colossians	(Col)
First Letter to the Thessalonians	(1 Thes)
Second Letter to the Thessalonians	(2 Thes)
First Letter to Timothy	(1 Tm)
Second Letter to Timothy	(2 Tm)
Titus	(Ti)
Philemon	(Phlm)
Hebrews	(Heb)
James	(Jas)
First Letter of Peter	(1 Pt)
Second Letter of Peter	(2 Pt)
First Letter of John	(1 Jn)
Second Letter of John	(2 Jn)
Third Letter of John	(3 Jn)
Jude	(Jude)

Revelation

Revelation	(Rv)

Glossary

Abba [page 14]
A word meaning "Father," expressing the unconditional trust of a child in a parent's love; the name Jesus used for God the Father, revealing the love and trust that exists between Jesus and God the Father.

Advocate [page 69]
A word meaning "one who is at our side," or "one who speaks for us"; title or name for the Holy Spirit, used by Jesus in John's Gospel.

Annunciation [page 111]
A word meaning "announcement"; the announcement to the Virgin Mary by the angel Gabriel that God had chosen her to be the Mother of Jesus, the Son of God, by the power of the Holy Spirit.

Anointing of the Sick [page 216]
The Sacrament of Healing that strengthens our faith, hope, and love for God when we are seriously ill, weakened by old age, or dying.

Apostles' Creed [page 18]
A summary of the faith of the Church handed down from the time of the Apostles.

apostolic succession [page 89]
The unbroken connection between the pope and Saint Peter and between the bishops of the Church and the other Apostles.

Ascension [pages 66, 67]
A word meaning "a going up," the return of the Risen Christ in glory to his Father.

assembly [page 140]
The community of the Church gathered to celebrate the sacraments and the liturgy.

Assumption [page 112]
The taking up of Mary's body and soul to heaven where she already shares in the glory of her Son.

Baptism [page 164]
The Sacrament of Christian Initiation in which we are joined to Jesus Christ, become members of the Church, are reborn as God's adopted children, receive the gift of the Holy Spirit, and original sin and our personal sins are forgiven.

Beatitudes [page 247]
A word meaning "ways of happiness or blessedness"; the sayings or teachings of Jesus that are found in the Sermon on the Mount and describe both the qualities and actions of people blessed by God.

bishop [page 226]
A successor of the Apostles; one who has received the fullness of the sacrament of Holy Orders and is a member of the order of bishops, or the episcopal college.

Body of Christ [page 100]
An image for the Church used by Paul the Apostle that teaches that all the members of the Church are one in Christ, the Head of the Church, and that all members have a unique and important role in the work of the Church.

Body and Blood of Christ [page 193]
The Eucharist; Christ's true and real presence under the appearances of bread and wine.

Book of Psalms [page 311]
The Old Testament book of the Bible containing 150 prayers in the form of poems and songs.

canon of Scripture [page 27]
The books identified and named by the Church as the inspired Word of God that have been collected together in the Bible.

capital sins [page 258]
Seven sins named by the Church that are the sources of other sins; pride, covetousness, envy, anger, gluttony, lust, and sloth.

charisms [page 100]
Graces, or gifts, given by the Holy Spirit to build up the Church on earth for the good of all people and the needs of the world.

Christ [pages 62]
Anointed One, title of Jesus identifying that he is the Anointed One of God, the Messiah who God promised to send to save his people.

Church [page 86]
The Body of Christ, the Temple of the Holy Spirit, the Bride of Christ, the new People of God the Father called together in Jesus Christ by the power of the Holy Spirit.

communion [page 224]
A word meaning "sharing with"; the unity in Christ of all the members of the Church, the Body of Christ.

Communion of Saints [page 99]
All the faithful followers of Jesus, both the living and the dead, those on earth, in purgatory, and in heaven.

confession [page 213]
The telling of sins to a priest in the Sacrament of Reconciliation, an essential part of the Sacrament of Reconciliation, another name for the Sacrament of Reconciliation.

Confirmation [page 166]
The Sacrament of Christian Initiation that strengthens the grace of Baptism and in which our life in Christ is sealed by the gift of the Holy Spirit.

conscience [page 256]
The gift of God that is part of every person that guides us to know and judge what is right and wrong.

consecrate [page 180]
Set aside and dedicate for a holy purpose.

contemplation [page 324]
An expression of prayer in which the mind and heart focus on the love and infinite goodness of God in loving adoration.

contrition [page 213]
Sorrow for sins, which includes the desire to make up for the harm our sin has caused; an essential part of the Sacrament of Reconciliation.

Covenant [page 30]
The solemn commitment of fidelity that God and the People of God made with one another, which was renewed in Christ, the new and everlasting Covenant.

covet [page 280]
To unjustly desire what rightfully belongs to someone else.

creed [page 18]
A statement of beliefs, a profession of faith; a summary of the principle beliefs of the Church.

Crucifixion [page 66]
The event of Jesus' saving death on the cross.

deacon [page 226]
One who has received the Sacrament of Holy Orders and belongs to the order of deacons, or the diaconate; coworker with the bishops and priests.

Decalogue [page 267]
The Ten Commandments.

disciple [page 62]
One who learns from and follows the teachings of another person.

distractions to prayer [page 312]
Thoughts and ideas that pull us away from prayer.

Divine Revelation [page 14]
God making himself and the divine plan of creation and salvation known over time.

E-F-G-H

epistle [page 74]
Lengthy and formal type of letter found in the New Testament.

Ephesians [page 76]
The people who lived in the city of Ephesus, which today is in the nation of Turkey.

eternal [page 52]
Having no end; timeless; everlasting.

Eucharist [page 192]
The Sacrament of the Body and Blood of Christ; the Sacrament of Christian Initiation in which we receive the Body and Blood of Christ, who is truly and really present under the appearances of bread and wine, and in which we are most fully joined to Christ and to the Church, the Body of Christ.

Evangelists [page 122]
A word meaning "announcers of good news"; Matthew, Mark, Luke, and John; the writers of the four inspired accounts of the Gospel, which are in the New Testament.

evangelization [page 338]
The Church's responsibility to share the Gospel with all people "so that it may enter the hearts of all men and renew the human race."

Exile [page 40]
The time in the history of God's people when many of them were forced to leave their homeland and live in the country of their conquerors.

Exodus [pages 17, 189]
The saving intervention of God in the history of God's people; the saving of the Hebrews from slavery in Egypt, making of the Covenant with them, and leading them to freedom in the land he promised them.

faith [page 16]
A supernatural gift and power from God; the gift of God's invitation to us that enables us to know and believe in him, and the power God gives us to freely respond to his invitation.

fidelity [page 38]
A word meaning "faithfulness," the virtue of keeping our promises and fulfilling our responsibilities to God and to other people.

forms of prayer [page 310]
The five types of prayer revealed in Sacred Scripture that are the norm for Christian prayer; adoration and blessing, petition, intercession, thanksgiving, and praise.

Gospels [page 122]
The first four books of the New Testament, which pass on the faith of the Church in Jesus Christ and in the saving events of his life, Passion, death, Resurrection, and Ascension.

grace [page 244]
The gift of God's life and love that makes us holy and helps us live a holy life.

heaven [page 126]
Everlasting life in communion with God the Holy Trinity, and with Mary, the angels, and all the holy people who live in eternal happiness.

holiness [page 242]
The quality, or condition, of a person who is living in communion with and in the right relationship with God, others, and with all of his creation; being in the state of grace.

Holy Orders [page 226]
The Sacrament at the Service of Communion through which a baptized man is consecrated to serve the whole Church as a bishop, priest, or deacon.

Holy Spirit [page 51]
The third Person of the Holy Trinity, the Advocate sent to us by the Father in the name of his Son, Jesus Christ.

Holy Trinity [page 50]
The mystery of one God in three divine Persons—God the Father, God the Son, God the Holy Spirit.

hope [page 38]
The theological virtue by which we desire and trust that God will fulfill all his promises, especially the promise of eternal happiness.

I-J-K-L

Immaculate Conception [page 112]
Mary's freedom from all sin, both original sin and all personal sin, from the first moment of her existence, or conception, and throughout her entire life.

Incarnation [page 65]
The term the Church uses to name the faith of the Church that the Son of God became fully human in all things except sin, while remaining fully divine.

inspiration of the Bible [page 26]
The Holy Spirit guiding the human writers of Sacred Scripture so that they would faithfully and accurately communicate the word of God, who is the principal author of the Scriptures.

invocations [page 308]
Brief prayers we can learn by heart and pray throughout the day.

Israelites [pages, 17, 26–29]
The Old Testament people to whom God revealed himself and with whom he made the Covenant.

judges of Israel [page 176]
The leaders of Israel before they had kings—Othniel, Ehud, Deborah and Barak, Gideon, Abimelech, Jephthah, and Samson are among the judges of Israel whose stories are told in the Book of Judges.

justice [page 282]
One of the moral, or cardinal, virtues; the good habit of giving to God and to all people what is rightfully due to them.

Kingdom of God [page 102]
The fulfillment of God's plan for all creation in Christ at the end of time when Christ will come again in glory.

Last Judgment [page 127]
The judgment at the end of time when all the saints will be invited to eternal life in heaven and our bodies will be reunited with our souls.

liturgical year [page 144]
The Church's yearly cycle of seasons and feasts that celebrate the mysteries of Jesus' birth, life, death, and Resurrection.

liturgy [page 140]
The Church's work of worshiping God.

Lord [page 332]
A title for Jesus that states he is truly God.

Lord's Day [page 157]
The name given to Sunday, the day of the Lord's Resurrection.

M-N-O

manna [page 188]
White breadlike flakes or grains with a taste like flour and honey.

Marks of the Church [page 88]
One, holy, catholic, apostolic; the four signs and essential qualities of the Church and her mission founded by Jesus Christ.

Mass [page 190]
The main sacramental celebration of the Church at which we gather to listen to God's word and through which we share in the saving death of Christ and give praise and glory to the Father.

Matrimony [page 228]
The Sacrament at the Service of Communion that unites a baptized man and a baptized woman in a lifelong bond, or covenant, of faithful love to serve the Church as a sign of Christ's love for the Church.

meditation [page 324]
An expression of prayer using our imagination, mind, and desire to live our new life in Christ.

Messiah [pages 64, 65]
A word meaning "Anointed One"; Jesus, the Anointed One of God, the Messiah, the Savior of the world.

moral decisions [page 254]
The decisions and choices we make to live as children of God and disciples of Jesus Christ.

moral virtues [page 43]
Prudence, justice, fortitude, and temperance; also called the cardinal virtues since other virtues "hinge" on them; human virtues acquired by human effort and practice.

morality [page 254]
A way of judging, or evaluating, whether our choices lead us to God or away from him.

mortal sin [page 258]
A serious failure in our love and respect for God, our neighbor, creation, and ourselves. Three things are necessary for a sin to be mortal, namely, (1) the thing we do or say must be gravely wrong; (2) we must know it is gravely wrong; (3) we must freely chose it.

mystery [page 50]
Unknown or unknowable. God is, and his loving plan for us is, a mystery. We only know who God is and what his plan for us is because he revealed it, or made it known to us.

Nicene Creed [page 19]
A creed, or brief statement of the faith of the Church, written in the fourth century.

obey [page 278]
To follow the advice and commands of others who use their lawful authority properly to guide us in living according to the Law of God.

oral tradition [page 290]
The passing on of stories and teachings by word of mouth.

original sin [page 54]
The sin of Adam and Even, by which they and all people lost the state of original holiness, and by which death, sin, and suffering entered the world.

P-Q

parable [page 200]
A form of story that compares one thing to another to help listeners understand the main point of the story.

particular judgment [page 126]
The judgment of one's life by God at the moment of a person's death at which a person is assigned to heaven, purgatory, or hell.

Paschal Mystery [page 66]
The Passion, death, Resurrection, and glorious Ascension of Jesus Christ; the "passing over" of Jesus from death into a new and glorious life.

Passover [page 154]
The Jewish feast that celebrates the sparing of the Hebrew children from death, and God's saving his people from slavery in Egypt and leading them to freedom in the land he promised them.

penance [see Reconciliation]
Prayer or act of kindness that shows we are truly sorry for our sins; an essential part of the Sacrament of Penance, or Reconciliation.

Pentateuch [page 26]
Word meaning "five containers," the first five books of the Old Testament: Genesis, Exodus, Leviticus, Numbers, and Deuteronomy; also called the Torah.

Pentecost [page 86]
A word meaning "fiftieth day"; the liturgical feast and holy day when the Church celebrates the coming of the Holy Spirit on the disciples and the birth of the Church.

People of God [page 98]
Biblical image for the Church; the people God has gathered and chosen to be his own; the people through whom God has revealed himself most fully and has invited all nations to live as the one family of God.

prayer life [page 320]
The habit of making prayer part of the rhythm of our day.

precepts [page 266]
Rules or laws that detail responsibilities and impose standards of conduct.

Precepts of the Church [page 270]
Positive laws made by the Church guiding the faithful to meet their minimal responsibilities in prayer and moral living for their growth in living the Great Commandment of love of God and neighbor.

priest [page 226]
One who has received the sacrament of Holy Orders, a member of the order of priests, or presbyterate; coworker with the bishop.

prophet [page 38]
One chosen by God to speak in his name; one who speaks divinely inspired words.

proverb [page 292]
A short, concise saying stating a well-accepted fact or criterion for making a wise decision.

prudence [page 42]
One of the four moral virtues, a virtue that helps us know what is truly good for us and how to choose the right way of achieving that good.

Psalms [pages 310, 311]
Prayer-songs found in the Old Testament Book of Psalms, or the Psalter.

public ministry of Jesus [page 86]
The work that God the Father sent Jesus, the Son of God, to do on earth with the help of the Holy Spirit.

R–S

Reconciliation [page 212]
The Sacrament of Healing through which we receive God's forgiveness through the ministry of a priest for sins that we have committed after Baptism.

Redeemer [page 65]
Jesus Christ.

Redemption [page 19]
The saving act of God setting humanity free from slavery to sin and from death through the power of the sacrifice of Jesus Christ on the cross.

respect [page 278]
The virtue, or good habit, of giving esteem to others due to them because they are images of God.

Resurrection [page 86]
The event of Jesus being raised from the dead to a new and glorified life.

rituals [page 152]
The combination of words and actions used in the celebration of the liturgy.

Rosary [page 114]
A prayer of meditation on the life of Mary and Jesus and the mystery of Salvation.

Sabbath [page 154]
The day of rest, the seventh day of the week, that the Israelites dedicated to God and that the Jewish people today dedicate to God as a day of rest and a holy day.

sacraments [page 140]
The seven main liturgical signs of the Church, given to us by Jesus Christ, that make his saving work present to us and make us sharers in the life of God, the Holy Trinity.

Sacraments at the Service of Communion [page 224]
The two Sacraments of Holy Orders and Matrimony.

Sacraments of Healing [pages 211–218]
Reconciliation, or Penance, and Anointing of the Sick.

Sacraments of Christian Initiation [page 164]
Baptism, Confirmation, and Eucharist.

Sacred Scripture [page 15]
Two words that mean "holy writings," the holy writings of God that the Holy Spirit inspired the people of God to write and that have been collected by the Church in the Bible.

Sacred Tradition [pages 14, 99]
The passing on of the Gospel in the Church through the power and guidance of the Holy Spirit.

sacrifice [page 359]
Freely giving up something of value out of love for God.

Salvation [page 62]
The deliverance of humanity from the power of sin and death by God through Jesus Christ who "died for our sins in accordance with the Scriptures."

Sermon on the Mount [page 334]
The summary of the teachings of Jesus on discipleship that are grouped in chapters 5, 6, and 7 of Matthew's Gospel.

sexuality [page 280]
The gift of being male or female—a boy or a man, or a girl or a woman.

sin [page 212]
Freely choosing to do what we know is against God's will or freely choosing not to do something we know God wants us to do.

soul [page 52]
The spiritual dimension of the human person that never dies, or is immortal.

T–Z

temptation [page 54]
Everything that tries to move us to do or say something we know is wrong or from doing something good we know we can and should do, all that moves us away from living a holy life.

Ten Commandments [pages 266–271]
The laws of the Covenant God revealed to Moses and the Israelites on Mount Sinai.

theological virtues [page 242]
The virtues of faith, hope, and love (charity); gifts of God that enable us to live a life of holiness, or a life in communion with the Holy Trinity.

venial sin [page 259]
A sin less serious than a mortal sin; a sin that does not have all the three things necessary for a sin to be mortal.

virtues [page 38]
Spiritual powers or habits or behaviors that help us do what is right and avoid what is wrong.

Wisdom [pages 291, 294]
A name for God in Sacred Scripture.

wisdom [page 42]
One of the seven Gifts of the Holy Spirit, which helps us to know God's plan of creation and salvation and to make moral decisions according to that divine plan.

Wisdom literature [pages 291–293]
The Old Testament books of Job, Psalms, Ecclesiastes, Wisdom, and Proverbs.

Word of God [page 15]
Title given to Jesus, the Son of God; the Bible, the inspired Word of God.

Works of Mercy [page 246]
Acts of loving kindness by which we come to the help of others in their bodily and spiritual needs.

worship [page 268]
Honor and respect we give God above all else; faith in, hope in, and love for God above all else.

worshiping assembly [page 140]
The community of the People of God, the Church, joined with Christ and gathered to give praise and thanks to God the Father through the power of the Holy Spirit.

YHWH [page 28]
The Hebrew letters for the name of God that he revealed to Moses.

Index

Credits

...ward
Cover Design: Kr?ny Freeman
Cover Illustrati...

PHOTO CF follows: (bkgd) background;
Abbrevia?bottom; (l) left; (r) right;
(t) top; ?
(c) cer?